JAPANESE AMERICAN ETHNICITY

THE PERSISTENCE OF COMMUNITY

Japanese American Ethnicity

THE PERSISTENCE

OF COMMUNITY

Stephen S. Fugita

David J. O'Brien

UNIVERSITY OF WASHINGTON PRESS
SEATTLE AND LONDON

Library of Congress Cataloging-in-Publication Data
Fugita, Stephen.
    Japanese American ethnicity : the persistence of
community / Stephen S. Fugita, David J. O'Brien
        p. cm.
    Includes bibliographical references and index.
    ISBN 0-295-97376-5 (alk. paper)
    1. Japanese Americans—Social life and customs.
2. Japanese Americans—Ethnic identity.   I. O'Brien,
David J.   II. Title
E184.J3F78   1991   90-25584
305.8956073—dc20   CIP

This book is dedicated to all those individuals who believed that documenting the Japanese American experience is an important task and took time from other pressing matters to share their experiences with us.

CONTENTS

ACKNOWLEDGMENTS

A project of this magnitude would never have reached completion without the dedicated help of many persons, especially the hundreds who took time out of their busy schedules to complete our interviews. At the risk of overlooking some of our unsung heroes, we would like to single out the following individuals and institutions for their support. In the first instance, the project could not have gotten off the ground without the financial support of the National Institute of Mental Health (RO1 MH31565). William T. Liu provided critical early support. Robert Albert, Karen Fugita, Alan Iba, Annie Iriye, Cynthia Kawachi, Cindy Rogers, Emi Takizawa, and Lynne Wada served as research assistants in either California or Ohio. Isadore Newman and McKee McClendon helped with statistical issues. The Asian American Studies Center at UCLA, the Fresno JACL/Nikkei Service Center, Percy Masaki, and Franklin Ng provided help with field offices and Japanese American community contacts in the three areas of California. The University of Akron, the University of Illinois at Chicago, and the University of Missouri-Columbia provided released time from teaching commitments and provided substantial resource assistance which was not covered by the NIMH grant. Beverly Riggin cheerfully typed the many drafts of this manuscript, and Irene Fort managed numerous details without which this project would never have been completed. Finally, we wish to thank three reviewers, S. Frank Miyamoto, Ivan Light, and Setsuko Matsunaga Nishi, whose insightful reviews resulted in a significantly improved book.

Tables 9:6 and 10:1 appeared originally in David J. O'Brien and Stephen S. Fugita, "Generational Differences in Japanese Americans' Perceptions and Feelings about Social Relationships between Themselves and Caucasian Americans," pages 223–240 in W. C. McCready (ed.), *Culture, Ethnicity, and Identity: Current Issues in Research* (New York: Academic Press, 1983). Tables 9:10 and 9:11 appeared originally in David J. O'Brien and Stephen S. Fugita, "The Mobilization of a Traditionally Petit Bourgeois Ethnic Group," *Social Forces* 63 (December 1984): 522–537. Tables 9:8 and 9:9 appeared originally in Stephen S. Fugita and David J. O'Brien, "Structural Assimilation, Ethnic Group Membership, and Political Participation among Japanese Americans," *Social Forces* 63 (June 1985): 986–995.

JAPANESE AMERICAN ETHNICITY

THE PERSISTENCE OF COMMUNITY

INTRODUCTION

During the nineteenth and early twentieth centuries, most scholars saw ethnicity as a relic of traditional society which would wane in the face of the forces of modernization. From this perspective, ethnicity was viewed as the embodiment of traditional primordial relationships that would be replaced by more utilitarian forms of association, such as those of the marketplace or bureaucracy (Glazer and Moynihan, 1975).

Since the end of World War II, however, we have witnessed the persistence and, in a number of instances, an actual revival of ethnicity as a significant form of identification and attachment even in the most advanced industrialized societies. Scholars have, quite correctly, pointed out that this phenomenon can be accounted for in large measure by the political utility of ethnicity in the modern state. In some instances ethnicity has become a catalyst to reinforce existing class identifications and in other instances it serves as a basis for collective mobilization when no other exists (Glazer and Moynihan, 1975; Nielsen, 1985; Olzak, 1983).

There is, nonetheless, a limitation to the preceding explanation in that it does not account for the substantial variations in the retention of ethnicity in the same society. In particular, the question remaining to be answered is: why are some groups apparently more successful than others in retaining their ethnicity while at the same time moving into the main-stream of modern society? Clearly, events outside the group itself play an important role in answering this question. No one doubts, for example, the role of the Holocaust in the persistence of Jewish ethnicity in the United States. Nevertheless, at best these external events only provide a necessary but not a sufficient condition for the development, change, and re-creation of ethnic community institutions. Our contention is that a significant amount of the variation in the capacity of ethnic groups to maintain viable community life, *while their members are becoming structurally assimilated into the institutional life of the larger society,* is due to the way the cultures and social organization of different ethnic groups inhibit or encourage their adaptation to changing structural exigencies.

This study seeks to explain why contemporary Japanese Americans are able to retain high levels of involvement in their ethnic community even though the vast majority of them have become structurally assimilated into mainstream American life. As a group, Japanese Americans fit Gordon's definition of being structurally assimilated, in terms of their ["large-scale entrance into cliques, clubs, and institutions of [the] host society, on [a] primary group level" (1964:71). Most Japanese Americans live in predominantly Caucasian neighborhoods, have Caucasian friends, participate in mainstream community affairs, and have begun to intermarry in significant numbers with Caucasian Americans. In 1979, for example, 50 percent of all new marriages involving Japanese in Los Angeles were with non-Asians (Kitano et al., 1984; Levine and Rhodes, 1981; Montero, 1978, 1980). Yet our data will show that compared with most second and third generation members of ethnic groups at similar stages of structural assimilation, Japanese Americans have retained a very high level of participation in ethnic voluntary associations and other forms of behavioral, rather than merely psychological, involvement in ethnic community life.

Certainly, external events have played a significant role in the preservation of the Japanese American community. Most important here are the continuous experiences of Japanese Americans with discrimination from the time of their arrival in the late nineteenth and early twentieth centuries to their internment in concentration camps during World War II. Nevertheless, although these events are important in explaining the motivation individuals have for maintaining Japanese American community life, they do not, in themselves, explain the actual process of community development and change.

Our central thesis is that the persistence of Japanese American ethnicity stems from elements in traditional Japanese culture that structure social relationships among group members in such a way that they are able to adapt to changing exigencies without losing group cohesiveness. These cultural principles have generated for Japanese Americans, as they have for the Japanese in Japan, a strong sense of peoplehood, allowing them to adopt major elements from other cultural systems without totally sacrificing social relationships within the group (see, e.g., Haglund, 1984; Reischauer, 1981).

A distinguishing feature of social relationships in Japanese American communities is that individuals perceive all members of their ethnic group—not just those in family, kin, or region—as "quasi kin." This is related to the group orientation of the original immigrants as it was reinforced by historical circumstances, and has produced extensive networks of voluntary organizations (e.g., Oguri-Kendis, 1979). Thus, Japanese American communities are much less likely to be isolated into self-contained cliques (Granovetter, 1973) such as those Gans (1982) found in his study of the Italian-American community in Boston's West End.

The ability of Japanese Americans to maintain their ethnic community through voluntary associations means that their ethnicity does not depend solely on continuing more exclusive strong ties (Granovetter, 1973). This, in turn, has permitted Japanese Americans to become involved in many aspects of life in the mainstream community without having to sacrifice the majority of their ethnic ties.

There are other specific ways in which the structure of social relationships among Japanese Americans has facilitated the development of their ethnic community life. First, as Light (1972) has pointed out, these relationships were crucial in developing their successful petit bourgeois economic accommodation to American society. Although the Japanese, like the Chinese, were "pushed" into this niche because of their exclusion from mainstream economic opportunities, their success in it was made possible by the existence of institutionalized quasi-kin relationships that formed the basis for trust on which enduring kinds of economic relationships could be developed (O'Brien and Fugita, 1982).

Second, although the less verbally assertive (compared with mainstream American norms) interactional style of Japanese culture has created some liabilities for individuals in upper-level bureaucratic positions (e.g., Hraba, 1979:332; Nomura and Barnlund, 1983), persons in this ethnic group, by and large, have been able to avoid the so-called ethnic mobility trap (Wiley, 1967). This is the predicament that individuals in many other ethnic groups have faced when they have had to choose between retaining ethnic values and attitudes on the one hand and adopting values and attitudes conducive to upward mobility on the other.

Although Japanese Americans, like other Asian Americans, have often avoided jobs that place a premium on core culture interpersonal skills and language mastery (Hraba, 1979:332), they have rapidly moved into professional and technical fields (e.g., Levine and Rhodes, 1981:48–52, 118–121; Peterson, 1971:116). This upward mobility can be attributed in part to the fact that a disproportionate number of Japanese Americans grew up in petit bourgeois family situations where they internalized the values of hard work, deferred gratification, and other perspectives conducive to success in mainstream society (Bland et al., 1978; Fujimoto, 1975; Goldscheider and Kobrin, 1980; O'Brien and Fugita, 1982). Moreover, the upward mobility of persons from petit bourgeois backgrounds is less likely to generate the kinds of intraethnic class cleavages that occur in groups whose initial economic adaptation is disproportionately working class in character.

Finally, although the social organization of Japanese American ethnic communities historically has had important economic consequences, it is not totally dependent on economic involvement for its survival. Our data will show that individual Japanese Americans identify with and participate in both formal and informal aspects of ethnic community life for noneconomic as well as economic reasons. Even third generation Sansei, who are not usually dependent economically on their ethnic community, generally feel responsible for supporting ethnic solidarity.

The general thrust of our argument, therefore, deemphasizes those perspectives that treat cultural phenomena as secondary to economic forces or as merely epiphenomena reflecting underlying interests (e.g., Bonacich and Modell, 1980; Bottomore and Rubel, 1956). At the same time, however, we want to avoid the tautological fallacies found in some earlier functionalist inquiries (Lockwood, 1956). It is obviously not enough to say that Japanese Americans are different because their culture is different. Rather, the critical task is to delineate precisely how cultural predispositions and traditional social organizational forms intersect with structural constraints to create certain kinds of adaptations which, in turn, have long-range consequences for succeeding generations of an ethnic group.

HISTORICAL DEVELOPMENTS AFFECTING JAPANESE AMERICANS

Because of the constricted time period of their immigration, the history of the Japanese in the United States is somewhat easier to describe than that of many other ethnic groups. The major wave of immigration from Japan to Hawaii and the West Coast took place between 1885 and 1924. As a result of the Immigration Act of 1924, immigration by Japanese virtually ceased until after World War II. This is important, for Japanese Americans themselves as well as for scholarly observers, because it has provided well-defined generational experiences to a greater extent than is true of ethnic groups that immigrated over a longer period. This is perhaps best reflected in the certitude with which layman and scholar alike describe the unique experiences of the first, second, and third generations with the terms Issei, Nisei, and Sansei. As Montero points out, "the Japanese are the only ethnic group to emphasize geogenerational distinctions by a separate nomenclature and a belief in the unique character structure of each generational group" (1980:8).

There are, however, important differences between the experiences of Japanese in Hawaii and those on the mainland. Immigration to Hawaii took place a few years earlier than immigration to the mainland, and the former consisted mainly of contract laborers while the latter was made up of a much more varied group of individuals. Among those who migrated to the mainland from 1886 to 1908, for example, there were significant numbers of students and merchants (Ichihashi, 1932:66–67). An even more important difference in the life experiences of Japanese in Hawaii compared with those on the mainland is that although almost all West Coast Japanese were interned in concentration camps during World War II, very few of their fellow ethnics in Hawaii suffered such an upheaval. For these reasons, caution must be exercised when making inferences about Japanese Americans in Hawaii on the basis of the experiences of Japanese Americans on the mainland, or vice versa.

The vast majority of Japanese immigrants to the mainland settled in the three Western states of California, Oregon, and Washington. Historical analyses have shown some differences in the settlement patterns in the different states, such as the greater urban concentration of Japanese in Washington than in California. Nonetheless, the overwhelming thrust of Japanese immigration was toward rural areas (Ichihashi, 1932:102–103).

The ancestors of the persons who were interviewed in this study were generally immigrants who landed in California at the end of the nine-teenth and early part of the twentieth centuries. Typically, they were independent small farmers seeking to avoid political instability and exces-sive taxation in Japan and to capitalize on new agricultural opportunities in the United States. When they came to the United States, technological developments, including irrigation and refrigeration for railroad cars, were creating new jobs in labor-intensive agriculture. The Japanese ini-tially worked as laborers in this sector of the economy, later moving into tenancy arrangements and, in some cases, into ownership of small-scale truck farms (Blackford, 1977; Fugita and O'Brien, 1978; Fuller, 1940; Modell, 1977:94).

In some ways it may be said that the Japanese were "forced" into the small-scale entrepreneurial, or "petit bourgeois," class position. After all, American labor unions, with the exception of the Industrial Workers of the World, discriminated against them and would not permit them to become union members (Foner, 1964:276–277). At the same time, how-ever, self-employment in agriculture offered them significant opportuni-ties to capitalize on their culture and social organization as economic resources (Fugita and O'Brien, 1978; O'Brien and Fugita, 1982). In turn, this economic accommodation has had a long-term impact on the unique pattern of Japanese American structural assimilation and ethnic commu-nity cohesiveness.

The Japanese immigrants were quite successful in small-scale agricul-ture (Carrott, 1983; Iwata, 1962; Mears, 1926). Their economic competi-tiveness, however, threatened many native white farmers, and this led to the passage of alien land laws in 1913, 1920, and 1923. At first, these acts made it illegal for aliens ineligible for citizenship (i.e., Japanese) to own land, but later they were even prohibited from leasing it. The intent of these laws was to eliminate the Japanese as competitors and push them back into the farm labor pool, thereby discouraging further immigration (Daniels, 1962; Ferguson, 1947; Ichioka, 1977; Iwata, 1962; Olin, 1966; Strong, 1934).

Nevertheless, Japanese farmers managed to circumvent the alien land laws by putting land in the name of a Nisei son or a close friend's son who had reached his majority (Iwata, 1962), or they turned to various forms of tenancy and lease arrangements with white landowners and thus realized a profit on quick growth crops with a minimum of capital invest-ment (Iwata, 1962; Kitano, 1976:20). Thus, even though 70 percent of Japanese farm operations in California in 1940 were leased (Iwata, 1962;

Eliot and Solberg, 1973; Poli and Engstrand, 1945), they grew 30 to 35 percent of the truck crops produced in the state during that period (Iwata, 1962).

World War II virtually destroyed the niche the Japanese had created in California agriculture (Eliot and Solberg, 1973; Solberg and Eliot, 1973). Shortly after the attack on Pearl Harbor, all West Coast Japanese and Japanese Americans were interned in concentration camps. One immediate effect on the structure of the ethnic community was to replace the authority of the Issei, which was suspect according to military officials, with that of youthful English-speaking Nisei leaders (Spickard, 1983). Japanese Americans also were physically removed from their isolated ethnic enclaves and rural settings. After the war, a large number of them did not return to these areas. It should be noted that official government policy encouraged the geographic dispersal of Japanese Americans, ostensibly to reduce the likelihood of arousing prejudices and discrimination by the white majority (Myer, 1971:132–135; Solberg and Eliot, 1973; U.S. Department of the Interior, 1946a, b).

Few persons could have predicted before World War II that Japanese Americans would have assimilated as rapidly as they did into mainstream middle-class American life after the war. After all, during the earlier period many scholars and journalists had described the Japanese as "unassimilable" (Ogawa, 1971). Yet the evidence on this score is hard to refute. Many persons, especially among the Nisei, became upwardly mobile following the war and entered professional and bureaucratic managerial positions (Levine and Montero, 1973; Peterson, 1970). Japanese Americans moved in much greater numbers into predominantly middle-class Caucasian neighborhoods, and, perhaps most telling, as the Sansei entered adulthood, they began to intermarry with Caucasians. At present, about 50 percent of all new marriages of Japanese Americans involve a non-Asian spouse (Kitano et al., 1984).

Despite the present geographical dispersal and high rate of structural assimilation of Japanese Americans, however, they have retained a high level of involvement in, and psychological identification with, their ethnic community. Whereas studies have shown that in many European ethnic groups, members who have left urban ethnic enclaves are unlikely to retain involvement in voluntary associations (according to one survey of third generation Italian-Americans, less than 5 percent of persons in the suburbs were members of an ethnic voluntary association; see Roche, 1982), 69 percent of the Japanese Americans in our sample belonged to at least one ethnic voluntary association. Other researchers have found that even though third generation Japanese Americans may retain little of the more visible characteristics of traditional Japanese culture such as language, they still seek friendships with other Japanese Americans with whom they share a "common interactional style" (Johnson, 1976; O'Brien and Fugita, 1983a; Oguri-Kendis, 1979). Thus, in different but very significant ways, their ethnicity persists.

JAPANESE AMERICAN ETHNICITY AND THE LOCAL AREA

Considerable scholarly attention has been given to the interface between Japanese American cultural and social organizational characteristics and the constraints imposed on them by the larger society at different times. Less attention has been given to the impact of differences in local areas on the development of Japanese American ethnicity. The only research explicitly addressing this in a directly comparative way is that of Harumi Befu (1965). His pioneering work, comparing two rural Japanese communities in Central California, showed that the economic opportunity structure of the local area strongly influenced the acculturation and assimilation of ethnic community members. As part of our analysis, we will examine how the basic structures of social relationships prescribed in traditional Japanese culture are adapted and operationalized in different local communities which vary in terms of ethnic population density and rural versus urban economic and social characteristics.

In recent years, scholars have offered two somewhat conflicting views on the relationship between ethnicity on the one hand and density and urban versus rural character on the other. Some have argued that urban environments—with their collage of ethnic, religious, and lifestyle groups—create a social atmosphere not conducive to keeping traditional values and organizational forms intact, including those of an ethnic group. Others have argued that the urban environment encourages the development and maintenance of ethnic ties because of the existence of a "critical mass" and intergroup friction, thus providing the resources and incentives to keep these traditional relationships and institutions viable (see Fischer, 1975, 1976:35–38, 1982:202–208). Our findings support the argument that Japanese American ethnic community life can persist in a variety of urban and nonurban and high- and low-density situations because it emphasizes preserving interpersonal relations rather than achieving specific instrumental ends. Nevertheless, the actual manifestation of

Japanese American structural assimilation and ethnic community involvement is different in different social contexts. Japanese Americans interact more with Caucasians in areas where there are smaller proportions of fellow ethnics. Yet persons in these areas have been able to preserve Japanese American ethnicity by their involvement in ethnic voluntary associations. Ironically, small-town Japanese Americans, like the small-town Jews in Rose's (1959) study, appear to be more self-consciously Japanese in outlook and behavior than their urban counterparts.

Alternatively, although urban Japanese Americans who live in areas with high concentrations of fellow ethnics experience less pressure to interact with Caucasians with any degree of intimacy, they are more affected by the various lifestyles and nuances of the urban milieu. Thus persons in this social context generally do not interact as much with Caucasians, but their ethnicity is less self-conscious and less closely linked to traditional Japanese American cultural and social organizational forms than is the case in rural areas. Nonetheless, both groups possess a unique interactional style and a well-developed social organization.

PLAN OF THE BOOK

The first three chapters of this monograph provide the theoretical framework for our analysis. Chapter 1 begins by examining traditional approaches to the study of ethnicity, including the assimilationist, structural, and emergent ethnicity perspectives. It points out Reitz's (1980) analytical distinction between structural assimilation and ethnic group membership retention. The chapter concludes by discussing why the traditional cultural and social organizational elements that immigrants bring with them from their homeland have critical consequences for future patterns of structural assimilation and ethnic group membership retention. Chapter 2 analyzes the cultural bases of social organization in traditional Japanese and Japanese American community life. The third chapter concludes the theoretical discussion by describing the historical processes through which these cultural orientations and social organizational forms became institutionalized in the "petit bourgeois" economic accommodation of Japanese Americans prior to World War II. It also deals with the specific consequences of this type of accommodation for later upward mobility into mainstream society as well as its effect on the persistence of ethnic community institutional forms.

The second part of the book reports on the findings of our survey of second and third generation Japanese Americans in California in 1979–80. Chapter 4 describes the methodology employed, including a sketch of the different social and economic characteristics of the three ethnic communities studied: Gardena, in suburban Los Angeles; Fresno, an agricultural area in the Central Valley of California; and Sacramento, the state capital.

Chapter 5 examines the socialization experiences of the Nisei and the Sansei, emphasizing the continuities and discontinuities between generations and between areas with respect to structural assimilation and ethnic group membership retention. Among the topics considered are rural versus urban backgrounds, attendance at Japanese language schools and predominantly Japanese churches, and educational experiences. The empirical data illustrate the high degree of continuity between generations with respect to social involvement with other Japanese Americans in voluntary associations even though the specific content of these associations has changed markedly over time.

Chapter 6 provides direct empirical evidence of the capacity of Japanese Americans to become involved in both ethnic and mainstream community life. Included in this analysis are data on participation in informal friendship networks with Japanese and non-Japanese as well as participation in ethnic and mainstream voluntary associations. Special emphasis is placed on the compatibility between Japanese cultural views toward social relationships and the development of relationships with both ethnic and nonethnic group persons.

Chapter 7 looks at economic activities and economic networks among Japanese Americans, with a focus on evidence of the persistence of the "petit bourgeois" accommodation among persons in the second and third generations and across the different areas from which the sample was drawn. Our data show that although the number of Japanese Americans who participate in the traditional "ethnic economy" has declined considerably, there remains a disproportionate number of persons involved in petit bourgeois pursuits. Moreover, our findings demonstrate that the petite bourgeoisie continue to have higher levels of involvement in ethnic community life and achieve higher incomes than their nonpetit bourgeois fellow ethnics.

Chapter 8 examines patterns of intermarriage between Japanese Americans and Caucasians. Although generally our data are consistent with what has been reported elsewhere, we find substantial areal differences in the extent to which Japanese Americans are likely to marry outside their ethnic group. Several reasons for these differences are studied, including the effect of variations in the relative density of the Japanese American populations in the three areas. The possibility of a self-selection process, with inmarried and outmarried persons feeling differentially comfortable in different community settings, is also discussed. Inmarried Japanese Americans are found to be different from their outmarried fellow ethnics in two critical ways. They are more involved in the voluntary associational life of the ethnic community and they are less likely to get a divorce. Nevertheless, the data support our general thesis about the viability of Japanese American community life in the face of structural assimilation. The level of involvement in the ethnic community of the intermarried still far exceeds that of third generation European ethnic group members.

Chapter 9 reports on the contemporary political attitudes and participation patterns of Japanese Americans. Among the most noteworthy findings here is the relatively high degree of continuity in political attitudes between generations, especially with respect to their support of the successful movement to obtain redress for the World War II incarceration. A major portion of this chapter is devoted to showing how having social network ties to both ethnic and nonethnic communities is an important political resource for members of this group. The chapter concludes with a discussion of a contemporary effort by the Nisei Farmers League to mobilize Japanese Americans in a farm–labor dispute.

Chapter 10 examines the perceptions Japanese Americans have of the "social boundaries" between themselves and Caucasian Americans. Among the more interesting findings in this chapter are the increases in perceived ethnic differences in several social contexts as one goes from the Nisei to the Sansei generation and the high degree of consensus among Japanese Americans on what characteristics most clearly differentiate them from other persons in the society.

Finally, Chapter 11 discusses the implications of our findings for general theories of ethnicity. The central theme is the need to reassess the role of preimmigration cultural and social organizational forms in determining the ability of an ethnic group to support ethnic community life in the face of structural assimilation.

ONE

Approaches to the Study of the Persistence of Ethnicity

The ability of Japanese Americans to retain substantial involvement in ethnic community life while also experiencing a high level of structural assimilation into the mainstream of American society poses some serious analytical problems for traditional approaches to ethnicity. Theories of ethnicity have been largely dominated by a concern with the European ethnic or black American experience. The former, in the main, follows a pattern of structural assimilation replacing ethnic community involvement while the latter exhibits a pattern of structural assimilation thwarted by continued resistance from the majority group (see, e.g., Glazer and Moynihan, 1970). Recently, some theoretical analyses have focused on the significantly different experiences of the "new immigrants," Hispanics and Asians (e.g., Bonacich and Modell, 1980; Portes and Bach, 1985) in theorizing about American ethnicity.

The central focus of this chapter is the capacity of different theoretical approaches to ethnicity to deal conceptually with the empirical reality of ethnic groups that exhibit high levels of both ethnic cohesiveness and structural assimilation. We will first examine the three major current approaches to the question of the retention of ethnicity and then suggest that a more useful starting point is Reitz's (1980) proposal to view structural assimilation and ethnic group membership retention as two analytically distinct processes. We will argue, however, that his explanation for the persistence of ethnicity is incomplete and that the cultural and social organizational makeup of the ethnic group at the time of immigration is a key factor in producing later adaptations in terms of *both* structural assimilation and ethnic group membership retention.

TRADITIONAL APPROACHES

Although the following three approaches are not mutually exclusive, scholars have generally taken one of them when studying why ethnicity persists in some cases and not in others: the assimilationist perspective, the structural perspective, and the emergent ethnicity perspective.

The Assimilationist Perspective

Under this general rubric we will group together several theories of ethnicity that differ substantially in their predictions concerning the outcome of the assimilation process, but that take an analytically similar view with respect to the relationship between assimilation and the persistence of ethnicity. The dominant emphasis of the assimilationist position is an implicit zero–sum relationship between assimilation and the retention of ethnic identification and ethnic community involvement (Gans, 1979; Sandberg, 1974). The extent to which members of an ethnic group are assimilated into American life, therefore, is seen as having a direct, negative effect on the capacity of ethnicity to survive.

The classical statements on ethnicity and assimilation reflect a more general belief in nineteenth and early twentieth century sociology of an inherent incompatibility between traditional ways of relating in preurban gemeinschaft communities and what were presumed to be more impersonal ways of relating in the urban gesellschaft. Within this frame of reference, ethnicity was seen essentially as a traditional form of identification and association which eventually would be superseded by more universalistic forms (see, e.g., the essays in Sennett, 1969). This perspective is perhaps best expressed in Robert Park's (1950) "contact hypothesis." In his view, traditional forms of identification, including ethnicity, which were formed in preurban settings inevitably must weaken as individuals leave the insulated, protected rural environment and are thrown in among persons with radically different backgrounds, values, and interests. Initially this contact will generate conflict, but eventually the process will result in the loss of traditional distinctions between groups. Speaking of race relations, Park observes (1950:150):

> In the relations of races there is a cycle of events which tends everywhere to repeat itself. . . . The race relations cycle which takes the form, to state it abstractly, of contact, competition, accommodation, and eventual assimilation, is apparently progressive and irreversible. Customs, regulations, immigration restrictions and racial barriers may slacken the tempo of the movement; may perhaps halt it altogether for a time; but it cannot change its direction; cannot at any rate reverse it.

Later, Park moderated his views on the inevitability of the unilinear assimilation process, suggesting that race relations can end in a relatively permanent caste system (e.g., Hraba, 1979:37).

A more contemporary version of the assimilationist perspective is found in the work of Milton Gordon (1964). He identifies seven stages of assimilation: (1) cultural or behavioral assimilation; (2) structural assimilation; (3) marital assimilation; (4) identificational assimilation (development of a sense of peoplehood based exclusively on the host society); (5) attitude receptional assimilation (absence of prejudice); (6) behavioral receptional assimilation (absence of discrimination); and (7) civic assimilation (absence of value and power conflicts) (1964:71).

Gordon's formulation of the assimilation process contains a crucial insight not found in the earlier work: the major barrier to be broken in the assimilation process is not cultural but structural. Most ethnic groups do, as Park anticipated, adopt many of the key values, attitudes, and outlooks of the majority group as time goes on. Gordon observes, however, that by the middle of the twentieth century, even though a good deal of cultural assimilation had taken place, there remained a substantial lack of what he terms structural assimilation: "large-scale entrance into cliques, clubs, and institutions of [the] host society, on [a] primary group level" (1964:71). In short, Gordon argues that the critical issue is not the assimilation of ideas but whether individuals in a minority group are able to interact with persons in the majority group on some basis other than pure marketplace exchange. Structural assimilation, then, by definition assumes some degree of basic acceptance of a minority group by majority group members.

Gordon noted that there were clear barriers to structural assimilation in the early 1960s, as evidenced by the continued separation of blacks and whites and the three major religious groupings (i.e., Protestants, Catholics, and Jews) on many social, institutional, organizational, and primary group levels. He concluded, therefore, that assimilation is not inevitable and that American society is essentially pluralistic in character (1964:132–159).

Moreover, Gordon notes that an ethnic group may become assimilated in some ways yet retain a viable sense of ethnic distinctiveness in others. Speaking of Jews in America, for example, he observes (1964:194–195):

> The acculturation process, thus, has drastically modified Jewish life in the direction of adaptation to American middle-class values, while it has not by any means "dissolved" the group in a structural sense. Communal life and ethnic self-identification flourish within the borders of a group defined as one of the "three major faiths" of America, while at the same time its members and, to a considerable degree, its institutions become increasingly indistinguishable, culturally, from the personnel and institutions of the American core society.

Nevertheless, the essential thrust of Gordon's work is similar to that of the earlier assimilationists. He does not see the process proceeding as simply or uniformly as did Park, yet he seems to share the view that once structural assimilation takes place it is only a matter of time until distinctive ethnic identity is lost: "Once structural assimilation has occurred, either simultaneously with or subsequent to acculturation, all other types of assimilation will naturally follow" (1964:81).

From our perspective, the most serious implications of these views is that they fail to deal theoretically with the fact that individual ethnic groups vary considerably with respect to the impact structural assimilation has on their capacity to retain the loyalty of their members and their participation in ethnic community activities. Most important, as we will see later, it is incorrect to assume that greater structural assimilation will necessarily lead to an equivalent reduction in the viability of ethnicity. This outcome is true of many ethnic groups, but not all. Moreover, certain kinds of structural assimilation, paradoxically, may be an effective means of maintaining the strength of an individual's identification with, and participation in, the ethnic community. The theoretical task before us, then, is to explain why such variations take place.

The Structural Perspective

The assimilationist perspective sees the process of structural assimilation as intimately linked to discrimination by the host society. Gordon (1964) notes, for example, that at a certain point in their histories many ethnic groups could not have moved out of their structural isolation from the mainstream society even if they had desired to do so. In fact, a major concern in his book is contemporary discrimination against some groups and their persistent isolation from the majority group. Although he expresses some ambivalence about the loss of ethnic and religious community life, he seems to imply that once such discrimination is removed, structural assimilation will take place and will result in the loss of traditional group identification.

The assimilationist perspective, however, does not propose a general theoretical framework to explain why certain groups, rather than others, remain structurally separated from the majority group or why structural assimilation occurs more rapidly in some cases than in others. Structural theories attempt to deal with these issues.

Structural theories focus on the relation between ethnicity and broader structural—mainly economic—features of the host society. Although writers in this tradition rarely go so far as to treat ethnicity as merely epiphenomenal, they do tend to view the persistence of ethnicity as resting on material conditions (e.g., Fendrich, 1983). This is seen, for example, in Hechter's (1975, 1978) development of the theory of the cultural division of labor. He explains the persistence of Celtic ethnicity in the British Isles as an economic struggle between persons on the "periphery" and the dominant English ruling group in the "core" region.

In Hechter's view, Scottish, Irish, and Welsh ethnicity has lasted over the centuries because "objective cultural distinctions are superimposed over class lines" (1975:30). Initially, according to his argument, economic statuses (i.e., class positions) were allocated according to core versus peripheral ethnic statuses and this was reinforced over time until a cultural division of labor was established in which Celtic ethnic affiliations were associated with subordinate class statuses in the marketplace. In turn, Hechter contends, this cultural division of labor reinforced objective class interests among persons in the various Celtic peripheral regions and this was a major contributing factor in the nationalism movements in Ireland, Scotland, and Wales (Hechter, 1975). Nielsen (1985) classifies an approach like that of Hechter's as a reactive-ethnicity model.

The intellectual origins of structural approaches to ethnicity can be found in Marx's writings (see, e.g., Bottomore and Rubel, 1956:51–87), but contemporary work in this tradition has produced varied interpretations, some running counter to those of the nineteenth-century thinker. For example, while Marx saw the persistence of ethnicity resting primarily on the machinations of capitalists who sought to play off one laboring group against another, Bonacich (1972) states that often it is the majority group working class that has the most at stake in maintaining the structural separation of minority ethnic groups. Her theory of the "split labor market" points out that capitalists are primarily motivated by considerations of profits and therefore have an incentive to hire "cheap labor" from indigenous or overseas minority ethnic groups. Native majority group workers, however, are directly threatened by this competition from lower-priced labor and thus have an economic incentive to exclude ethnic minorities from the workplace and to keep them socially and politically isolated as well.

Structural theories provide us with fresh insights not found in the assimilationist perspective. The most important of these is that ethnicity must be understood within a broader context of economic and political relationships in the larger society and, in fact, the world. While we may take issue with structural explanations for the persistence of ethnicity in a given instance, we cannot ignore that economic interests play an important role in shaping the nature of an ethnic community. In Chapter 3 we will note how the special economic niche occupied by the Japanese immigrants in California played a crucial historical role in the development of Japanese American ethnicity. The legacy of this economic accommodation has significantly affected both the structural assimilation and the retention of ethnicity among Japanese Americans today.

Scholars having a structural perspective generally take into account cultural elements in explaining the unique niche occupied by a particular ethnic group. Thus, for example, Hechter (1975) describes at length the cultural differences between the Celts and the English that preceded their later struggles involving economic dominance. Bonacich's (1973) concept of the "middleman minority" focuses on the economic role certain ethnic groups play as intermediaries between elites and the masses, but she takes care to point out the unique cultural and social organizational characteristics that made these groups prime candidates for that role.

Nevertheless, the basic thrust of the structural perspective is to propose that the persistence of ethnicity ultimately has an economic basis. Researchers working out of this tradition may debate among themselves the exact causal mechanisms linking economics and ethnicity, but this literature is quite consistent in arguing that ethnic community life rests on some type of economic foundation. For our purposes, the most important implication of this view is expressed in Bonacich and Modell's (1980) claim that the viability of the Japanese American community is based on its capacity to maintain economic interdependence among its members. This is an issue we will examine at length in later chapters.

Even though they differ on many other points, the assimilationist and structural perspectives are similar in their analytical approach to the relation between structural assimilation and the persistence of ethnicity. Structural theorists do not specifically focus on structural assimilation, since they see economics as the core issue, but they do argue that when members of the same ethnic group are concentrated in a particular economic or class position, their ethnicity will be reinforced (see Bonacich and Modell, 1980). They imply that as ethnic group members assimilate and become more dispersed throughout the organizational and institutional structures of society, they will be less likely to have common class interests and therefore will be less cohesive in their ethnicity. Thus, in the main, we would argue that the structural position suggests, like the assimilationist's, that structural assimilation signals the end of ethnicity.

The Emergent Ethnicity Perspective

The original conceptualization of ethnicity as a process was developed by the historian Oscar Handlin (1951). He noted that the various ethnic identifications and cultures associated with Americans whose ancestors came from Europe were shaped as much by processes that occurred in the New World as by the cultural content they brought with them from the Old World. He observes (1951:186) that at the time of their arrival in the United States:

> it was no easy matter then to define the nature of such groupings. Much later, in deceptive retrospect, a man might tell his children, Why we were Poles and stayed that way—or Italians, or Irish or Germans or Czechoslovaks. The memories were in error. These people had arrived in the New World with no such identification. The terms referred to national states not yet in existence or just come into being. The immigrants defined themselves rather by the place of their birth,

the village, or else by the provincial region that shared dialect and custom; they were Masurians or Corkonians or Apulians or Bohemians or Bavarians. The parents back across the Atlantic, troubled by a son's too quick abandonment of the old ways, begged that he keep in himself the feeling of a Poznaniak. (They did not say Pole.)

A central theme of the emergent ethnicity perspective, then, is to turn away from the process of assimilation and focus on evolving adaptive responses and ethnic identifications whose specific cultural content will change as the ethnic group faces different structural exigencies (e.g., Glazer and Moynihan, 1970:4–5; Nahirny and Fishman, 1965; Yancey et al., 1976). The concept of emergent ethnicity suggests that the reasons individuals have for maintaining ethnic identification and ethnic community involvement change with each succeeding generation. Thus, persons of a later generation may no longer be compelled to participate in an ethnic community out of economic necessity yet they may find interaction with fellow ethnic group members satisfying because of the opportunity to share experiences with others within a mutually understood and preferred interactional style (e.g., Johnson, 1976; O'Brien and Fugita, 1983a).

But there is also evidence that ethnicity may become a very important basis for pursuing interests within a democratic political system, and thus there are some purely utilitarian reasons why individuals may want to retain or perhaps even to re-create or reshape ethnic affiliations (e.g., Glazer and Moynihan, 1970, 1975; Hirschman, 1983; Nielsen, 1985; Novak, 1972; Olzak, 1983; Trottier, 1981).

One of the contributions of the emergent ethnicity perspective is that it increases our sensitivity to the role of historic events in shaping the direction and meaning of a given ethnic community. It is better able to handle, for example, the impact of the Holocaust and the creation of the state of Israel on American Judaism (e.g., Goren, 1982:108–114; Mathias, 1981; Molotch, 1983) or the impact of the Turkish massacre on the persistence of Armenian identity and community in the United States (e.g., Mirak, 1980).

In the case of Japanese Americans, several clearly identifiable historical events have dramatically changed the institutional character of their ethnic community life. Among the most important was the so-called gentleman's agreement between the United States and Japan in 1907–8 which, with the exception of spouses, severely restricted immigration. This, combined with the Immigration Act of 1924, which almost totally cut off Japanese immigration, produced a very clear-cut generational profile in the Japanese American community (Ichihashi, 1932:243–260). Also important because of their impact on community structures and processes were the alien land laws passed during the same period. These reinforced the need to develop mutual self-help networks in economic affairs (Ichihashi, 1932:261–282).

The most dramatic and devastating event in the history of the Japanese American community was the forced evacuation and relocation of its citizens to concentration camps during World War II. For all practical purposes this destroyed the highly developed, Issei-dominated ethnic community (Spickard, 1983). Following the war, the War Relocation Authority's policy of discouraging Japanese Americans from recreating their prewar ethnic enclaves speeded up their dispersal into the larger society. This, of course, encouraged the structural assimilation of Japanese Americans (Starn, 1986) and, as is shown in later chapters, helped to recreate a much different ethnic community.

Conceptually, the most important implication of the emergent ethnicity perspective is that there need not be a zero-sum relationship between structural assimilation and the retention of ethnicity. Rather, scholars using this perspective have proposed that ethnic groups, in varying degrees, transform the nature of their ethnicity to meet the new exigencies that continually arise (e.g., Banton, 1981).

STRUCTURAL ASSIMILATION AND ETHNIC GROUP MEMBERSHIP RETENTION

Jeffrey Reitz's (1980) theoretical distinction enables us to begin to go beyond the limitations of the assimilationist and structural approaches. He proposes that the traditional approach to the problem of the relation between assimilation and retention of ethnicity is invalid (cf. Gordon, 1964). The core problem, in his view, is that scholars have seen assimilation and retention of ethnicity as opposite sides of a coin, whereas they are two analytically distinct processes. Reitz notes (1980:101):

> Structural assimilation is not the opposite of ethnic group membership retention. There are two distinct social processes involved in the two concepts. On the one hand, individuals may or may not retain membership in an ethnic minority group on the primary group level. On the other hand, they may or may not gain acceptance into the institu-

tions of the dominant society. The two variables are quite distinct and should be treated separately. A key issue is the question of precisely how the two are related. Does acceptance into the institutions of the dominant society either require, or lead to, abandonment of membership in an ethnic minority group? Does structural assimilation affect ethnic cohesion?

Reitz makes a further distinction between two types of ethnic group membership retention. The first is "ethnic identification," which refers to whether or not an individual sees himself, or herself, as being a member of a particular ethnic group, without necessarily having any contact with fellow ethnic group members. This concept, therefore, pertains to a "psychic" membership in an ethnic group or, put differently, the extent to which ethnicity is a salient part of self-identity. The second type of ethnic group membership refers to *social interaction* with other members of an ethnic community (Reitz, 1980:92–100; see also Gans, 1979). The distinction between identification and actual interaction with an ethnic group is especially important in the development of our thesis with respect to Japanese Americans. Many European ethnic groups have maintained fairly high levels of psychic identification among their members, but most of these groups have not been able to maintain within-group interaction by the time the third generation has reached adulthood (e.g., Alba, 1976, 1981; Goering, 1971; Roche, 1982). Reitz (1980) recognizes this issue and devotes considerable attention to the more perplexing question of why some groups retain higher levels of interaction among their members than others.

He observes that one important source of variation between ethnic groups with respect to their capacity to maintain interaction among their members is simply that groups vary in terms of where they are in their particular "life cycle." Thus the more cohesive communities in his Canadian sample generally have a disproportionate number of recent immigrants (1980:139).

Nevertheless, Reitz's data suggest that stage in the life cycle of an ethnic group only accounts for approximately half of the variance between groups with respect to retention of within-group interaction (1980:141). In fact, his data show quite clearly that different ethnic groups have different life cycles (1980:143). Therefore, the remainder of his book is devoted to identifying other sources of differences in the retention of intraethnic interaction.

Reitz's explanatory argument centers on the difference in economic positions of ethnic groups. For example, he finds that the most cohesive ethnic groups in his sample, the Italians and the Chinese, are more apt than other non-French Canadians to be segregated into ethnic occupations: "In these groups, as much as one third of the labour force works in a setting in which its own ethnic tongue is spoken. These settings include not only ethnic businesses, but also work groups within Anglo-Saxon controlled organizations in which members of a particular ethnic group are concentrated" (1980:154–155).

Reitz goes on to say, following Hechter's (1975, 1978) general line of reasoning, that occupational specialization along ethnic lines—the "cultural division of labor"—can reinforce both working- and middle-class ethnicity, depending on whether economic forces have generated a "niche" for a particular ethnic group. In the case of Italian Canadians, ethnic segregation into working-class occupations tends to create an "ethnic mobility trap" (Wiley, 1967) in which individuals are faced with a dilemma: behavior conducive to mobility within the ethnic group is incompatible with behavior necessary for upward mobility in the mainstream society (Reitz, 1980:162–167). Alternatively, Jews typically have been segregated into "middleman" occupational categories, and this has reinforced a strong middle-class ethnic identification and involvement more conducive to upward mobility (Reitz, 1980:179–185).

It would appear, then, that Reitz ends up with an essentially structural argument, although he emphasizes, in contrast to most of the structural thinkers referred to earlier (e.g., Bonacich and Modell, 1980), that ethnicity may persist even after economic supports are no longer operative. He does, however, have some theoretical difficulty dealing with those ethnic groups that at one time had significant economic bases, but now persist without them. He posits two explanations for persistence under such conditions: social discrimination and the propensity of organizations to survive even when their original purposes have been met.

The first explanation, social discrimination, seems plausible since persons who are denied access to the most intimate forms of interaction with the majority group might be expected to have more incentive to involve themselves with their fellow ethnics. Yet this explanation has some limitations. The resource mobilization literature, for example, has pointed out that the degree of objective deprivation is not highly correlated with the capacity of persons to mobilize. The key element is the ability of "political entrepreneurs" to find and utilize resources creatively (see e.g., Jenkins, 1983; Jenkins and Perrow, 1977; McCarthy and Zald, 1977; Olzak, 1983). It follows from this that discrimination may or may not increase group solidarity. There are other factors, beyond structural conditions themselves, that need to be taken into account in explaining why some ethnic groups and not others succeed in mobilizing. Moreover, the social discrimination argument tends to downplay the possibility that an ethnic group wishes to remain socially apart from the mainstream on the primary group level. This is seen, for example, in numerous contemporary campaigns in the Jewish community to ensure its survival (e.g., Cohen and Fein, 1985; Goren, 1980:597; Sklare and Greenblum, 1979:301).

The most compelling evidence with respect to the limits of the social discrimination argument, however, is seen in the case of Japanese Americans. On the one hand, researchers have found a consistent trend toward greater interaction between Japanese Americans and other groups, highlighted by an intermarriage rate of over 60 percent of all new marriages, including 50 percent with non-Asians (Kitano et al., 1984). On the other hand, our data in Chapter 6 show a high rate of involvement of Japanese Americans in ethnic community voluntary associations, even among the third generation. In short, although social discrimination is clearly a factor in ethnic group solidarity, it is by no means a sufficient cause for the persistence of ethnic community involvement.

Reitz's (1980) second noneconomic explanation for persistent ethnicity, the propensity of organizations to seek survival, is certainly plausible. Yet if there were some universal law operating, we would expect to have a much higher survival rate of ethnic voluntary associations in the United States. But it appears that some groups have been better able than others to maintain their organizational infrastructure.

Several researchers have suggested that ethnic voluntary organizations tend to survive primarily when they are supported by dense concentrations of ethnics in an urban area. This theme has been developed in Fischer's concept of the subcultural theory of urbanism (Fischer, 1975, 1976, 1982; Fischer et al., 1977). Contemporary studies of European ethnics in the suburbs show an extremely low rate of involvement in such organizations, oftentimes less than 5 percent (Goering, 1971; Roche, 1982). At the same time, however, certain ethnic groups, including American Jews and Japanese Americans, have been able to maintain much higher levels of involvement in ethnic voluntary associations even in areas where they are relatively small in numbers (O'Brien and Fugita, 1983b; Rose, 1959).

Undoubtedly, part of the explanation for the higher retention of voluntary associations among groups like the Jews and the Japanese is that they had a greater number of organizations at the time of immigration than was true of many European ethnic groups (Benkin, 1978; De Santis and Benkin, 1980; Fugita and O'Brien, 1978; O'Brien and Fugita, 1982; Rosentraub and Taebel, 1980). A more fundamental reason for variations in the persistence of ethnic voluntary associations, however, can be found in differences in the respective cultures the immigrant groups brought with them to the United States. This is the topic to which we will now turn.

CULTURAL ELEMENTS IN THE PERSISTENCE OF ETHNICITY

Since the mid-1960s there has been a growing tendency among sociologists to play down the role of cultural elements in influencing the outcomes of social change. In large measure, this has been a reaction to the postwar dominance of Parsonian sociology, which, in effect, used values as a major explanatory variable. As the critics have pointed out, such explanations, besides having a conservative ideological bias, are not explanations at all but tautological exercises in which observable behavior is explained in terms of values that the behavior is supposed to reflect. The critics have proposed that scholars should examine the structural conditions that create such values. This has given rise to a variety of Marxist and quasi-Marxist approaches as well as more general structural approaches, such as those we discussed earlier (see, e.g., Collins, 1975; Demerath and Peterson, 1967).

Structural approaches have provided a much needed balance to sociological inquiry in general and to ethnic research in particular by demonstrating that many distinctive traits of a group of people that have been attributed to culture are more the product of structural conditions, especially those of a material nature. A major limitation of such approaches, however, is that they fail to explain why groups cope differently when faced with similar structural constraints. More specifically, in terms of our present inquiry, why do ethnic groups similar in level of structural assimilation vary widely in their retention of ethnic community life? In the most general sense, the answer to this question was given by Max Weber when he proposed that at certain points in the history of any people—be they a nation, a religious group, or a class—key ideas are advanced about how to approach the world. Even though much later it might be difficult to recognize these key ideas, they set in motion a series of events that generate quite predictable responses. This is seen, Weber argued, in the "rationalization of the West," which reached its fruition in the development of the modern Western marketplace and bureaucracy but which had its origins in the "this-wordly" interests of Judaism many hundreds of years earlier (see Gerth and Mills, 1946:51).

A further implication of the Weberian worldview is that cultures differ with respect to their adaptability to certain kinds of exigencies. Change, then, is not merely a matter of gaining or losing traditional cultural content but also how the internal mechanisms of a culture respond to specific kinds of external pressures. In the case of the rationalization of the West, Weber argued that mechanisms inherent in the Judeo-Christian tradition that were essentially "this-worldly" served to adapt traditional religious beliefs to the changing circumstances of modern times. This contributed, in his view, to the "inner-worldly asceticism" of the Calvinists (Gerth and Mills, 1946:61).

We will argue that ethnic cultures also vary with respect to how their internal mechanisms permit adjustment to the changing conditions brought on by structural assimilation. Specifically, we will show that key cultural ideas, manifested in well-defined social organizational forms, created a specific kind of adaptation by the Japanese to the exigencies of American society both at the time of their immigration and later. While recognizing the role of structural forces in placing Japanese Americans in a particular economic niche in American society, it is our position that their ability to exploit the opportunities in such a niche is based on the culture the immigrants brought with them from Japan. The key elements in this culture are not language, religion, or other aspects of ethnicity, which sociologists typically emphasize when they describe ethnic culture (and acculturation), but rather a set of guidelines for structuring social relationships.

Our thesis is that these cultural guidelines for structuring social relationships play a critical role in understanding both the structural assimilation and the contemporary retention of ethnicity among Japanese Americans. They have provided support for the development of "petit bourgeois" ethnic enterprises, and involvement in these enterprises has promoted the development and retention of values, such as hard work and deferred gratification, which have been conducive to rapid upward mobility into the professions (Bland et al., 1978; Goldscheider and Kobrin, 1980). This in turn, we will argue, contributed to the rapid structural assimilation of

Japanese Americans in both economic and noneconomic spheres of American life after discriminatory barriers were lowered following World War II (Levine and Montero, 1973; Levine and Rhodes, 1981).

At the same time, this cultural orientation and the social organizational forms that have emerged from it have supported an ethical imperative for individual Japanese Americans to preserve social relationships in the ethnic community even though much of the specific cultural content the immigrants brought with them from Japan has disappeared. This, we will show, explains why, for example, third generation Japanese Americans perceive themselves as having a "unique interactional style" and why they continue to be more involved in ethnic voluntary associations than their counterparts in most other ethnic groups (e.g., Johnson, 1976; Fugita and O'Brien, 1985; O'Brien and Fugita, 1983a).*

*Third generation Italian Americans, for example, do not reflect this cohesiveness (see Roche, 1982).

TWO

The Structure of
Social Relationships
Among Japanese Americans

In this chapter we will explore the historical, cultural, and social organizational factors contributing to the persistence of individual involvement in Japanese American community life despite high levels of structural assimilation. We will argue that although contemporary Japanese American social organization has been significantly influenced by adaptations to the American experience, there remains a remarkable degree of continuity in certain principles for structuring social relationships. These principles have permitted them to adapt the content of ethnic community associational life to changing circumstances, including those demanded by structural assimilation, without losing the basic form of relationships among community members.

HISTORICAL FACTORS SHAPING THE JAPANESE AMERICAN COMMUNITY

Although our argument centers on culture and social organization, it is important to appreciate the role historical influences have played in the adaptation of Japanese Americans to American society, especially discrimination. Not only were the Japanese one of the few groups who were legally blocked from becoming naturalized citizens, but they remain the only ethnic group to have experienced wholesale incarceration because of their ethnic background.

From the time the Issei first emigrated in large numbers at the turn of the century, discrimination has influenced the kinds of accommodations the Japanese have made to American life. In many ways, for example, they were pushed into the petit bourgeois niche because discrimination prevented them from obtaining mainstream jobs in the private and public sectors (O'Brien and Fugita, 1982). This is not, as we will discuss in Chapters 3 and 7, a sufficient explanation for the development and maintenance of the complex set of relationships necessary to support an ethnic economic enterprise (Light, 1972). Nevertheless, the Japanese might have used other strategies for achieving economic mobility if this level of discrimination had not existed. This interpretation is supported by the fact that Japanese Americans moved in large numbers into professional occupations once discriminatory barriers were lowered after World War II.

The general impact of discrimination before the war was to force the emergence and institutionalization of a parallel community. This does not mean that Japanese Americans were completely isolated from Caucasian society. For example, with the exception of a few segregated elementary schools in the Sacramento area, virtually all Nisei were educated in integrated schools. Moreover, they often took an active part in the athletic and organizational life of their schools. But virtually all of their significant social interactions outside of school were with other Japanese Americans. It is probably most accurate to say, then, that the Nisei grew up in two worlds, one white and one Japanese.

Being restricted to their own social circles reinforced a Japanese cultural disposition to form voluntary associations (Norbeck, 1972). The Issei, not surprisingly, were much more likely than the Nisei to form groups with strong traditional Japanese cultural content. In fact, one of the most ubiquitous Japanese organizations, the Japanese Association, was a semiofficial organ of the Japanese government (Ichioka, 1977). The Nisei, however, were more likely to participate in organizations with American cultural content although the interpersonal style involved in the maintenance of these groups was quite Japanese. Examples of this were the many Nisei baseball and basketball teams which competed not only in local Japanese American leagues but often statewide or even throughout the Pacific Coast.

The creation of an extensive ethnic community infrastructure served two main purposes: (1) it was the basis for the continual resocialization of members in Japanese ways, and (2) it provided a means by which families could keep in touch with each other, thereby reinforcing Issei social control over the community.

The culmination of the discriminatory treatment against Japanese Americans was, of course, the World War II evacuation, incarceration, and resettlement. Not only were they collectively imprisoned and stigmatized for up to four years, but the institutions and structure of their community were almost totally destroyed. Moreover, they were cut off from any normal contact with mainstream American life. As has been well documented, they endured many physical and economic losses. This event so altered their lives that even today when the Nisei talk among themselves, they divide their lives into two distinct periods, "before the war" and "after the war" (see Commission on Wartime Relocation and Internment of Civilians, 1982; O'Brien and Fugita, forthcoming).

Not only was the incarceration a deeply degrading experience for individuals, but it was a collectively shared hardship that minimized prewar socioeconomic differences among the Japanese. Thus the incarceration was a unique shared event in the lives of almost all Japanese Americans who were old enough to be aware of what was going on. Evidence for the contemporary importance of the internment issue is found in the broad-based support in the ethnic community for the successful redress movement (see Chapter 9; Hohri, 1988; O'Brien and Fugita, 1984).

In the years immediately following the war, Japanese Americans attempted to rebuild many of their community institutions so that they could meet their own social, psychological, and economic needs. This occurred even though many de jure discriminatory barriers were falling. Initially, they were released from the internment camps to settle only in the Midwest and East. Since they had all been from the West Coast prior to the internment, they were not only unfamiliar with their new homes but faced an extremely uncertain future. In order to deal with this, most of them quickly sought out other Japanese who had settled in the local area and started to reestablish some of the community mechanisms they had maintained before the war. Not surprisingly, the resultant postwar community was altered in many significant ways.

Among the Issei, most were never able to rebuild either their economic viability or their community leadership roles. Given their heavy losses during evacuation, the capital needed to repurchase a tuna fishing boat or farming equipment was often too great. The time spent in camp also disrupted the socialization of their offspring and the social control they were able to exercise over them. This gave the Nisei much greater autonomy and permitted a restructuring of the Japanese American community along lines more consistent with their more Americanized experiences and worldviews. This restructuring of the ethnic community facilitated the adaptation of Japanese American institutional structures to a society into which the majority of persons were rapidly becoming structurally assimilated.

PRINCIPLES OF SOCIAL ORGANIZATION AMONG EUROPEAN ETHNIC GROUPS AND JAPANESE AMERICANS

Even though the history of exclusion and discrimination experienced by Japanese Americans may continue to be a powerful motivation for the persistence of ethnic community life, it does not explain the mechanisms through which the community has adapted to the pressures brought on by the high levels of structural assimilation in the postwar period. To understand how these mechanisms have adjusted to changing exigencies it is necessary to focus on some core cultural elements in the Japanese American tradition and the manner in which these elements have encouraged the development of certain kinds of social organizational responses to social, political, and economic constraints.

One way to gain insight into the elements of Japanese American culture most central to our thesis is to compare the legacy of "peoplehood" the Japanese immigrants brought with them to the New World with the backgrounds of most European groups. There was a relative absence of such a legacy among most of the European immigrant groups that have served as examples for the bulk of theorizing and descriptive work on ethnicity in America.

As noted in Chapter 1, a large portion of the new arrivals from Europe had no sense of belonging to what we would think of as their respective ethnic groups. Their identities were not tied to nation-states because these either were not yet formed or were just coming into being. They defined themselves much more locally, by village or province (Handlin, 1951; Rolle, 1972:2; Sarna, 1978). Handlin observes (p. 8):

Always, the start was the village. "I was born in such a village in such a parish"—so the peasant invariably began the account of himself. Thereby he indicated the importance of the village in his being; this was the fixed point by which he knew his position in the world and his relationship with all humanity.

There has been, of course, considerable variation among individual European immigrant groups with respect to how much cultural baggage they brought with them from their respective village experiences. At one extreme were the immigrants who arrived from the poor villages of southern Italy, among whom were the ancestors of the Boston West Enders studied by Gans (1982). These persons emerged from a cultural tradition Banfield characterizes as "amoral familism," in which there was intense distrust of all persons outside one's immediate nuclear family (1958:10). This type of cultural tradition, therefore, emphasized strong-tie relationships and was clearly antithetical to the development of voluntary associations (see Gans, 1982; Granovetter, 1973). Gans observed that the vast majority of West End residents did not participate in local community life even though they lived in an extremely homogeneous ethnic environment. He goes on to say (1982:108):

> West Enders are not adept at cooperative group activity. . . . West Enders are reluctant to place themselves in a leader–follower, officer–member relationship, which would detract from the individuating function of the group and would also require members to assume a subordinate, if not dependent role toward the leader. Consequently, only a highly charismatic leader seems able to attract followers and retain their loyalty for any length of time.

Thomas and Znaniecki's (1927) account of the Poles in Chicago points out that not all the European immigrants were as isolated organizationally as the West Enders. In the nineteenth century, the Polish immigrants were quite well organized within their respective parish boundaries. Even the mutual benefit societies, which dealt with insurance and other economic matters, functioned relatively autonomously at the parish level (Renkiewicz, 1980). In this case, the parish boundaries seemed to coincide with the territorial frame of reference of the village and the parish in the old country. However, Thomas and Znaniecki (1927) report that it was extremely difficult for political entrepreneurs in this ethnic group to form voluntary associations, or coalitions of voluntary associations, that went beyond the local parish boundaries. They concluded that "Priest Barzynski in spite of all his ability and influence could not even induce all of the parishes in Chicago to form one social body; their solidarity has never gone beyond cooperation in a few public manifestations of a national character" (1927:1575).

Perhaps the best evidence for the impact of the peasant village orientation on the survival strategies of the European immigrants in the New World is found in their use of the political machine in urban politics. The immigrants in their respective enclaves were not organized by any appeals to larger entities or sense of peoplehood, but rather by the *particularistic affective bonds* between the local precinct captains and the voters on their blocks. Banfield and Wilson (1963:117–118) describe how these bonds were established and the kinds of "exchanges" involved in maintaining them:

> Even though the precinct captain asks for something that is almost worthless to the voter (i.e., his vote), he must offer something in return. What he offers is usually a personal nonmaterial incentive, "friendship." A Chicago captain explained, "I never take leaflets or mention issues or conduct rallies in my precinct. After all, this is a question of personal friendship between me and my neighbors." Much has been made of the "favors"—turkeys at Thanksgiving, hods of coal at Christmas, and so on—with which the machine in effect buys votes. Such material inducements are indeed given in some instances. The voter, however, is the one contributor to the machine's system of activity who is usually given nonmaterial inducements, especially "friendship." The reason for this is, of course, that people will exchange their votes for "friendship" more readily than for cash or other material benefits; and the machine cannot afford to pay cash for many of the votes it needs.

In short, the success of the political machine in organizing the European immigrants can be attributed in large measure to the skill of its leaders in utilizing principles of social organization, mainly strong ties, which were extensions of the basic cultural orientation of the peasant villager. By the same token, the critics of the political machine, the so-called reformers during the Progressive Era, were largely middle-class WASPS who saw the ethnic village perspective as incompatible with more universalistic norms of efficiency and fairness (e.g., Hofstadter, 1955).

At this juncture, it is important to emphasize that the kinds of relationships developed by the European immigrants in their ethnic enclaves undoubtedly were essential for their survival in the New World. Indeed, given the historical experience of most of these persons—the absence of a clear sense of peoplehood or national identity—it is hard to imagine how they could have been organized on any other basis. Moreover, a persuasive case may be made that historical attempts to impose middle-class WASP ways on these ethnic communities caused a good deal of personal damage, in terms of cultural confusion or "anomie," as well as hampering the development of positive self-images among the children of immigrants (cf. Novak, 1972).

The types of identification patterns found among most European ethnic groups were also found among many Asian groups. The Chinese, for example, have been described as "familist" because of the centrality of family and lineage in the social organization of their peasant village life. As a result, they also lacked a developed sense of national identity (Fei, 1939; Freedman, 1964; Johnson, 1962; Nee and Wong, 1985).

Nevertheless, it is also fair to say that a particularistic, exclusively strong-tie focus was incompatible with many aspects of structural assimilation into mainstream American society. While the moral value of ethnic versus mainstream American ways may be debated, it is clear that those ethnic group members who elected to retain their traditional peasant village worldview were at a serious disadvantage in mainstream society and suffered what Wiley (1967) refers to as an "ethnic mobility trap."

Indeed, historians tell us that perhaps the most significant influence in the overall process of structurally assimilating large numbers of the European peasant immigrants was the subsuming of ethnic interest under the larger umbrella of the Catholic Church. Again, one may debate what were the "real" causes of specific historical decisions such as the Catholic Church hierarchy's ruling that a single American Catholic Church, and not a proliferation of ethnic Catholic Churches, would survive; the Irish won and some of the less powerful ethnic groups lost. But, it seems clear, in hindsight at least, that ethnic communities that were not able to give up their more particularistic outlook had serious problems in moving into the mainstream of society, especially into higher status positions (Ellis, 1969:41–83; Herberg, 1960:138–161).

In any event, structural assimilation, especially as it was fostered by upward mobility through education and placement in higher-status occupations, has meant for most Americans of European ethnic stock an abandonment of the traditional ethnic community solidarity and its replacement with only a residual of that community in the form of a psychological identity and selective retention of ethnic symbols (Alba, 1976, 1981; Gans, 1979).

Since the European ethnic experience in America has provided the empirical data for most general theories of ethnicity, it is not surprising that scholars have tended to see a zero-sum relationship between ethnic community cohesion and structural assimilation. The basic flaw in generalizing from this experience to that of all ethnic groups in America, let alone in other countries, is that it assumes that all these groups are similar in terms of the sources of their internal solidarity (A. Cohen, 1981; G. B. Cohen, 1984; Thurlings, 1979).

If all ethnic groups had the same sources of community cohesion, we would be forced to explain variations in cohesiveness under similar levels of structural assimilation strictly in terms of unique historical events or specific actions of political entrepreneurs. However, a convincing argument can be made that significant differences in the bases of ethnic community solidarity exist.

A critical difference between European ethnic groups that have failed to retain ethnic community solidarity and those groups, such as the Jews and the Japanese, that have maintained a high degree of solidarity is that, in contrast to the cultural orientation of peasant village life, the latter came to the United States with a strong sense of peoplehood. Castile (1981:xviii) summarizes in general theoretical terms what we will describe in specific terms in the Japanese American case:

> . . . *the* defining characteristic of a persistent people is a continuity of common identity based, Spicer suggests, on "common understandings concerning the meaning of a set of symbols." . . . The symbols may in fact change, as does all else in the adapting entity, but, as long as a continuity is maintained in the symbol system sufficient to define a collective identity separate from that of surrounding peoples, endurance occurs. . . .

One of the most salient characteristics of the Japanese immigrants at the turn of the century was their clear perception of peoplehood. By almost any standard, the Japanese were among the most homogeneous people in the world (e.g., Haglund, 1984; Nakane, 1970:141–142). Reischauer notes, for example, that as early as the seventh century, they saw themselves as a single people living in a unified nation (1981:8). By the Meiji era, the uniqueness of the Japanese people was institutionalized in the Constitution and the Imperial Rescript on Education (Ichioka, 1971). This perception of uniqueness and homogeneity is probably due in part to the long-term physical isolation of the Japanese from other peoples in the world. But, as Reischauer points out, similarly situated island peoples, such as the British, have experienced much greater social, political, and religious heterogeneity (1981:34–35; see, e.g., Hechter, 1975, for historical data on the British situation to compare with that of the Japanese). Thus, as Nakane (1970:142) observes, the Japanese have not been conditioned to the kinds of crosscutting strata in their social organization that would weaken their national identity.

In addition, by the time of the Meiji Restoration, Japanese villages were quite closely integrated with one another and intervillage mobility was common. Further, Japan was emerging as a major economic and military power in the nineteenth century. Patriotism and striving for national glory were stressed in the educational system (e.g., Nee and Wong, 1985; Smethurst, 1974).

A fundamental difference between the West and Japan is in the emphasis placed on individualism versus collectivism (e.g., Hsu, 1975; Zander, 1983). The Japanese attach much greater importance to the smooth functioning and preservation of the group as a whole compared with the interests of any given individual. Interpersonal harmony is sought above all else. Consensus is more important than either personal autonomy or abstract rules (Haglund, 1984; Nakane, 1970:10, 45–58). Kiefer observes that historically, "a basic assumption of all group interaction was that each individual had no legitimate interests which conflicted with those of the group, that group and individual interests were the same, and that person and role were considered for practical purposes identical" (1974:123).

The cultural roots of Japanese conceptions of the proper relationship between individuals and groups are found in a variant of Confucian ethics that places a high value on harmony, asceticism, and obligation (Davis, 1983). These values, in turn, have created a normative system that gives, from a Western individualistic perspective, an inordinate amount of attention to norms about interpersonal relationships, especially those concerned with the obligations of specific roles and statuses. For example, group harmony is supported by meticulous norms of deference and self-effacement (e.g., Johnson et al., 1974). Speaking of middle-class family life in postwar Japan, for instance, Kiefer (1974:119–120) observes:

Relationships between parents and children . . . tend to be intense and emotionally demonstrative until the age of about five or six. After this, they are characterized by an emotional reserve which strikes the Westerner as almost cold, but is merely careful. Older children and adults must keep their emotions under control at all times in the interest of social harmony, and discipline in this skill must begin as soon as the child is psychologically mature enough to begin learning it.

The process of maintaining group solidarity through commitment to role relationships rather than through particularistic affective ties to individuals produces a situation Kiefer terms "structural intimacy" (1971). Again, from a Western perspective, this appears to merge individual identity with the role a person plays. Its advantage is that it generally produces much more stable groups than if solidarity depended more on emotional attachments to specific individuals.

The Japanese emphasis on group harmony helps to explain what Westerners may incorrectly interpret as either false modesty or nonassertiveness. Since the underlying ethical imperative is to preserve relationships among group members, preventing embarrassment to all individuals in a group is seen as very important. Clever repartee that is difficult to respond to in a predictable, socially appropriate way is deemed undesirable and destructive to the group (e.g., Johnson, 1976; Lyman, 1977; Nomura and Barnlund, 1983; Zander, 1983).

In both traditional Japanese and Japanese American cultures there are institutionalized means for discouraging overt displays of individual power and self-aggrandizement. Status is, of course, important for individuals in both settings, as it is in all human societies. In fact, the Japanese generally are more concerned about an individual's formal ranking than are Caucasian Americans, and tailor their interpersonal interactions to fine-grained distinctions in this regard (Haglund, 1984; Nakane, 1970:25–40). These rankings, however, are established in more subtle and indirect ways than is typically the case in American society. The successful person in either traditional Japanese or Japanese American communities is one who displays, along with his or her other talents, an appropriate amount of modesty, self-effacement, and identification with the group so as not to create conflict or embarrassment (e.g., Johnson et al., 1974).

Thus, to a degree that is astounding to most American observers, the Japanese place primacy on the group, not the individual. This general orientation has survived very much intact among Japanese Americans, although its behavioral manifestations have changed and some unique forms have emerged.

A second major characteristic of Japanese social organization has been its emphasis on mutually dependent hierarchical relationships. The prototype of this arrangement is the institution of the *iemoto* ("origin of the household" or "household root"). Hsu describes the core structure of this relationship (1971:38):

> Each master has several disciples with whom he maintains mutual dependence. He commands great authority over his disciples. He owes to them the best he has to offer (livelihood, instruction, justice, social responsibility), and most of whatever he requires. This relationship and its characteristic ideas are not economic, nor political, nor militaristic, nor religious. They can be applied to any field of endeavor, whether it be running a bean paste factory or an army or a university.

Two major characteristics of the *iemoto* are relevant to the basic thesis of this book. First, it explicitly encourages the development of superior-subordinate role relationships in larger and larger social groupings. In marked contrast to the almost exclusive reliance on strong-tie cliques of family and kin found in many European peasant ethnic enclaves (see, e.g., Gans, 1982; Granovetter, 1973), the *iemoto* in traditional Japanese society connected all persons to one another through clearly defined role relationships from the emperor down to the ordinary farmer and his family (Hsu, 1971). This suggests that the Issei came to the United States with a tradition supporting the view that individuals should have associational ties outside their immediate family and kin. The modern prototype of this norm is, of course, the Japanese corporation.

Second, even though the *iemoto* is expansive in character in that it connects individuals to larger and larger social networks, it is nonetheless framed in what Hsu (1971) calls "pseudo-kinship" terms. This means that individuals experience the kinds of "structural intimacy" (Kiefer, 1971) associated with kinship in settings much larger in scope than blood kin relations. Thus, in traditional Japanese society, "although a majority of Japanese individuals have to move away from their first kinship base, their culture enables them to secure permanent circles of intimacy without moving too far away from it. And the all-inclusive and interlinking mutual dependence between members of any two levels in a large hierarchical organization has the effect of extending the feeling of intimacy beyond those situated near each other" (Hsu, 1971:38).

Thus the *iemoto* provides a basis for establishing quasi-kin ties in what Westerners typically would think of as secondary relationships. Involvement in associational life in Japanese society may be "voluntary" in the sense that individuals can choose whether to enter or leave, but once in these associations they relate to one another according to the quasi-kin principle. Hsu refers to this as "kin-tract," and describes it as "a fixed and unalterable arrangement voluntarily entered into among a group of human beings who follow a common ideology for a set of common objectives. . . . It is partly based on the kinship model so that, once fixed, the hierarchical relationships tend to be permanent, and partly based on the contract model, since the decision for entering, and occasionally for quitting a particular grouping rests with the individual" (1975:62).

We can see, then, that the structure of social relationships in traditional Japanese culture and social organization contains, almost paradoxically, a high degree of both permanence and flexibility. The permanence stems from the institutionalization of stable role relationships and the corresponding devaluing of individuality. Yet there is an enormous amount of flexibility in how such relationships may operate to meet the exigencies of specific situations. This explains, for example, how the Japanese were able to adopt significant aspects of Chinese culture and later significant aspects of Western technology and fashion without losing a sense of their own identity as a unique people (Hsu, 1975; Nakane, 1970:ix; Reischauer, 1981).

There are few signs of the hierarchical aspects of the *iemoto* still present in the contemporary Japanese American community. One reason is that the emphasis on ranking runs counter to the American norm of casual egalitarianism. Also, the small size of most Japanese American communities discourages hierarchical distinctions. Nevertheless, the quasi-kin aspects of relationships within the ethnic community are still very much in evidence. Moreover, they do not run into any resistance from the larger American culture.

The ability of the Japanese to adapt their social organizational forms to a wide variety of circumstances is reinforced by an emphasis on relativism in Japanese culture. Reischauer states that "the Japanese certainly have less of a sense of sin than Westerners or of a clear and inflexible line of demarcation between right and wrong. There are no obviously sinful areas of life. Most things seem permissible in themselves, so long as they do not do some damage in other ways" (1981:141–142).

The adaptive nature of Japanese social forms has played a role in facilitating the current high level of structural assimilation of Japanese Americans. There is no inherent contradiction in Japanese culture between maintaining a sense of distinctive "peoplehood" while adopting a variety of cultural elements from a host country. Indeed, as Reischauer points out, in traditional Japanese culture "ethics blends off into politeness and good manners" (1981:143). To be a "good Japanese" is to "fit in" and "not to make trouble." Within this context, then, it is not surprising to find that the Japanese in America have seen being a good American as an expression of being a good Japanese (Hosokawa, 1969; Lebra, 1972).

Supportive of this emphasis on harmony in Japanese social forms is the general compatibility of Japanese and middle-class American interpersonal styles. Even though the emphasis on interdependence in Japanese social relations is quite different from the much greater emphasis on personal autonomy in American culture, most Americans tend to evaluate the Japanese interpersonal style positively. This is not to say, however, that their interpersonal style has been adaptive for Japanese Americans in all situations. The less assertive Japanese approach to social interaction may hinder upward mobility, for example, in American bureaucracies (Hraba, 1979). Nevertheless, there has been little direct pressure on Japanese Americans to discard their traditional way of interacting in order to become accepted by the majority group. In short, although the Japanese, like other immigrant groups, have had to abandon many traditional practices, some of the elements most central to their survival as a distinctive ethnic community (e.g., the structure of social relationships) have essentially remained intact.

This has meant, then, that traditional forms of social organization have provided Japanese Americans with specific mechanisms for maintaining ethnic community cohesiveness in the face of pressures from both within and outside the ethnic community. A central finding in all the empirical analyses reported in subsequent chapters is that despite substantial changes in adherence to many traditional elements of Japanese culture, including major intergenerational differences in types of religious identification (i.e., Buddhist vs. Christian) and facility with the Japanese language, there is a great deal of continuity with regard to the involvement of individual Japanese Americans in ethnic community life.

VOLUNTARY ASSOCIATIONS IN JAPANESE AMERICAN COMMUNITY LIFE

One of the most important findings reported in subsequent chapters is the extent to which Japanese American ethnic community life rests on the participation of individuals in voluntary associations. Japanese Americans are much more likely to be involved in voluntary associations with fellow ethnics, ranging from mutual benefit associations to fishing clubs, than European ethnics have been at roughly equivalent stages of structural assimilation. While most European immigrant groups arrived with an almost exclusive orientation toward strong-tie relationships with family and kin, with the exception of the church, the Japanese arrived with a long tradition of involvement in associational life. Extensive networks of voluntary associations existed in the farming villages of Japan in the nineteenth and early twentieth centuries (Embree, 1939:112–157, 163–170; Norbeck, 1972). This tradition served as a template for the Issei who created a large number of self-help groups in the Japanese enclaves in California at the turn of the century (Ichihashi, 1932:220–227).

Also, in contrast to the experience of many European immigrants, the Japanese government showed considerable interest in protecting the rights of its citizens in America and in facilitating their adjustment to the New World by supporting the formation of a Japanese Association in almost every ethnic enclave of any size. Not only did they handle legal and immigration issues, but these associations also disseminated information about practical matters such as the latest techniques in scientific farming (e.g., Ichioka, 1977).

Another kind of voluntary association that helped the immigrant Japanese adapt to the exigencies of economic life in the United States was the *tanomoshi*, or rotating credit association (see Light, 1972; Miyamoto, 1939). Although this type of association was probably not as widespread as Light's (1972) book would suggest, it is important in terms of our general thesis because it was based on the kind of quasi-kin relationship described earlier (Ichioka, 1988:154). These associations were used to raise capital for small business ventures, usually for labor-intensive "ethnic enterprises," such as truck farms or grocery stores.

Essentially, the *tanomoshi* involved a group of individuals who contributed a specified amount of money on a regular basis. Someone in the group periodically was selected by drawing lots or by a bidding procedure, and this person would take the "pot" and use the money for his or her business or purchase. Given the widespread public support of discrimination against the Japanese at that time, there were few realistic legal remedies if a participant absconded with the money. Thus the real foundation of the *tanomoshi* was the trust ethnic community members had in one another. This trust was based on the quasi-kin *iemoto* principle described above. It should be noted, however, that the threat of community ostracism also acted as a powerful social control mechanism which reduced unethical behavior.

A number of *tanomoshi* still exist in the Los Angeles area, although they now serve more social than economic functions. The proliferation of Japanese American investment clubs in Southern California may be seen as an adaptation or residual form of this institution (Fugita and O'Brien, 1978; Light, 1972).

An important type of voluntary association in the Japanese American community today is the so-called area club, which is found in many rural sections of California. These clubs, such as the Lone Star Japanese Community Club, the Del Rey Friendship Society, and the North Fresno Community Club are both geographically and ethnically based. Families must either be current or former residents of the area and be Japanese or at least married to a Japanese. Sometimes this latter requirement is surreptitiously enforced through a 100 percent positive (i.e., "black ball") voting procedure. Japanese families new to the neighborhood are invited to join. Some remain members of their old clubs even after they have left the area. Most Nisei are members, and Sansei are likely to join as they start raising their own families. Typical events that the clubs sponsor include graduation parties, an Issei appreciation night, a year-end party, and dance lessons. The Nisei look upon them as good vehicles to socialize their children and their children's children in Japanese values as well as providing them with an opportunity to meet other Japanese youth. It is hoped that this will decrease the likelihood of intermarriage.

The most important voluntary associations in Japanese American communities are the churches. Despite the high degree of structural assimilation in many areas of life, most Japanese Americans who attend a church belong to a congregation whose members are of the same ethnic background (Oguri-Kendis, 1979). What is perhaps most striking about this situation is the high degree of continuity across generations and across rural and urban areas even though there are substantial differences in affiliation with Buddhist versus Christian churches. These findings are further evidence for the perpetuation of the basic principle of Japanese culture that the preservation of social relationships among group members is of fundamentally greater importance than the specific content of such relationships.

At the same time, of course, we would expect that the American experience would produce changes in aspects of traditional Japanese voluntary associations, especially given the situational sensitivity and emphasis on relativism found in Japanese culture. One important effect of living in American society has been to make it much easier for Japanese Americans to create horizontal peer relationships *within* generations in voluntary associations (cf. Nakane, 1970:59–60). In addition, the content of many of the Japanese American voluntary associations reflects a distinctly American flavor, such as the ubiquitous bowling and golfing leagues. One persistent cultural element consistent with the *iemoto* form which supports the maintenance of ethnic organizations is the emphasis on family standing in the community. This pushes individuals to accept burdensome roles in terms of time and energy commitments to ethnic organizations. Not only do the individuals want to "pay back" the community but they also want to contribute to their family's standing within the ethnic community (e.g., Suzuki, 1980). In this way, they may secure greater community acceptance for their children.

Perhaps most important, the quasi-kin style of relating is very rewarding to those who have been socialized into it. The ethnic community may be the only place where some Japanese Americans believe they can find a group-oriented, low conflict, and trusting interpersonal environment (Johnson, 1976; Watanabe, 1973).

THE STRUCTURE OF SOCIAL RELATIONSHIPS AND THE MOBILIZATION OF JAPANESE AMERICANS

In his classic work on social networks, Granovetter (1973) points out that ethnic loyalty in itself does not necessarily lead to collective mobilization. In fact, in some instances it can inhibit mobilization, as was the case in the Italian American West End of Boston. Ethnicity in this situation was a negative force with respect to collective action because it encouraged individuals to form exclusively "strong ties" within isolated cliques of families (Granovetter, 1973). One of the distinguishing features of mechanisms that structure social relationships among Japanese Americans, however, is that they tend to encourage wider and wider relationships between "quasi kin."

In effect, the whole ethnic group becomes a network of "distant relatives." This establishes, therefore, a significant potential for the development of an extensive network of social ties connecting a large number of families and cliques to one another, even among those who live in dispersed geographical areas. This gives Japanese Americans a greater capacity to make collective responses to needs as they arise. A case in point is the Nisei Farmers League (Fugita and O'Brien, 1977; O'Brien and Fugita, 1984), whose formation and effectiveness will be described in Chapter 9. In addition, Japanese and Japanese American principles for guiding social relationships also provide a set of normative principles for running voluntary associations. The value placed on minimizing public conflict and the emphasis on preserving relationships, even if it means sacrificing individual instrumental goals, clearly facilitate the adaptability of Japanese American organizations.

The mechanisms that structure Japanese American social relationships do not require a withdrawal from mainstream society. As we will see in Chapter 6, Japanese Americans participate in voluntary associations in the larger society while also participating in ethnic community voluntary associations. Thus, Japanese Americans are linked to each other and to groups in the larger society. This means, therefore, that persons in this ethnic group have a large potential set of political resources (Fugita and O'Brien, 1985). This is a point we will elaborate at length in Chapter 9.

PSYCHOLOGICAL BENEFITS AND COSTS OF SOCIAL RELATIONSHIPS IN THE JAPANESE AMERICAN COMMUNITY

Since social relationships among Japanese Americans take on a quasi-kin character, individuals feel a greater trust toward their fellow ethnics who are geographically, generationally, or areally distant than would be the case with persons in ethnic communities where relationships tend to center on strong-tie cliques. Given that all members of the ethnic group are, in effect, quasi kin, there is one less "screen" to penetrate in the movement toward interpersonal involvement. The social penetration process (Altman and Taylor, 1973) is therefore more rapid, and the speed with which meaningful relationships develop is faster.

But there are some real "costs" individuals experience as participants in these kinds of relationships. Since there is greater understanding and trust, there is also a greater sense of responsibility and obligation to other individuals and to the community as a whole. These relationships "count more" in both a positive and a negative sense. The individual Japanese

American is not only more cognizant of pressures to maintain positive relationships but is also more concerned about being embarrassed, or, if he or she steps too far out of line, of being ostracized from the ethnic community. Many Nisei, for example, were admonished by their parents about violating group norms: "They'll laugh at us." Also, because of the emphasis on harmony and mutuality in relationships, negative feelings are frequently created when particular individuals stand out even in a positive way (Nomura and Barnlund, 1983).

Moreover, the extensiveness of relationships within the ethnic community means that the negative consequences of violating group norms are very difficult to avoid. Information about deviant behavior passes quickly from one Japanese American community to another. Thus the deviant has few opportunities to escape and get a new start someplace else, unless, of course, he or she wishes to leave the ethnic community altogether. The cost of living in this ethnic community can also be seen in the comparisons Japanese Americans make between their cautious style of interpersonally relating and the way Caucasians are assumed to be better able to express their feelings or to deal with conflict in a direct fashion.

The greater potency (both positive and negative) of ethnic social relations means that ethnic community members are able to extract more costly (in both material and psychological terms) resources from fellow ethnics to meet both individual and group goals. Thus individuals feel more concerned not only about minimizing possible transgressions of community norms but also with paying back individuals or the community for past support. This suggests that a positive or negative self-image for the individual Japanese American will largely depend on the extent to which that person feels successful in meeting his or her obligations. This has significant implications for the persistence of ethnic community organizations that can capitalize on this sentiment.

To summarize, we have argued that although the history of discrimination and social isolation plays an important part in accounting for the persistence of Japanese American ethnic community life, a more complete explanation for the adaptation of ethnic community institutions *under conditions of high levels of structural assimilation* must consider the role of core Japanese cultural and social organizational elements. In the next chapter we will examine some of the ways in which these traditional elements have helped to shape the distinctive economic adaptation of the Japanese to American society.

THREE

The Petit Bourgeois Economic Accommodation

In Chapter 2 we examined how Japanese ways of structuring social relationships affected the overall accommodation of the Issei immigrants, and their descendants, to American society in the early twentieth century. This chapter will focus on how these factors affected their economic accommodation. Specifically, we will examine how characteristic ways of structuring social relationships facilitated the entrance of the Japanese into the small business or petit bourgeois niche. The Japanese, like the Jews and the Chinese, historically have been overrepresented in this type of economic activity (e.g., Goldscheider and Kobrin, 1980; Light, 1972). As is true of these other groups, the choice of this kind of economic accommodation was made in part because of their exclusion from other types of economic activity. This option, however, would not have been possible without a supportive cultural and social organizational base in the ethnic community. In turn, the experience of disproportionate involvement in the petit bourgeois niche, as well as the absence of any substantial involvement in industrial laboring-class activities, has had profound consequences for both the structural assimilation and retention of ethnic community life among Japanese Americans.

The Nature of the Petit Bourgeois Niche

Bechhofer and Elliot have pointed out that the petite bourgeoisie fall outside the traditional classification of "capitalist" or "proletariat." They define them in the following way (1981:182–183):

These are neither bourgeois nor proletarians. At the same time it is clear that they are unlike the routine white-collar workers in industry, commerce or public administration and they are different too from the bureaucratized professionals or salaried intelligentsia. The one thing they all have—the crucial thing—is petty productive property, and it is property with which they work themselves. It is their labour and very frequently that of their families and kin, that they mix with this property, and though a good many also become the employers of hired labour, the scale of that exploitation is typically very small and is an extension of, rather than a substitute for, their own labour.

Traditionally, the petite bourgeoisie were viewed as a residual category in the stratification systems of capitalist societies. It was assumed by Marx, for example, that small producers would eventually be pushed into the working class as technological development and competition drove out less efficient and weaker producers (e.g., Bottomore and Rubel, 1956:188). In certain economic activities that continue to be highly labor intensive and low in remuneration, however, the petite bourgeoisie have persisted in advanced capitalist societies (Bonacich, 1980). They remain quite strong even in some socialist and communist economies (Bechhofer and Elliot, 1981).

The petite bourgeoisie occupy a rather complex position in relation to both the working and the large capitalist classes. They are aware of their dependent status with regard to the large corporations but are also envious of the latter's success. At times, the petite bourgeoisie are mocked and at other times pandered to by those above them. During economic dislocations, the petite bourgeoisie may be praised by the upper classes because of the "buffer" function they perform in absorbing discontent from below (Blalock, 1967:79–84). They may be resented by the working class for having more material goods or for exploiting workers in their shopkeeping roles (Bonacich, 1973). At the same time, they are sometimes romanticized by the laboring classes because their economic adaptation is seen as a way of escaping the drudgery of working-class life (Mayer, 1953).

Mayer suggests that the peculiar position of the petite bourgeoisie results in strained relationships with other classes: "The lower middle class [i.e., the petite bourgeoisie] has a compliant but also strained relationship with the upper establishment, which it aspires to and resents. Its relations with those 'beneath' it—the underclass of essentially unskilled and ethnically disadvantaged trapped workers—are becoming increasingly strained as well" (1975:423).

The unique position of the petite bourgeoisie is also reflected in a constellation of values setting them apart from both the proletariat and the large capitalist classes. At the core of these values is a distinctive kind of "rugged individualism" distrustful of both big business and big labor and extolling the virtues of hard work, thrift, and achievement (e.g., Lipset, 1981:131–135; Szymanski, 1978:82–83). These values, as we will illustrate later, play a crucial role in the upward mobility and structural assimilation of persons who have grown up in petit bourgeois settings.

One body of literature, which draws its conclusions primarily from studies of white small businessmen in Europe and the United States, sees this "rugged individualism" as leading to extreme social isolation (e.g., Bechhofer and Elliot, 1981; Mayer, 1975). In Bechhofer and Elliot's words, a "loner" mentality is produced: "Most small businessmen are 'loners,' not joiners and large politically effective associations among them are rare. Resisting 'organization' becomes normative" (1981:190).

Clearly, many petit bourgeois households, such as the French bakers studied by Bertaux and Bertaux-Wiame (1981), are relatively isolated from one another. They have highly personalized relationships only with family members and the few hired workers they employ. Another body of literature, however, which draws upon the experiences of Asians and Hispanics in the United States, suggests that although most small businessmen are "rugged individualists" in the sense of subscribing to the values of hard work, achievement, and autonomy, many of them are also quite dependent on extensive social networks offering contacts and other resources indispensable to the success of their businesses (e.g., Bonacich and Modell, 1980; Light, 1972; Wilson and Portes, 1980). Two crucial features appear to distinguish this type of petite bourgeoisie from the more isolated type.

First, those petite bourgeoisie who are more socially connected are members of ethnic groups that are, or have been, in some way socially "stigmatized" and discriminated against by their respective host societies. This was the case with the Jews in Europe and the Chinese in Southeast Asia. The Japanese and Chinese in America were excluded from labor unions and management opportunities in the large corporations and public bureaucracies (Bonacich, 1973; Bonacich and Modell, 1980; Foner, 1964).

Nevertheless, as Light (1979) points out, situational constraints in themselves do not explain the disproportionate involvement of certain ethnic groups in small businesses. If restricted opportunities alone were a sufficient cause, we would expect a much greater involvement in these activities by blacks, who also have been excluded from both working-class and large capitalist positions. Light (1979) demonstrates, however, that blacks have been notably absent from such activities. Thus a second element necessary for the interdependent petite bourgeoisie or ethnic economy to emerge is the presence of particular types of cultural and social organizational forms. This is the subject of the next section.

CULTURAL ELEMENTS IN THE PETIT BOURGEOIS ACCOMMODATION

Light's (1972) classic work on ethnic involvement in petit bourgeois enterprises proposes that a key element in the success of groups like the Chinese and the Japanese was their social "trust" of fellow ethnic group members. The operation of this moral relationship is perhaps best illustrated by the presence of the *hui* and the *tanomoshi* in the Chinese and Japanese immigrant communities, respectively. Although these financial mechanisms typically did not involve large amounts of capital, the very fact that individuals were willing to lend money to fellow ethnics having little in the way of conventional collateral or other means of securing loans illustrates the depths of the social trust found in these groups (see Miyamoto, 1972, for a discussion of both the advantages and disadvantages to the individual of an economic system built on interpersonal claims).

The original source of this trust, in Light's view, was the proliferation of "ascriptive ties" found throughout the Chinese and Japanese communities (1972:60):

> Among both Chinese and Japanese, trustworthiness resided in ascriptively defined subcommunities of region and kinship. Regional and kinship ties had moral significance, in that persons thus linked

together were ethically bound to behave honorably in financial transactions. Since all Chinese and Japanese were organized into such ascriptively bordered moral communities, the two Oriental communities could depend on extensive social trust in the community at large. This social trust enabled the rotating credit associations to attain the flexibility in formation and the large size necessary to [sic] commercially useful credit agencies. Had the Oriental communities been composed of isolated individuals, they would not have been able to employ rotating credit, since isolated individuals lack the necessary social trust. Since, however, both the Chinese and Japanese communities were subordered on the basis of ascriptive ties infused with moral significance, the proportion of social isolates was quite low.

In the case of the Japanese, one of the initial bases of ascriptive ties, the *kenjinkai* (province) of the immigrant's origins, was gradually weakened as the Nisei influence in the Japanese communities increased during and after World War II (Spickard, 1983). But, as noted in Chapter 2, the Japanese communities retained intricate networks of interconnected families so that the principle of ethnic honor, a Japanese group-based standard capable of disciplining individual conduct, remained to ensure the flow of labor and capital into the "moral economy" (cf. Levine and Rhodes, 1981:10). There are many well-documented struggles between Nisei and Issei over what the former saw as too "parochial" forms of ascription, but the younger generation never sought to diminish the interconnectedness of families and kin within the ethnic community. They retained a more general form of ascriptiveness in which Japaneseness and family remained central while provincial ties receded in importance (Light, 1972:178).

The cultural values highlighted earlier played three overlapping and yet analytically distinct roles in the formation of petit bourgeois enterprises among the Japanese in the United States. First, the strong sense of obligation, commitment, and family honor found in the ethnic enclave provided the proper motivation for family members to tolerate the long hours necessary to be successful in petit bourgeois enterprises. In businesses like restaurants or truck farms, for example, the only way a family with little capital could make money was for all of its members to contribute enormous numbers of hours at what would be considered, in a pure wage-per-hour sense, quite exploitive. For the individual, the advantages of this "exploitation" were the strong obligations of other family members to help him or her in other situations (Benedict, 1968).

The second way in which the cultural values found in the ethnic community were important in the development of petit bourgeois enterprises among groups like the Japanese, the Chinese, and the Jews was to supply the social trust necessary to ensure relatively harmonious relationships between different ethnic enterprises that depended on one another in the various phases of the production and distribution process. Wirth (1928), for example, noted that a central element in the survival of Jewish entrepreneurs in Chicago's ghetto was the propensity of Jews to buy and sell from one another. Bonacich (1973) notes a similar process among Jews in the clothing business in New York. Social connectedness was especially important given the small size and risks associated with these types of enterprises.

Among the Japanese growers, packers, shippers, and retailers in the Southern California truck farming market, this social interconnectedness resulted in what Modell (1977) terms a "vertically integrated ethnic economy" (see also Bloom and Riemer, 1949:92–96). Moreover, in many trades, the Japanese were horizontally integrated. For example, ethnic farmers' cooperatives bought supplies at favorable prices, attempted to control labor rates in the local area, and regulated within-group competition (e.g., Ichioka, 1971).

The third, and final, way in which the cultural values of the ethnic community were important in the development of petit bourgeois enterprises was in relationships between ethnic and nonethnic businessmen and consumers. The cultural admonition to protect the honor of one's family and that of the Japanese people became a very important lever Japanese businessmen used to minimize unscrupulous practices by fellow ethnics and to prevent giving Japanese businessmen a bad name. In this way, a positive united front was presented to outsiders. This was especially important when the Japanese were involved in economic conflicts with other groups (e.g., Miyamoto, 1939; Tsuchida, 1978).

Light (1972) has suggested that culturally distinct ethnic groups have an advantage in certain small businesses. This "protected market" thesis points out that only fellow members of the ethnic group can cater to the unique tastes of the group with regard to products such as foodstuffs. While this is certainly true, it cannot explain the overall success of groups such as the Japanese. After all, the economic niche the Japanese most often entered was truck farming, which involved mostly vegetables and berries (e.g., Iwata, 1962). Not only was the produce geared to the tastes of the majority group, but the overall output was of such size as to require sales to the larger society. The Japanese market was much too small. The same was true of their efforts in the fishing business. Even in the restaurant line, most of their operations emphasized low-priced "American" food.

JAPANESE AMERICAN INVOLVEMENT IN CALIFORNIA AGRICULTURE

Bonacich (1973) and Bonacich and Modell (1980) have correctly pointed out that the full story of the petit bourgeois accommodation of groups like the Japanese, the Chinese, and the Jews must include a consideration of situational factors that make other kinds of economic adaptations less feasible. These factors played a major role in the involvement of the Japanese in California agriculture at the end of the nineteenth and the early part of the twentieth centuries.

The largest influx of Japanese immigrants to the West Coast occurred from 1900 to 1918. Most of these persons became farm workers (e.g., Iwata, 1962). The proximate reasons for farm owners bringing farm workers from Japan were the Chinese Exclusion Act of 1882, which eliminated a traditional source of cheap labor, and the movement of white laborers into nonagricultural jobs. At this time, labor-intensive agriculture was expanding rapidly because of the development of refrigerated railroad cars, federally subsidized irrigation projects, and new and more effective agricultural marketing organizations (e.g., Fugita and O'Brien, 1978; Fuller, 1940). There also were problems in Japan that encouraged emigration during this period, including considerable political instability and a harsh tax policy that fell particularly hard on the agricultural sector. Thus U.S. farm labor wages, although low compared with other sectors of the American economy, were substantially higher than those in Japan. Moreover, the Japanese laborers saw themselves as "sojourners" merely spending enough time in the New World to accumulate capital and return to their native land (e.g., Bonacich, 1973; Fugita and O'Brien, 1978).

Nevertheless, the movement of individual Japanese laborers into tenant and leasing arrangements, a form of petit bourgeois enterprise, was hastened because the laborers could not achieve upward mobility through other routes. The Japanese were not able to move into management or government bureaucracies because of language difficulties and widespread discrimination (e.g., Hraba, 1979:332). As Bonacich and Modell (1980) point out, in many instances even the second generation Nisei were forced to work in ethnic enterprises because of discrimination in mainstream occupations. There are, for example, many documented cases of college-educated Nisei unable to find jobs in engineering, teaching, or other vocations for which they had trained. Reluctantly, they went back to the ethnic farm or fruit stand to make a living (e.g., Ichihashi, 1932:356–358).

In addition, the Japanese were largely excluded from the American labor movement. The American Federation of Labor (AFL) was blatantly racist. After winning a long and bitter strike in Oxnard in 1903, for example, the Japanese and Mexican workers applied for membership in the AFL, but Samuel Gompers replied to the leadership, "Your union must guarantee that it will under no circumstances accept membership of any Chinese or Japanese" (Foner, 1964). The radical Industrial Workers of the World (IWW) tried to recruit Asian laborers but lost its effectiveness as a union after the mass arrests during the "red scare" of 1917 (Labor Unions in American Agriculture, 1945:58; Yoneda, 1967, 1971).

Thus, in some respects, the Japanese became participants in an ethnic economy because they had few alternatives. In fact, both Light (1972) and Bonacich and Modell (1980) point out that at least by the time of the second generation's maturity, many Japanese Americans felt resentful about their forced participation in ethnic petit bourgeois activities. Bonacich and Modell describe this situation the following way (1980:85–86):

> The Nisei were highly motivated to obtain a college education, and they hoped, after thus training themselves, to secure white collar positions, particularly in the professions and at managerial levels in general-community concerns. On attempting to gain employment in the non-ethnic world, however, they faced racism and discrimination. Consequently, they were forced back into seeking work in the firms run by their parents and their parents' colleagues. Now, not only were they overeducated for the menial jobs available, but they were forced to remain in unfortunate dependency to the same people upon whom they had always been dependent.

Nevertheless, the critical point in terms of understanding the Japanese American experience is their capacity to exploit successfully the few opportunities to be found in the petit bourgeois sector. Discrimination and other structural constraints, in themselves, do not explain the success of the Japanese or, for that matter, the success of the Chinese or the Jews in these enterprises. As Light (1979) persuasively argues, it is the capacity of these groups to establish and maintain social organizational arrangements based on social trust that permits them to succeed in small business. In Wilson and Portes's (1980) view, groups successful in establishing extensive petit bourgeois enterprises are able to use the concentration of ethnics in "enclaves" to their advantage. By collectively controlling certain industries, these groups can create some of the same monopolistic advantages normally found only in the "center" economy.

During the early part of the twentieth century, the Japanese in California were able to produce just such center economy advantages. They were able to adapt their traditional social organization to the exigencies of American intensive farming. In most farming areas, for example, cooperatives were established, occasionally with the the aid of the Japanese government, to pass on information about new farming techniques, to control labor rates, to purchase implements and supplies from wholesalers at cheaper prices, and to serve as collective marketing mechanisms (Liu, 1976; Yoder, 1936). In addition, the *tanomoshi* sometimes allowed individuals to obtain capital when the banks discriminated against them (Ichioka, 1977; Light, 1972:29).

The extensive network of ascriptive ties in the ethnic community became a very powerful source of both vertical and horizontal integration between individual ethnic entrepreneurs and their families. In agriculture this meant that the Japanese were able to control a large portion of the production of certain vegetables and berries and to set the wages paid to their farm workers. For example, a Japanese farmer would deal with a Japanese haulman who would deal with a Japanese packer-shipper who would deal with a Japanese fruit stand operator. Other examples of horizontal integration were found in the shoe repair, laundry, and gardening businesses. Japanese guilds in these fields not only regulated internal competition among the ethnic entrepreneurs in areas such as rates and territories but also organized collective self-defense efforts (e.g., Modell, 1977:113–120).

Perhaps the most impressive manifestations of the ability of the Japanese community to support ethnic businesses were found in its responses to strikes by farm workers. Although there were some attempts by Japanese farm workers to organize unions, and even historical accounts of a socialist union, the Fresno Domei Kai (Fresno Labor League) (Ichioka, 1971), the ethnic community was largely successful in preventing individual Japanese laborers from participating in these organizations when they were not otherwise prohibited by racism. For instance, in 1937 the white food clerks union in Los Angeles tried to organize Japanese workers but failed. Subsequently, Japanese-owned stores were blacklisted and picketed by the union (Modell, 1969).

When Japanese farmers hired farm laborers, usually Mexicans, to pick their berries or other crops, the Japanese community was sometimes called upon to back up the farmers in labor disputes. A classic illustration of this occurred in the El Monte Berry Strike of 1933. Japanese American youths were excused from school, and they, along with friends and relatives of the growers, came out to help harvest the crops when the laborers left the fields. Most of the major Japanese organizations, such as the Japanese Associations, the Little Tokyo Businessman's Association, and the local Japanese American Citizens League (JACL) chapters, supported the growers (Fugita and O'Brien, 1978; Hoffman, 1973; Lopez, 1970; Modell, 1977:122–123; O'Brien and Fugita, 1982; Spaulding, 1934; Wollenberg, 1972). A similar ethnic community response occurred in the Venice Celery Strike of 1936 (Tsuchida, 1978). More recently, as we will describe in greater detail in Chapter 9, the ethnic community played a much less unequivocal but nonetheless important role in the lobbying efforts of the Nisei Farmers League (NFL) in the Central Valley of California in the 1970s (Fugita and O'Brien, 1977, 1978; O'Brien and Fugita, 1984).

Numerous writers have noted that the petite bourgeoisie possess values differing in significant ways from those of their fellow citizens who are either working class or grande bourgeoisie. Bechhofer and Elliot (1981:193), for example, observe that there is a very strong association between the "moral economy" of the petit bourgeois experience and what today would be considered "right wing" values, including the following:

> . . . the urge to "roll back the state," to allow market forces not government intervention to shape economic activity; hence the opposition to organized labour depicted by the less sophisticated as preventing the establishment of free contracts between employers and employees, by those with a broader understanding as "necessary," even as "valuable," but now in need of some reform; hence too the distaste for big business and its capacity to squeeze subsidies and concessions from governments. In all this the small businessman becomes a symbol representing, it is claimed, the virtues of an old order to which we

must return if our economic fortunes are to mend and our society and polity be restored to health.

Other scholars have found that this penchant for looking backward has resulted in a disproportionately large petit bourgeois support for right wing, even fascist, movements. Examples here include the small shopkeepers' support of Hitler, their rallying behind Senator Joseph McCarthy in the 1950s, and their support of the so-called radical right movement in the early 1960s (Lipset, 1981:143–148). Our own research on the Nisei Farmers League, a contemporary organization started by small, independent Japanese American farmers in California, reveals a similar right-wing outlook (see Chapter 9; Fugita and O'Brien, 1977, 1978; O'Brien and Fugita, 1984).

Nevertheless, the values produced by the petit bourgeois experience, such as hard work, sacrifice, and thrift, also facilitate the upward mobility of subsequent generations (e.g., Bechhofer and Elliot, 1981). Petit bourgeois parents pass these values on to their children partly through role modeling and reinforcement, but more important is the children's participation in the ethnic enterprise itself. Here they directly experience the connection between work and the family unit's economic well-being (Bland et al., 1978).

Benedict (1968) observes that family firms are a rational way to do business in a developing economy, which is where the petit bourgeois niche is most frequently made. The children's experience in this setting provides them with a viable template for success even if, as is usually the case, they choose to pursue careers outside the labor-intensive small shop or truck farming situation. The role relationships and interactional patterns in the family-owned ethnic enterprise encourage trust and a sense of reciprocal obligation between members of the firm, and provide individuals with larger incentives for success. Finally, the capital generated in the business frequently provides a resource the children may use to promote their careers; for example, by paying for college or professional school education.

The mutual support systems found in the network of Japanese American truck farms manifested the kinds of "efficiencies" to which we have just referred. Not only the family but the whole ethnic community played a part in the development of tangible organizational mechanisms as well as the reinforcement of the petit bourgeois values of hard work, trust of family and kinsmen, and the desire for occupational mobility (Light, 1972:62–80).

Once the petit bourgeois niche had been successfully created by the Issei, they were anxious not to lose it (Modell, 1977:135–136). This is illustrated by a 1935 oratorical contest designed and pushed by the Issei to encourage the young Nisei to continue in farming. The name of the contest was "Japanese in Agriculture." Eleven Japanese American Citizens League districts in Southern California from San Luis Obispo to San Diego held preliminary contests in their local communities to prepare for the finals in Los Angeles. The latter was a major community event attended by at least 800 people and received heavy coverage in the local vernacular press (*Rafu Shimpo*, 1935).

The values reinforced by the petit bourgeois experience have produced, in successive generations of ethnic groups like the Jews, the Japanese, and the Chinese, rates of educational attainment much higher than those of groups involved in other types of economic accommodation, even when the educational backgrounds of parents are considered (Bland et al., 1978; Goldscheider and Kobrin, 1980). The strong family and community ties characteristic of the petit bourgeois groups also serve to inhibit juvenile delinquency and other deviant activities, further encouraging mobility among persons in these groups (Fujimoto, 1975; Kitano, 1976:157–158; Light, 1972:187–189; Modell, 1977:85–86).

Paradoxically, then, although the ethnically based petit bourgeois experience approximates the extreme case of group centeredness, insofar as the "moral economy" is based on institutionalized feelings of obligations to fellow ethnics, the values learned in this type of milieu facilitate individual mobility in subsequent generations. Thus, when the opportunity structure becomes more open for these groups, as it did for the Japanese after World War II, they tend to take advantage of the more attractive occupational opportunities in the larger society. A natural consequence of this mobility, then, is greater structural assimilation. In addition, having the option of this type of mobility means that ethnic group members do not have to utilize the kinds of collective movements that generate intensive conflict with majority group persons. This contrasts with the case of American blacks, who, lacking an institutionalized system for economic cooperation and the petit bourgeois infrastructure, as well as facing more severe discrimination than most petit bourgeois groups, have had to use civil rights protest and affirmative action programs, which frequently result in resentment on the part of working- and middle-class whites (see, e.g., Glazer, 1975; Killian, 1975:114–118; Wilson, 1980:116–120).

Clearly, then, the petit bourgeois accommodation has contributed significantly to the high rates of upward mobility among Japanese Americans, especially their disproportionate involvement in the professions and in middle-level corporate or government bureaucracies (Levine and Montero, 1973). At one level, this upward mobility provides a necessary, but not sufficient, condition for certain kinds of structural assimilation into the larger society. A college education, for example, increases a person's understanding of the cultural symbols and feelings of self-efficacy conducive to participation in voluntary associations in the larger society as well as involvement in core culture occupations (e.g., Hraba, 1979:189; Smith, 1975; Verba and Nie, 1972). In addition, middle-class and upper middle-class occupations provide the material resources for individual members of the ethnic group to buy homes in predominantly white suburbs. All of these effects, in turn, produce the social propinquity that increases the likelihood of intimate forms of assimilation such as intermarriage.

Nevertheless, there is no a priori reason why upward educational or occupational mobility must necessarily lead to higher levels of structural assimilation. Many Orthodox Jews in New York, for example, become highly educated and enter professional careers and yet elect to remain almost totally immersed, both geographically and socially, in an ethnic ghetto (Gendrot and Turner, 1983). In a similar fashion, Chinese merchants throughout Southeast Asia have often separated themselves from the host societies in which they work, while adopting "protective coloration" (e.g., Bonacich, 1973; Coughlin, 1960:11).

In the case of Japanese Americans, however, upward mobility has been associated with high levels of structural assimilation. Following the World War II internment of this ethnic group, most discriminatory barriers against them were removed and the Nisei and Sansei capitalized on their new occupational opportunities to build middle-class lives. In most instances this meant moving into Caucasian neighborhoods and associating with majority group members in several spheres of life (Fujimoto, 1975; Hirschman and Wong, 1981; Kitano, 1976; Montero, 1977, 1978, 1980). Most revealing in this respect are the high rates of intermarriage between Japanese Americans and non-Asians (Kitano et al., 1984).

Ironically, the war with Japan ultimately increased the pace of structural assimilation of Japanese Americans in that it disrupted the insular occupational and geographic patterns of the ethnic ghettos. Most, but by no means all, of the Nisei leadership made a decision to respond to the wartime incarceration with—at least on the surface—a "100 percent

American" attitude. This facilitated the entry of Japanese Americans into the mainstream of American society following the war (e.g., Spickard, 1983). Especially important in this regard were the young Japanese American men in the concentration camps who volunteered for the much decorated all-Japanese 100th Battalion and 442nd Regimental Combat Team (Wilson and Hosokawa, 1980:235–244).

THE PETIT BOURGEOIS EXPERIENCE AND THE RETENTION OF ETHNICITY

The petit bourgeois-based ethnic economy, particularly when it is a reaction to blocked opportunities in other job settings, encourages the maintenance of ethnic ties. In its most fully developed horizontally and vertically integrated forms, it creates tightly woven interdependencies between individuals and families. Indeed, from the structuralist point of view, it is this economic interdependency that is at the root of ethnic solidarity (Bonacich, 1972; Bonacich and Modell, 1980:257–258; Modell, 1977:135–136).

Our view of these matters, however, is most compatible with Light's (1972, 1979) and is different in emphasis from that of the structuralists. We believe that it is the prior solidarity of the ethnic group, manifested in its cultural and social organizational traditions, that makes the petit bourgeois accommodation possible in the first place. At the same time, we recognize that the petit bourgeois experience itself plays a crucial role in institutionalizing the ethnic community in the New World. Put simply, the petit bourgeois tradition not only encourages a great deal of interaction between ethnic members but leaves with those who have experienced it an interpretive framework of rewarding interaction with fellow ethnics. Ethnicity, then, is not merely an ideal to be preserved but rather a pattern of social networks that accomplish specific objectives. This kind of experience occurs to some extent in all ethnic groups, but it is much greater in petit bourgeois groups because of the long history of economic interdependencies between individuals and families.

Moreover, a tradition of a petit bourgeois-based ethnic economy gives a contemporary ethnic group the significant advantage of having had successful experiences in developing and maintaining voluntary associations. This leaves the ethnic community with a complex infrastructure that remains even when most of its members have left the small capitalist niche. Reitz (1980) has demonstrated how this "organizational momentum" significantly increases ethnic group solidarity.

Finally, the petit bourgeois accommodation is less likely to produce the ethnic mobility trap often found in nonpetit bourgeois ethnic groups. In many such groups, in order for individuals to achieve upward mobility they are placed in the position of eschewing traditional "ethnic peasant values." Historically this was the case, for example, in many of the European ethnic enclaves in the nineteenth and early twentieth centuries. The second generation often felt forced to give up traditional ethnic ways of looking at the world in order to better "fit in" to the mainstream society (see, e.g., Thomas and Znaniecki, 1927; Whyte, 1981). It is usually only in the third generation of these groups that the now structurally assimilated individuals want to regain their ethnicity (cf. Novak, 1972). However, the ethnicity they reassert, although clearly an important part of their self-identity (Alba, 1981; Alba and Chamlin, 1983; Gans, 1979), usually consists of little in the way of actual involvement in an ethnic community in a behavioral sense (Goering, 1971; Roche, 1982).

Ethnic groups that historically have been disproportionately involved in petit bourgeois activities, however, are fundamentally different. While successive generations may struggle with prior ones over some traditional values, such as language use, there remains a fundamental continuity in the constellation of core values pertaining to the petit bourgeois ethic. These values are not only consistent with but reinforce the collectivistic community concepts that were crucial in establishing the initial economic and social accommodation of the first generation. Subsequently, they become an important source of social mobility and structural assimilation for the second and third generations if the opportunity structure is at least moderately open.

Therefore, our basic argument is that there will be a greater degree of continuity in the meaning of ethnicity in successive generations of Japanese Americans than is typically found across generations in many other ethnic groups. Scholars viewing intergenerational ethnicity retention among Japanese Americans from an assimilationist perspective generally have focused on the persistence of what we would see as more peripheral cultural content, such as facility with the Japanese language or membership in the Buddhist church (the latter being seen as a more traditional expression of Japaneseness than belonging to a Christian denomination) (Connor, 1977; Feagin and Fujitaki, 1972:89; Levine and Rhodes, 1981; Montero, 1977, 1978). The structuralists, such as Bonacich and Modell (1980), also focus on the decline in adherence to these aspects of ethnicity among successive generations of Japanese Americans, although the causal mechanism they emphasize is the lesser role of the petit bourgeois accommodation. In our view, however, both these perspectives fail to understand that a central feature of Japanese American ethnicity is the preservation of social relationships, and on this score there is a remarkable degree of continuity across generations. The empirical support for this view will be found in subsequent chapters, which describe our survey findings.

FOUR

The California
Survey

The origins of the California-based survey of Japanese Americans conducted in 1979–80 are found in the earlier work of one of the co-authors of this book, Stephen Fugita. He became interested in a conflict between the predominantly Mexican, Mexican American, and Filipino United Farm Workers Union and the Japanese American-dominated Nisei Farmers League (NFL) in the Fresno area of the Central Valley of California in the early 1970s (for descriptions of the UFW-NFL conflict, see Chapter 9 of this work as well as Fugita, 1978; Fugita and O'Brien, 1977; Fugita and O'Brien, 1978; and O'Brien and Fugita, 1984). The conflict erupted when the UFW, under the leadership of Cesar Chavez, made a concerted effort to organize farm workers on ranches in the Fresno area, including those owned by Japanese Americans. The Nisei Farmers League emerged as a growers' response to the UFW organizing campaign. The organization first focused on counterpicketing and later became involved in political lobbying efforts in a controversial state referendum in 1976 in which the UFW and its allies were seeking to gain additional money from the state legislature to fund the California Agricultural Labor Relations Board (ALRB). A coalition of agricultural interests, which included the NFL as a major participant, was successful in defeating the referendum. The president of the NFL, Harry Kubo, was head of this statewide growers' public relations and lobbying organization.

Clearly, the Nisei Farmers League was an economic interest group engaged in a struggle with another interest group. Nevertheless, there were intense debates within several Japanese American communities in California as well as in other parts of the country about the appropriate role of Japanese Americans in the conflict. Significantly, the UFW-NFL controversy surfaced during the period when some third generation Japanese Americans, particularly on West Coast college campuses, were involved in movements to establish and develop Asian American studies programs, similar to the ethnic studies programs created in response to pressures from blacks and Mexican Americans (e.g., Murase, 1976). This movement used symbols linking Asian Americans to the struggles of "third world people of color." This ran head-on into the conservative "defense of private property" and antiunion views of the Nisei Farmers League. While the activists on the campuses were attempting to create a new Asian American identity emphasizing shared interests with third world peoples, the Nisei Farmers League was stressing the need for Japanese Americans to support Japanese American farmers against a union dominated by persons whose roots are very close to the third world. Particularly irksome to the NFL growers were the public displays of support for Cesar Chavez by Japanese Americans they saw as "uninformed urban liberals" (Fugita and O'Brien, 1977).

The controversy between the Nisei Farmers League and the third world-oriented college students and the liberals became quite heated in the Japanese American press and in meetings of a number of local chapters of the Japanese American Citizens League (JACL). Indeed, a cursory examination of what was appearing in print during this period would show that the Japanese American community was experiencing a good deal of intergenerational as well as interareal (i.e., between rural spokesmen supportive of the NFL and urban Japanese Americans with more liberal, pro-UFW sympathies) conflict (Fugita and O'Brien, 1977; O'Brien and Fugita, 1984).

The idea of conducting a survey of a cross section of representative Japanese American communities in California emerged during the authors' ethnographic and historical analyses of the controversy surrounding the NFL-UFW struggle. Specifically, we wanted to know if, in fact, ordinary Japanese Americans experienced conflicts between ethnic loyalties and their sympathies for the struggles of other minorities. If such conflicts occurred, we reasoned, they would most certainly surface in the NFL–UFW issue. Further, we hypothesized that generational and areal factors would shape individuals' responses to the issue.

As it turned out, our data did not reveal the kinds of "cross pressures" we had anticipated. Nevertheless, the study had called for a research design that not only addressed significant social, psychological, and political dimensions but also captured the generational and areal diversity of Japanese American communities in California. This diversity, along with the required broad scope of the study, permitted us to address the question of the viability of ethnic community life.

THE AREAS SAMPLED

As a general site for research on Japanese Americans, no single state could be as representative as California. It contains the largest portion (37.5 percent) of the Japanese American population in the United States (U.S. Bureau of the Census, 1988: table 2), followed closely by Hawaii (34.2 percent) (U.S. Bureau of the Census, 1988: table 2), and has played a historical role in Japanese immigration and community development (see, e.g., Ichihashi, 1932). In addition, the state contains the diversity of community contexts within which persons in this ethnic group currently live, ranging from urban to rural settings.

Anyone who is familiar with Japanese American community life in California will be quick to point out that each community has a unique history. Thus any selection of individual communities from those available in the state is bound to contain some biases. When we were working on our sampling design, for example, some of our consultants urged that we also include a subsample from Orange County, thus ensuring that we would interview "yuppie" Japanese Americans. Limited resources prevented us from drawing additional interviews from this area.

Nonetheless, the areas selected do reflect a diversity of the urban, suburban, and rural social contexts in which Japanese Americans currently live. The two areas sampled in the Central Valley, Fresno and Sacramento, were large enough in geographic area, essentially county units, to include many third generation Sansei who had moved from areas where their parents lived. The most serious selective migration bias is likely to have occurred in Gardena. Our suspicion is that the high concentration of Japanese Americans and Japanese nationals in this distinctively ethnic area may contain, on average, less assimilation-oriented individuals who have opted for more cultural and interpersonal contact with their fellow ethnics than would be true of the group as a whole.

Fresno

The first area selected was at the center of the NFL-UFW conflict: Fresno and Fresno County in the Central Valley of California. This region has a distinctive rural atmosphere, reflecting its status as the most productive agricultural county in the United States (California Department of Food and Agriculture, 1975), accounting for a substantial portion of the country's grapes and tree fruits. Also, since agriculture in this area is labor intensive, as opposed to capital intensive as in the Midwest and some other parts of California, there is a large farm labor population. At various times this population has consisted of Arabs, "Arkies," Chinese, Filipinos, Hindus, Japanese, Mexicans, and "Okies." The presence of farm laborers and their families in the Fresno area is very visible to even the casual observer. The large population of Mexicans and Mexican Americans as well as Japanese, Armenian, and other ethnics gives the area a distinctive ethnic complexion which is perhaps somewhat surprising to the student of ethnicity from the East or Midwest who is used to finding "ethnics" in cities and WASPS in the countryside.

The first Japanese came to the Fresno area in the early 1880s, working primarily as grape pickers. They gravitated to farm labor because of their agricultural experience in Japan and the need for a cheap and transitory labor force in the Valley (Iwata, 1962). The first generation (Issei) made up about 60 percent of the grape harvesters in the Fresno area during the early part of the twentieth century (U.S. Immigration Commission, 1911). They and their offspring, the Nisei, moved quite rapidly from farm laborers to farm tenants and finally, in many instances, to farm owners. Many Japanese American farmers in the Central Valley lost their land during the World War II evacuation, but a substantial number of descendants of the immigrants still operate farms today (Fugita and O'Brien, 1977, 1978; O'Brien and Fugita, 1984). The size of most Japanese American farms in the area today, however, is relatively small compared with the many huge corporate agribusiness operations found in the Valley. The mean size of farms of the members of the Nisei Farmers League, for example, was 53 acres in 1976, while the average size of all

California farms in 1975 was 571 acres (California Department of Food and Agriculture, 1975; Fugita and O'Brien, 1977).

Today, the city of Fresno contains the remnants of a once thriving Japantown, or Nihonmachi, in the central business district. Shops, restaurants, and hotels catering to a Japanese clientele developed in this section of town at the turn of the century. At its peak, Nihonmachi consisted of 187 Japanese businesses, providing a migrant laborer or farmer virtually all he might need in the way of services, goods, and recreation. Following World War II, the Japanese did not concentrate in the area nearly as much as before the war, in large measure because of the War Relocation Authority's (WRA) policy of dispersing Japanese Americans to reduce the chances of rekindling anti-Japanese sentiment (Albert, 1980:114–115; Myer, 1971; Starn, 1986). Later, construction of a freeway through the area and the increased opportunities for Japanese to find better housing elsewhere contributed to the further decline of Nihonmachi.

Nevertheless, a number of businesses remain. A large Buddhist Church, which serves as the mother church to the numerous temples in the small towns surrounding Fresno, remains very active, as does the Nikkei Service Center of the Japanese American Citizens League, which administers a hot lunch program for elderly Issei and provides a setting in which they can socialize and participate in cultural activities. In addition, this area still has a Japanese department store, hardware store, two service stations, a fish market, a supermarket, flower shops, barbershops, and restaurants, as well as some newer businesses recently started by Japanese nationals.

Japanese Americans are a relatively small proportion (1.26 percent) of the population of Fresno County (6,471 out of a total population of 514,621), which contains significant numbers of blacks, Mexican Americans, Armenians, Scandinavians, and other Asian groups (U.S. Bureau of the Census, 1983b: table P-7).

Prior to and during World War II, relationships between the local Japanese American population and other residents of Fresno County were often strained, and at the time of the evacuation clearly abrasive. During the initial resettlement period, several violent incidents took place in the area (e.g., Daniels, 1962:159–160). The postwar period in the main, however, has been characterized by the absence of rancorous conflict. The Japanese American population is relatively small and is widely dispersed throughout the area.

Gardena

To provide a basis of comparison of Japanese American community support for the NFL, we also selected a sample from an urban setting in the
greater Los Angeles area. The city of Gardena, approximately 15 miles
south of downtown Los Angeles in the Southbay region, contains the
largest concentration of persons of Japanese ancestry outside of Hawaii.
In the very small geographical area that constitutes the city, 5.3 square
miles, Japanese Americans make up 21.5 percent of the population,
which also includes a substantial number of whites (35.7 percent), blacks
(21.9 percent), and Mexican Americans (15.4 percent). Japanese Americans make up over 30 percent of the population in three of the census
tracts in Gardena (Gardena Special Census, 1978).

Japanese have lived in Gardena almost as long as they have in Fresno.
The first immigrants settled there in 1902 to grow strawberries. By 1907
there were 253 Japanese living there, most of whom were directly or
indirectly involved in agriculture. By the advent of World War II, the
crop rotation requirements of strawberries had encouraged most of the
Japanese farmers to switch to more diversified truck farming (Mason,
1969).

Following the World War II incarceration, rapid urbanization, rising
land costs, and the difficulty of obtaining capital dissuaded most Japanese Americans from returning to truck farming. The majority went
into the gardening and nursery businesses as well as entering the rapidly
expanding industrial and public service sectors of the greater Los Angeles economy.

Although strictly speaking Gardena is a suburb and its Japanese American population largely middle class, it has a distinctive urban ethnic
ambiance which is dominated by Japanese American cultural symbols
and artifacts. Visitors enter the city through a Japanese arch or "tori
gate." Once inside the city, one is constantly made aware of its Japanese
character by a proliferation of Japanese shops, grocery stores, gas stations, and insurance agencies. Even the local McDonald's has a Japanese
motif.

In addition, Japanese nationals who come to work in Southern California frequently live in Gardena or shop in its many stores owned by
Japanese Americans. Although there is little informal interaction between
Japanese nationals and Japanese Americans, the financial resources of the
former have facilitated the development of numerous local Japanese

American businesses. Recently, for example, a Japanese motif shopping mall, Pacific Square, was built in part with Japanese national capital but is operated by Japanese Americans. It serves both Japanese Americans and Japanese nationals.

Gardena contains many Japanese churches as well as the large (over 5,000 members) and influential Japanese Cultural Institute. There are numerous judo clubs, kendo classes, investment clubs, retirement centers, cultural lectures and centers, senior citizen apartments, Boy Scout troops, athletic leagues, and VFWs that have a dominant Japanese American membership or cultural orientation.

A striking feature of life in Gardena is the extent to which a person can become absorbed in a Japanese American lifestyle. One can go to school with other Japanese, have exclusively Japanese friends, and easily find a Japanese mate. One can worship with a Japanese congregation, work in a Japanese store, have one's children play in a Japanese baseball league, take dancing lessons with other Japanese Americans, buy a house from a Japanese realtor, and have one's car repaired in a Japanese garage.

Gardena has a "Japanese ghetto" reputation, and those Japanese who grew up there and elect not to leave for predominantly Caucasian suburbs as well as those who choose to move into the area probably prefer greater ethnic exclusivity. Among the communities in the survey, the Gardena Japanese American community comes closest to Fischer's characterization of the urban ethnic subculture (Fischer, 1975, 1976:35–38, 1982:202–208). Finally, because of their numbers and cohesiveness, Japanese Americans have been able to elect fellow ethnics to mayoral and city council positions. In addition, informal and formal networks in the ethnic community provide a mechanism for individuals to have political influence in larger legislative bodies.

Sacramento

The final area in the survey initially was selected because it was almost the same distance from Fresno as Gardena (although in the opposite direction) but was still within the Central Valley (at its northern end). More relevant for the purpose of this study is that Sacramento in many ways can be considered "halfway" between Gardena and Fresno on the rural-urban continuum.

As the center of state government, Sacramento is more cosmopolitan than Fresno. Although there are significant farming operations in the area, the major source of employment for persons living in the city and its suburbs is government offices. Sacramento is essentially a middle-class city with mostly quiet, tree-lined streets. Since it is only 80 miles from San Francisco and has a sizable white-collar population, it has developed many middle-class urban amenities. Still, the relatively moderate pace of life in this city is much more like that of a midwestern city such as Columbus or Indianapolis than one of the major coastal cities.

The Japanese arrived in Sacramento in the early 1880s. By 1910, 1,437 persons of Japanese extraction lived in the city itself and 3,874 in Sacramento County. By 1930 there were 3,347 residing in the city and 8,814 in the county. These numbers, compared with those in other areas of California, represented a substantial concentration of Japanese, and this contributed to the vehement anti-Japanese sentiment in the area prior to World War II. This attitude was a continuation of the nativist fears of an "oriental menace" that were expressed during the earlier Chinese immigration to the area (Daniels, 1969:18, 24).

The first area where the Japanese immigrants lived in Sacramento is now the site of the Capital Mall. The first businesses, a boarding house and two hotels, were started in 1891. By 1911 there were 209 Japanese businesses in Sacramento, most of them located in the small area known as Japantown (U.S. Immigration Commission, 1911). Individual Japanese could have virtually all their material and social needs met within this ethnic enclave. Thus the turn-of-the-century Japanese section of Sacramento, like other large Japanese American enclaves, came close to what Breton (1964) has termed an "institutionally complete" ethnic community.

Upon release from the concentration camps after World War II, most of those who had previously lived in Japantown did not return to their former homes. The area had become rundown during the war and the opportunity structure had opened up for many Japanese, making it possible for them to move into professional and bureaucratic occupations and into middle-class Caucasian residential areas. In 1958 the remnants of Japantown were torn down as part of a city urban renewal project (Cole, 1974).

At present, there are small pockets of Japanese businesses in downtown Sacramento. Also, some initiatives have been taken to create a downtown ethnic community. Recently, for example, plans were laid to build a convalescent hospital for the Issei as well as child care and cultural centers. In addition, as in Gardena and Fresno, there are numerous Japanese American Buddhist and Protestant churches, ethnic associations and clubs, and the Japanese American Citizens League (JACL). There is even a highly oversubscribed children's summer cultural program called Jan Ken Po.

The number of Japanese Americans living in the Sacramento area is substantial today (14,160), but it remains a relatively small proportion of the total population (1.4 percent of a population of 1,014,002 in the Sacramento SMSA in 1980) (U.S. Bureau of the Census, 1983c: table P-7). Japanese Americans live in most parts of Sacramento, but there is some concentration on the South Side. They are very involved in the life of the larger community, holding a variety of memberships in civic, business, and professional associations. The acceptance of Japanese Americans in the area as well as their capacity to marshal political influence is perhaps best reflected in the fact that this area has sent the first mainland Japanese American to the U.S. House of Representatives.

Areas Not Included in the Survey

The communities sampled in this study represent a cross section of Japanese American ethnic communities in California. The reader should be cautioned, however, that there are at least two other types of Japanese American communities with quite different historical legacies as well as contemporary demographic profiles. The findings in the subsequent chapters may not be applicable to them.

First, there is the large Japanese American community in Hawaii. The major immigration to Hawaii from Japan occurred several years earlier than immigration to the mainland (Ichihashi, 1932:6–8). Thus the ages of the generations in Hawaii differ somewhat from the ages of corresponding generations in California. More important, interethnic relations between Asians and Caucasians have been quite different in Hawaii compared with the mainland, partly because of the much larger Asian communities on the Islands and the fact that Japanese Americans are the largest of the Asian groups. Hawaiian Japanese Americans have had very different experiences than their California counterparts. Most significant in this regard is that Hawaiian Japanese Americans were not incarcerated during World War II.

The second type of Japanese American community not considered in this survey encompasses the small eastern and midwestern communities such as those found in New York, Cleveland, and Minneapolis. These communities have not received much attention in the literature, but what is known about them suggests that their relatively small numbers and geographical as well as cultural distance from the center of Japanese American life in California and Hawaii have weakened their community institutions (Albert, 1980).

SAMPLING PROCEDURES

Our sample was drawn from a list of all Japanese male names in the telephone directories in the three areas. Japanese males seldom change their surnames, and their names are distinctive enough so that with some training they can be accurately identified (Tinker, 1973). Telephone books were employed because Japanese are not geographically concentrated, except to some extent in Gardena, and thus any kind of cluster sampling would have been more costly than our resources permitted. Moreover, 95 percent of the households in the United States have telephones (Alwin, 1977). A more serious problem in using telephone directories as sampling frames, however, is the matter of unlisted numbers. Nonetheless, recent findings indicate that although there are statistically significant differences between persons having listed numbers compared with those who have unlisted telephones, when the number of unlisteds is around 20 percent (approximately the national average) the magnitude of error associated with generalizing demographic characteristics using only listed phone numbers is between 1 and 2 percent (Rich, 1977). In our three research sites, the numbers of unlisteds reported by Pacific Bell Telephone were: Gardena, 15 percent, Fresno, 24 percent, and Sacramento, 25 percent.

The present intermarriage rate (with non-Asians) among Japanese Americans is about 50 percent of all new marriages (Kitano et al., 1984). Therefore, we encountered a serious problem in trying to identify the universe of Japanese American females from our telephone book sampling frame, because most women who had intermarried with Caucasians or other Asians would have non-Japanese last names. In order to deal with this difficulty we would have had to generate a new list of females using other techniques. The limitations of the resources we had to work with prevented this, and thus we elected to restrict our sample to males.

The fact that women are not represented in the sample produces some serious biases, and thus in a strict sense we cannot interpret our results as reflecting the attitudes and behavior of the Japanese American community in general. For example, the proportion of persons in the sample who are married to Caucasians is substantially smaller than it would be if we had been able to draw a truly representative sample of Japanese American women (see Chapter 8). According to the 1980 census, Japanese males are more likely than Japanese females to be college graduates (35.2 percent for males only compared with 26.4 percent for the total ethnic group; see U.S. Bureau of Census, 1983c: table 160). On the other hand, Japanese American females, in general, have higher educational levels and are more likely to participate in higher-paying occupations than American women as a whole (Wong and Hirschman, 1983). The educational level of the men in our survey is quite high, with 43.9 reporting that they are college graduates (see Chapter 5).

⌐ It is difficult to ascertain precisely what sorts of biases an all male sample might produce on attitudinal and behavioral items measuring ethnic community participation. One that does come to mind, however, is Yanagisako's (1977, 1985) point that women play the major role in maintaining interhousehold linkages in the Japanese American community. The implications of this for the interpretations of our findings on the effects of intermarriage on ethnic community solidarity will be discussed in Chapter 8.

Two other biases in the sample should be mentioned. First, there is a somewhat smaller percentage of Japanese American men in our sample than those in the 1980 census for California who describe their occupations as being involved in farming, forestry, or fisheries. The figures are 9.0 percent versus 11.8 percent (U.S. Bureau of the Census, 1988: table 33), respectively. On the other hand, the number of persons in our sample who claim to be self-employed is considerably higher than the percentage reported for the census sample of Japanese American men in California. The figures here are 28.2 percent for our sample and 11.1 percent for the 1980 census (U.S. Bureau of the Census, 1983a: table 162).

Since generation was a major variable of interest in the study, a decision was made a priori to obtain approximately equal numbers of Nisei and Sansei. Individuals were randomly selected from a list of names generated from the telephone books in each of the areas until approximately equal numbers of persons in the two generations were interviewed. This procedure produced a total sample of 634; 211 in Gardena (105 Nisei, 106 Sansei), 212 in Fresno (103 Nisei, 109 Sansei), and 211 in Sacramento (105 Nisei, 106 Sansei). The overall refusal rate was 26.5 percent; 37.8 percent in Gardena, 13.8 percent in Fresno, and 21.2 percent

in Sacramento. The ordering of the refusal rates in the three areas con-
forms with the order one would expect on the basis of the positions of the
areas on the rural–urban continuum (Sudman, 1976:65).

ETHNIC COMMUNITY CONTACTS, FIELD OPERATIONS, AND INTERVIEWING
PROCEDURES

In each of the research sites, an effort was made to work through ethnic
community information channels in order to maximize the cooperation
of potential respondents. This involved contacting community influentials, leaders of churches and ethnic associations, and writing a brief story
in the Japanese American and local area newspapers describing the nature
of the survey and alerting persons to the possibility that they might be
called upon to be interviewed.

Field offices were established in each of the three research sites as the
interviewing operation moved from Gardena to Fresno to Sacramento.
The field office for Gardena was located at the Asian American Studies
Center at UCLA; the Fresno office was headquartered in the Nikkei Service
Center in downtown Fresno; and the field office in Sacramento was
established in the office of the Sacramento Japanese American Citizens
League.

Letters were sent to persons whose names had been randomly selected
from the telephone book lists. They were then telephoned by project
personnel to schedule interviews. These were conducted face to face,
either in the respondent's home, his place of employment, or at the local
field office. Because the survey questions dealt specifically with ethnic
issues, only Japanese American interviewers were employed (see Hatchett and Schuman, 1975–76; Schaeffer, 1980; Schuman and Converse,
1968; Sudman and Bradburn, 1974:102–112, for a rationale for this procedure). The interviewers, primarily college students, were given extensive
training. Interviewer quality and perceptions by the respondent of the
interview situation were randomly checked in 20 percent of the sample
through a callback procedure.

THE CONTENT OF THE INTERVIEW

The first part of the interview dealt with the respondent's early socialization experiences, including his educational and occupational experiences,
whether he had attended a Japanese language school, whether he had

various Japanese American cultural experiences, and whether he had a rural or urban background. The purpose of these items was to measure the impact of the different early experiences, of persons in different generations and in the different areas, on contemporary levels of involvement in the ethnic community and assimilation into the larger society. Since, as delineated in Chapter 3, a major historical fact of life for Japanese Americans was involvement in petit bourgeois ethnic enterprises, the second portion of the interview dealt at considerable length with the respondent's current work experiences. Specifically, we were concerned with whether or not he was self-employed and the extent to which he was economically linked to other Japanese Americans.

The third portion of the interview dealt with specific questions on the respondent's attitudes about interactions with Caucasians, feelings about belonging to the Japanese American community, and perceptions and evaluations about Japanese values and whether they were changing. A central focus of this phase of the interview was an attempt to identify attitudes about the current state of Japanese American involvement in the larger society and the viability of the ethnic community.

The fourth phase of the interview dealt with different aspects of the respondent's interaction with Japanese Americans and Caucasians in both formal and informal settings, including marriage, friendship, voluntary associations, and the use of stores and other services. Responses to these questions provided us with behaviorally linked measures of the extent of assimilation and involvement in the Japanese American community.

The fifth, and final, phase of the interview was concerned with a number of specific issues currently facing Japanese Americans, including the NFL-UFW conflict and the proposal then before the U.S. Congress to approve reparations for Japanese Americans detained in concentration camps during World War II. The latter issue was subsequently resolved in 1988 when a redress bill, the Civil Liberties Act of 1988, containing an apology and provisions for monetary compensation, was passed by Congress and signed into law by President Reagan.

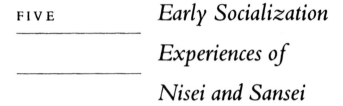

FIVE　　*Early Socialization*

Experiences of

Nisei and Sansei

Much of the research on Japanese Americans done from either the assimilationist or structural perspective has focused on comparing the more visible elements of acculturation and assimilation across generations (e.g., Bonacich and Modell, 1980; Connor, 1977; Levine and Rhodes, 1981; Montero, 1980). Substantial differences between Nisei and Sansei on these elements have been reported, and researchers generally have interpreted these findings as signifying the loss of ethnic group identification and cohesion.

We do not take issue with the findings of loss of the more visible elements of traditional Japanese culture, but propose that the more important fact is the persistence of the underlying structure of social relationships across generations. As Hechter (1975) has emphasized, the critical conceptual dimension of ethnicity is solidarity, and thus care should be taken not to equate ethnicity with the retention of particular cultural elements. This is especially true when one is comparing different generations of persons in the same ethnic group.

Although changes in the cultural content of the socialization process would be expected as a natural outgrowth of assimilation, such changes will not necessarily weaken the essential social organizational mechanisms that maintain relationships among persons in the group. The critical issue here is the extent to which the core social organizational base of ethnic community life can be adapted to meet the changing circumstances of successive generations. Our central thesis is that this basis of solidarity among Japanese Americans is indeed adaptable and thus has persisted in spite of substantial changes in the specific cultural aspects of Japanese American life.

An example of the adaptiveness of Japanese social organizational forms has been insightfully discussed by Yanagisako (e.g., 1977). She argues that strong kin networks linking families persist in the Japanese American community even though the linking function is now carried on by women instead of men. Traditionally, men represented their families to the outside world, including acting as social linkages. In the American context, however, this violates the cultural ideal of independent nuclear families. Yanagisako (1977) contends that if Japanese American males had continued to act as social linkages between families, this would make both them and their families appear too dependent. Women, on the other hand, are able to perform this function much more unobtrusively and thus maintain the traditional Japanese interfamily connectedness while appearing to adhere to "appropriate" American norms.

CHARACTERISTICS OF THE ETHNIC COMMUNITY IN WHICH THE NISEI AND SANSEI WERE SOCIALIZED

The Nisei, as noted in Chapter 2, grew up in two worlds. They spent much of their time in the white world of school, but virtually all of their primary relationships were with fellow Japanese (Daniels, 1985; Leonetti, 1983). They were not totally isolated from the main currents of American life, but their most intimate relationships and institutional affiliations were found within the ethnic community. Hosokawa (1969:164) recalls the feelings of many Nisei at that time:

Nisei life in this period was relatively uncomplicated. For most of them, the Japanese community was the center of activity, and by staying within its confines, one avoided the barbs of prejudice. For recreation, one went to a movie, fished, organized a beach party, took a drive, played ball or watched others play. There was nothing more pleasurable than stuffing oneself at a Chinese dinner—bean cake and pork, sweet and sour ribs, cold boiled chicken, shrimp chow mein, egg foo young, rice, barbecued pork loin—in the company of family and friends. It was not an unhappy life.

Because of their limited experience with the outside world, the Nisei's worldview tended to be somewhat narrow. As they reached college and work age in the 1930s, however, they began to look beyond the Issei-dominated ethnic community, which they considered too parochial. Kitagawa (1967:14) observes:

> The Japanese community was not participating in the ongoing life of either America or Japan. Such being the case, there was little possibility that any new ideas would emerge. The Japanese in America was exclusively preoccupied with the cold business of making a living and raising his family, trading and associating almost exclusively with his fellow countrymen. His community could not escape becoming ingrown.

In a similar fashion, Miyamoto relates: "The Nisei . . . considered their Issei fathers to be authoritarian, distant, and conservative. Mothers were thought to be overly anxious about their children and given to endless preaching. And the community was viewed as parochial in its concerns" (1972:230).

The values the Issei parents attempted to inculcate in their children had roots in Meiji-era Japanese village life. These values were transmitted by a cohesive Japanese American family which was usually deeply embedded in a local ethnic community. As Levine and Rhodes (1981) point out, the Japanese American community is most appropriately conceptualized as a system of families. Miyamoto observes:

> . . . since status in the community depends upon the observation of these basic ideals, another means of parental control exists in an appeal to the children's sense of respect for the family name. Every caution and every reprimand, therefore, is accompanied by a reminder of the necessity for preserving the status of the name, and of attempting to raise it if possible. What others will think of one's behavior looms large in the minds of the Japanese and controls their behavior extensively. This pressure, undoubtedly, is of basic importance in explaining the strong Japanese interest in keeping up a front and preserving "face." Family control, therefore, is not simply parental control, but

community control as well. It is family in relation to the community
that becomes the decisive force in regulating the behavior of individuals within the group. [Quoted in Hosokawa, 1969:163.]

Yamamoto and Wagatsuma (1980) characterize typical Americans as
living in a more impersonal social environment where people are more
"substitutable." Japanese Americans, on the other hand, have more stable
social networks of "named" people. Even today, according to Yamamoto
and Wagatsuma, Nisei are much more aware of and much more likely to
keep track of the reputation and successes of a fairly wide range of blood
and quasi-kin relatives than is the case with most Americans.

Some of the specific values supported by the social arrangements just
described were cohesiveness, mutual aid, and a generally patriarchal set
of authority relationships (e.g., Kitano, 1976:33). Respect for age, senior-
ity, obligation, and responsibility was sometimes subtly and many times
not so subtly insisted upon. A Nisei (Thomas, 1952:211) recalls:

It was always an ordeal for us to have Issei visitors in our home. We
had to go through a certain form of greeting and follow all the rituals
which we didn't even understand. Then we had to sit still in the corner
and not dare to speak up in the presence of elders. We didn't have a
Buddhist shrine in our home, though, and that was one consolation.
In some of the homes the Nisei children had to go through a regular
ritual in regard to this Buddhist shrine.

These norms were followed without much open resistance (Yamamoto
and Wagatsuma, 1980). Almost always, cohesion and the minimizing of
conflict took precedence over individual interests (e.g., Kiefer, 1974:14).

Contingent love, as a social control technique, was less important in the
Issei-Nisei family than were role relationships and their attendant responsibilities. As noted before, emphasis was placed on elevating and preserving the good name of the family. The baishakunins (go-betweens), who
were frequently used to check into the history of a prospective bride's and
groom's families before a marriage, were common manifestations of this
concern. Shame and disgrace were important group-oriented social control devices used to keep individuals in line.

This family-community relationship was, in some ways, quite similar
to the one Ouchi (1984) describes as characteristic of modern Japanese
corporations. These organizations are embedded in a dense network of

trade associations, government officials, and government-endorsed but privately run discussion councils that have a "social memory" ensuring that both selfish and cooperative actions are remembered and repaid. Thus, when it is to their mutual advantage, highly competitive corporations will cooperate.

Yamamoto and Wagatsuma (1980) have pointed out that from a Japanese perspective to be individualistic in the Western sense is to be selfish in the worst meaning of the term. When a Japanese is individualistic and is thinking only of self, he or she is failing to be an actualized person. To be ethical, one cannot fully exist without performing an appropriate social role.

The resultant sense of always being responsible for one's action in the context of community censure or praise is captured by Caudill and De Vos (1956:1117), who point out the following similarities and differences between Japanese American and white middle-class achievement orientations:

> The ultimate destinations or goals of individuals in the two groups tend to be very similar; but Japanese Americans go toward these destinations along straight, narrow streets lined with crowds of people who observe their every step, while middle class persons go toward the same destinations along wider streets having more room for maneuvering, and lined only with small groups of people who, while watching them, do not observe their every movement.

If a person failed, it brought shame or ridicule not only to him or her but to the entire extended family. Thus Japanese Americans emphasize detailed knowledge of norms, rituals, and relative status as a guide to social performance (Kiefer, 1974:27).

It should be pointed out that these tight family and community relations were not found in all areas of family life. Because of the language differences between the Issei and Nisei, communication was often partial at best. Further impeding meaningful dialogue was the patriarchal family structure, which emphasized avoiding family conflict and embarrassment. Thus what communication did take place was generally about safe topics.

Nevertheless, the critical point is that the Nisei grew up in a situation in which the vast majority of their close friends and organizational memberships were within the confines of the ethnic community. They belonged to mostly Nisei organizations such as the Young Buddhists Association and the Japanese American Citizens League, since the more traditionally Japanese-oriented Issei organizations did not meet their more youthful, Americanized needs. The majority of these organizations had mainstream content, such as softball and basketball leagues and ballroom dancing under the aegis of an ethnic church, although all of the individuals involved in them were Japanese.

The childhood and adolescent years of the Sansei, most of whom were born soon after the concentration camp experience, were dramatically different from those of the Nisei. After the war, the majority of Japanese no longer lived in a socially and economically self-contained ethnic community. The evacuation and relocation had destroyed the Issei-dominated, petit bourgeois ethnic enclaves, although they were to some degree recreated in several West Coast areas. The larger society had become much more receptive to the occupational and assimilation aspirations of the Nisei, most of whom were just beginning their careers. Thus they were no longer trapped into working in the ethnic economy, and many of them took positions with corporations and government agencies, which were rapidly expanding during the postwar era.

By 1947 in Chicago, for example, only 1 percent of the Nisei were in unskilled laborer positions while 35 percent were white collar workers and 9 percent were managers and professionals (Caudill and DeVos, 1956). Thus the Sansei were socialized in situations where their Nisei parents generally were economically mobile and substantially better off than they (i.e., the Nisei) had been as children.

A significant factor in producing the contrasting milieus in which the Nisei and Sansei were raised was the change in the amount of discrimination each faced and its impact on the kinds of economic accommodations made by persons in the respective generations. Most Nisei grew up in a petit bourgeois economic context which reinforced the patriarchal family both as a unit of production and as a unit of consumption. The Issei husband-father not only was seen as the head of the family, which was, of course, consistent with generalized American norms during that period, but also was seen as the head of the family business. When the Issei head of the household-business retired, the traditional primogeniture rule was applied and the oldest son inherited the rights and responsibilities of leadership of both the family and the family business.

The lessening of discrimination after the war, however, dramatically altered the macrostructural supports for the traditional petit bourgeois accommodation, and with this occurred a corresponding weakening of supports for traditional Japanese family business arrangements. Specifically, the substantial numbers of Nisei who moved into professional and managerial positions in the mainstream of American economic life no longer occupied a position of leadership in a family business enterprise. Moreover, their participation in mainstream economic activities, along with greater contact with Americans outside their ethnic community, further eroded support for traditional Japanese family arrangements.

Although subsequent generations of Japanese Americans have usually made what might seem to outside observers a remarkably smooth accommodation to Americanized family arrangements, tensions have sometimes arisen between the more traditional patriarchal family form of the Issei generation and the more egalitarian form of the Nisei generation. For example, if an Issei parent, following the traditional rule of primogeniture, has left his property to his or her eldest son, the other children, evaluating their experience by mainstream American norms, may feel themselves treated unfairly and become resentful about being "left out of the will" (e.g., Yanagisako, 1985:245).

Despite these changes in family structure, however, there is a high degree of continuity between generations on several psychological levels. Connor (1974a, 1974b) has shown that even the third generation Sansei retain certain core Japanese traits, as reflected in a greater deference, less need to dominate, a greater tendency to affiliate, less aggressiveness, and a greater need for succor and order than other Americans. Moreover, compared with the general population they have closer family ties, a greater sense of duty and obligation, and a great fear of failure in social role performance. Finally, Caudill and Frost (1974) suggest that these traits will persist into the fourth (Yonsei) generation, since Sansei mothers still use some traditional Japanese approaches to child rearing.

Percentage of Japanese in the Neighborhood When Growing Up

After the war, Japanese Americans began interacting with Caucasians in most spheres of life. Many Nisei moved from poorer, segregated inner city neighborhoods to middle-class white suburbs. During this period, housing discrimination against the Japanese went from being very common to relatively rare. Kitano reports (1976:191):

Housing is not a major problem for the Japanese. There are still areas that practice covert discrimination, but, in general, the Nisei and Sansei can buy homes in "desirable" neighborhoods, depending on their income and occupation. The progress in housing can be inferred from the mixed reaction of Nisei and Sansei to Proposition 14, a controversial 1964 California ballot measure on discrimination in housing. Many Japanese took the side of the California Real Estate Association, which opposed fair-housing laws.

Table 5:1 reports data from the California survey on neighborhood integration. It shows that the percentage of Japanese living in the respondent's neighborhood while he was growing up drops off significantly from the Nisei to Sansei generation in all the communities sampled. Overall, going from the Nisei to the Sansei generation, there is a 10 percent reduction in estimated percentage of Japanese in the respondent's neighborhood when he was growing up. This amount of change is not as great as one might expect, however, because the relevant early socialization years for most Sansei were in the 1950s and early 1960s. During this period, many Japanese families were still living fairly close together in central city locations.

Given the greater number of housing options available to the Sansei today, we expect that their children, the Yonsei, will be even more likely to live in neighborhoods containing very low concentrations of Japanese

TABLE 5:1. Mean Percentage of Japanese in Respondents' Neighborhoods While Growing Up, by Generation and Area ($N = 586$)

	AREA							
	Gardena		Sacramento		Fresno		Totals	
Generation	%	N	%	N	%	N	%	N
Nisei	49.2	96	40.9	96	29.8	101	39.8	293
Sansei	41.3	92	29.5	100	19.6	101	29.8	293
Totals	45.4	188	35.1	196	24.7	202	34.8	586

Generational effect: χ^2 (1, $N = 584$) = 14.63, $p < .001$
Area effect: χ^2 (2, $N = 583$) = 21.15, $p < .001$.
Interaction effect: χ^2 (2, $N = 583$) = .15, $p =$ n.s.

Americans. The greatly diminished size of the local Japantown, or Nihonmachi, is also a visible reminder of the dramatic postwar movement of Japanese Americans into Caucasian neighborhoods. Nevertheless, the increased availability of freeways and inexpensive telephonic communications will lessen the effects of the decrease in neighborhood concentration on the continued involvement of persons in the ethnic community. Especially important here, as we will see in the next chapter, is the persistence of Japanese American voluntary associations in areas where there are few fellow ethnic group members.

Educational Attainment

The socialization dimension having the greatest impact on acculturation and structural assimilation in all ethnic groups is educational attainment (e.g., Hraba, 1979). It has been shown that Japanese Americans who are better educated are more structurally assimilated (Levine and Rhodes, 1981:89–91; Montero, 1977:45–66).

When they arrived in this country, the Japanese immigrants were, by and large, quite well educated compared with many of their counterparts from other nations. The Issei were the product of the Meiji-era requirement of universal education (e.g., Nee and Wong, 1985). Their median educational attainment was 8 years (Ichihashi, 1932; U.S. Department of the Interior, wra, 1946a:80). By 1940, the median educational level of the Nisei was 12.2 years compared with 10.1 years for American-born whites living on the Pacific Coast (U.S. Department of the Interior, wra, 1946a:93). In 1980, 26.4 percent of persons of Japanese extraction over age twenty-five in the United States were college graduates compared with 16.2 percent of the corresponding age group in the total U.S. population. The corresponding figures for males only were 35.2 percent for Japanese and 20.07 percent for the general U.S. population (U.S. Bureau of the Census, 1983a: table 160) (see also Montero and Tsukashima, 1977; Peterson, 1971).

Table 5:2 shows that the persons in our sample have somewhat higher educational levels than Japanese American males in general. This discrepancy may reflect a tendency of less educated persons to refuse to be interviewed, but it is also due in part to our exclusion of the Issei generation from this sampling frame. In any event, it is clear that the Nisei are well educated compared with other persons in their age cohort, and that the Sansei have gone even further in this direction; two-thirds of the

TABLE 5:2. College Graduates, by Generation and Area (*N* = 581).ᵃ

| | AREA | | | | | | | |
| | Gardena | | Sacramento | | Fresno | | Totals | |
Generation	%	N	%	N	%	N	%	N
Nisei	23.8	105	29.4	102	23.5	102	25.6	309
Sansei	50.0	80	71.0	100	70.7	92	64.7	272
Totals	35.1	185	50.0	202	45.9	194	43.9	581

By generation: χ^2 (1, N = 581) = 88.4, $p < .001$.
By area: χ^2 (2, N = 581) = 9.13, $p < .01$
By generation and area: χ^2 (2, N = 581) = 3.99, p = n.s.

ᵃIncludes only respondents 25 or older.

latter over the age of twenty-five are college graduates (see Levine and Rhodes, 1981:51, for supporting information).

Rural Versus Urban Early Socialization Experiences

As noted in Chapters 2 and 3, the historical experience of the Japanese in the United States is deeply rooted in a rural context. Like most groups that have been involved in agriculture, the Japanese show a widespread exodus from rural to urban areas.

The heavily agricultural experience of Japanese Americans is reflected in the data presented in Table 5:3, which shows that even among the Sansei almost half (48.3 percent) spent the majority of their childhood in a rural area. Obviously, the figures here are biased by the fact that we selected a rural location, Fresno, as one of the sample sites. Nevertheless, even in urban Gardena, over one-fifth of the younger generation spent the majority of their childhood in a rural setting. In addition, as shown in Table 5:4, the majority of persons in our sample (58 percent) spent some portion of their childhood on a farm.

Attendance at Japanese Language Schools

One of our measures of the intergenerational maintenance of traditional Japanese culture during early socialization was whether the respondents had attended a Japanese language school. These schools, established by

TABLE 5:3. Persons Who Spent the Majority of Their Childhood in Rural Areas, by Generation and Area ($N = 633$).

	AREA							
	Gardena		Sacramento		Fresno		Totals	
Generation	%	N	%	N	%	N	%	N
Nisei	53.8	104	64.1	103	82.5	103	66.8	310
Sansei	21.7	106	40.7	108	81.2	109	48.3	323
Totals	37.6	210	52.1	211	82.1	212	57.3	633

By generation: χ^2 (1, $N = 633$) = 21.33, $p < .001$.
By area: χ^2 (2, $N = 633$) = 88.76, $p < .001$.
By generation and area: χ^2 (2, $N = 633$) = 8.56, $p = .01$.
By generation in Gardena: χ^2 (2, $N = 210$) = 21.77, $p < .001$.
By generation in Sacramento: χ^2 (1, $N = 211$) = 10.59, $p < .001$.
By generation in Fresno: χ^2 (1, $N = 212$) = 0, $p =$ n.s.

TABLE 5:4. Persons Who Have Ever Lived on a Farm as a Child, by Generation and Area ($N = 629$).

	AREA							
	Gardena		Sacramento		Fresno		Totals	
Generation	%	N	%	N	%	N	%	N
Nisei	57.8	102	68.0	103	80.6	103	68.8	308
Sansei	28.8	104	41.7	108	71.6	109	47.7	321
Totals	43.2	206	54.5	211	75.9	212	58.0	629

By generation: χ^2 (1, $N = 629$) = 28.05, $p < .001$.
By area: χ^2 (1, $N = 629$) = 47.60, $p < .001$.
By generation and area: χ^2 (2, $N = 629$) = 2.90, $p =$ n.s.

the Issei, served not only to perpetuate use of the Japanese language but, even more important, to inculcate Japanese social and moral values (Lebra, 1972). They were never substitutes for the public schools. The closest analogues to them among European ethnic groups would be the Hebrew schools and afterschool catechism classes. All such efforts were seen by their founders as ways of preserving a subculture in the midst of a frequently hostile environment.

Most Nisei, however, did not take Japanese language school as seriously as their Issei parents would have liked. After all, it took up much of their limited recreational time. One Nisei reports (Thomas, 1952:184):

It was in the Japanese school that I was taught all about manners, respect for elders, and other stuff like that. I used to take kendo and the instructors were from Japan. They were very strict about us being courteous to the old folks and we had to make the proper greetings to them. The instructors always reminded us that we should be very proud of our Japanese blood because we came from a great race. But none of this stuff sunk deeply. They couldn't come right out and say for us to be devoted to the Emperor, but they used to tell us all the time how boochie-land [Japan] was. They told us how the white race would always look down on us and that we should never be ashamed of being Japanese, because our ancestors had a glorious history.

Another Nisei vividly recalled (Masumoto, 1987:141):

They disciplined us pretty well. The one incident that I'll never forget, towards the end of the school year we always practiced for gaku ekai, that's graduation, the eighth grade graduation and we would all put on something. Some people would learn speeches and a lot of people had to learn something and say it. They had some plays or something like that and the teacher would have to figure it all out. . . . we would put on skits and we would have to polish everything up and memorize things. There was one boy that was standing up on the stage and practicing his speech. Well, in his storytelling he's supposed to say, "Hyaku dete ike!" (Hurry, get out!) but he said it softly . . . "Hyaku dete ike." And so the sensei (teacher) said "that's not the way to do it, you can't do it like that . . ." So she then yelled "Hyaku dete ike!" And you know what happened? One kid was in the basement all this while, I don't know what he was doing down there, playing when he wasn't supposed to I guess. Well, he just ran out of there and flew into the hall . . . because the sensei had yelled and he thought he was getting in trouble and you know how the sensei seemed to know things all the time. Oh, everyone laughed when he really ran out of there.

TABLE 5:5. Persons Who Attended a Japanese Language School as a
Child, by Generation and Area ($N = 597$).

| | AREA | | | | | | | |
| | Gardena | | Sacramento | | Fresno | | Totals | |
Generation	%	N	%	N	%	N	%	N
Nisei	89.2	102	87.8	99	86.1	101	87.4	302
Sansei	55.9	93	36.0	100	42.1	102	44.4	295
Totals	73.3	195	61.8	199	64.0	203	66.3	597

By generation: χ^2 (1, $N = 597$) = 125.96, $p < .001$.
By area: χ^2 (2, $N = 597$) = 6.58, $p < .05$.
By generation and area: χ^2 (2, $N = 597$) = 1.68, $p = $ n.s.

Table 5:5 shows the percentage of Nisei and Sansei in each area who
attended Japanese language schools as children. Among persons in the
Nisei generation it is clear that attending these schools was the norm.
Over 87 percent of them attended Japanese language schools. Aside from
an interesting areal difference, which we will discuss later, the most
significant finding is the dramatic reduction in attendance among the
Sansei in what is an important enculturating institution. Slightly more
than 44 percent of persons in the younger generation attended a language
school. Nevertheless, if these Sansei were compared with third generation European ethnics, the frequency of their exposure to a formal language school would be considered quite high.

Often the young Nisei rebelled at their parents' urgings to attend
Japanese language school. By and large, however, parents seemed to
accept their children's reluctance to continue this traditional aspect of
Japanese American enculturation. The following Nisei attitude was quite
typical (Masumoto, 1987:144):

Everyone began sending their kids to Japanese school in Sanger. I
asked our daughter to go and she said, "No, I don't want to go to
school seven days a week." I don't know if it was wrong that I asked
her, I should have sent her but I guess it also was laziness on my part
because that meant I would have to make an effort to send her. I don't
think I worked at it that hard. And it's kind'a sad 'cuz as I grew up I
was sorry I couldn't remember how to read and write more. I was

sorry I didn't remember and yet I didn't try to push it on to her because I thought, well, how much did I learn? I really didn't retain it.

Attendance at Buddhist Versus Christian Churches as Children

A common theme in studies of Japanese Americans is that involvement in Buddhist churches reflects greater continuity with the Japanese cultural experience whereas involvement in Christian churches represents a significant step toward assimilation into the mainstream of American society (e.g., Feagin and Fujitaki, 1972; Connor, 1977). In fact, during the initial period of immigration to the United States, many white Christian denominations attempted to facilitate the assimilation of the Japanese (Miyamoto, 1972). Buddhist church leaders would sometimes accuse these Japanese Christian converts of "selling out" to white pressure. Others, both Japanese and non-Japanese, saw adoption of Christianity as a key indicator of successful adaptation.

The association between Buddhism and traditional Japaneseness was reinforced by the officially sanctioned paranoia during World War II in which being a Buddhist made an individual Japanese American and his or her family more suspect in terms of presumed loyalty to the United States. After Pearl Harbor, many persons hurriedly concealed or destroyed their family altars and sutra books (Kashima, 1977).

Occasionally, religious differences led to conflict within the ethnic communities. Most of the time, however, these differences were associated with a kind of friendly rivalry between active social groups. The Buddhist temples and Christian churches sponsored similar activities, such as festivals and sports teams for the youth. In part, this lack of conflict between religious institutions in the community is a product of the Japanese culture's flexible and low key approach to religion. A Nisei reported that: "The rest of my family were Buddhist but religion didn't make much of a difference. I don't remember any time when it did. Two of our oldest children were married in a Christian ceremony and the other two married Buddhists and were married in a Buddhist way" (Masumoto, 1987:150).

The findings from the survey, shown in Table 5:6, indicate that there is a significant overall generational decline in the proportion of persons who attended a Buddhist church as a child. This trend has been a source of concern for the Nisei Buddhist leadership, many of whom are deeply concerned about the survival of their church (Kashima, 1977). There are,

TABLE 5:6. Buddhist Church Attendance Among Respondents Who Attended Church While Growing Up, by Generation and Area (*N* = 522).

| | AREA | | | | | | | |
| | Gardena | | Sacramento | | Fresno | | Totals | |
Generation	%	N	%	N	%	N	%	N
Nisei	63.4	82	62.5	80	72.6	84	66.3	246
Sansei	39.3	84	50.0	86	72.6	106	55.4	276
Totals	51.2	166	56.0	166	72.6	190	60.5	522

By generation: χ^2 (1, *N* = 522) = 5.94, *p* < .05.
By area: χ^2 (2, *N* = 522) = 19.10, *p* < .001.
By generation and area: χ^2 (2, *N* = 522) = 4.64, *p* = n.s.

however, important differences between areas in the likelihood of having attended a Buddhist church during childhood. We will comment on these later.

We can summarize our findings up to this point by saying that they are clearly consistent with the general thesis of assimilation theorists that there has been a substantial decline in adherence to many traditional Japanese cultural practices as successive generations of Japanese Americans have become more assimilated into the mainstream of American life (e.g., Connor, 1977; Montero, 1977, 1980).

Ethnic Composition of the Church Attended as a Child

Despite the obvious evidence of an intergenerational decline in involvement in many traditional Japanese and Japanese American institutions (i.e., Japanese language schools and the Buddhist religion), the most intriguing finding is the remarkably high degree of continuity across generations in involvement in predominantly Japanese American churches as youths. The relevant figures are found in Table 5:7. Although there has been a marked shift in denominational loyalties in the succeeding generation, there remains in the childhood experiences of the Sansei a fundamental similarity with the experience of their elders. In both instances, they were likely to worship with fellow ethnic group members. Further, in the case of the Sansei, this was usually not the result of discrimination from

TABLE 5:7. Respondents Who Attended a Predominantly Japanese Church When Growing Up, by Generation and Area (N = 629).

| | AREA | | | | | | | | | | | | | | | |
| | Gardena | | | | Sacramento | | | | Fresno | | | | Totals | | | |
Generation	Jpn (%)	Cau (%)	DNA (%)	N	Jpn (%)	Cau (%)	DNA (%)	N	Jpn (%)	Cau (%)	DNA (%)	N	Jpn (%)	Cau (%)	DNA (%)	N
Nisei	71.2	11.5	17.3	104	75.5	3.9	20.6	102	71.8	9.7	18.4	103	72.8	8.4	18.8	309
Sansei	67.6	13.3	19.0	105	69.2	10.3	20.5	107	88.0	8.3	3.7	108	75.0	10.6	14.4	320
Totals	69.4	12.4	18.2	209	72.2	7.2	20.6	209	80.1	9.0	10.9	211	73.9	9.5	16.5	629

By generation: χ^2 (2, N = 629) = 2.74, p = n.s.
By area: χ^2 (4, N = 629) = 11.34, p < .05.
By generation and area: χ^2 (4, N = 629) = 14.08, p < .01.
By generation in Gardena: χ^2 (2, N = 209) = .32, p = n.s.
By generation in Sacramento: χ^2 (2, N = 209) = 3.23, p = n.s.
By generation in Fresno: χ^2 (2, N = 211) = 12.33, p < .01.

DNA = Did not attend.

majority churches, as is often the case with blacks; other indicators, such as intermarriage rates, point to a fairly high degree of social acceptance of Japanese Americans by whites in the post–World War II period. Oguri-Kendis (1979) has demonstrated that the Sansei will drive long distances from the suburbs to maintain their participation in an ethnic church.

In short, in the area of religion, there is significant discontinuity between Nisei and Sansei with respect to specific cultural content (i.e., Buddhism versus Christianity) but substantial intergenerational continuity in maintaining social relationships with other Japanese Americans. This contrasts markedly with the situation in a number of European ethnic groups, such as the Irish or the Germans, where religious differences have resulted in the development of quite separate ethnic communities in the United States with hyphenated titles such as "Irish-Catholics" or "German-Lutherans."

Areal Differences in Early Socialization Experiences

In Gardena, the larger proportion of Japanese in the respondents' neighborhoods while growing up indicates that this area comes closest to being the sort of "ethnic ghetto" students of European ethnicity have described (see Table 5:1). It is not surprising that the overall educational level of persons in Gardena is significantly lower than that of respondents in Sacramento or Fresno (see Table 5:2). We suspect that if we had sampled Japanese Americans in Orange County (which contains many of the affluent suburbs in the greater Los Angeles area), we would have found educational levels similar to or perhaps even higher than those in Sacramento or Fresno.

With respect to what effects rural versus urban social contexts have on continuities or changes in Japanese American ethnicity, the data presented in this chapter provide some complex results. On the one hand, the urban subsample is more traditionally Japanese with respect to the proportion of persons in the younger generation who attended a Japanese language school as a child (see Table 5:5). On the other hand, there is much greater continuity between the generations in Fresno with respect to having attended a Buddhist church as a child and having lived in a rural area as a child. The relationship between rural versus urban setting and the contemporary nature of Japanese American ethnicity involves a number of complex issues which will become clearer in the next chapter.

CONCLUSION

As predicted by both assimilationist and structural theories, most of our data show a significant decline across generations in the more visible elements of Japanese early socialization experiences. As children, the Sansei are less likely than the Nisei to have lived in neighborhoods with high concentrations of other Japanese Americans and to have attended a Japanese language school or a Buddhist church. Yet the most compelling findings are the indications of intergenerational continuity. Specifically, although there have been substantial shifts in denominational affiliation and even though both formal and informal discriminatory barriers against Japanese Americans have been markedly reduced since World War II, the Sansei are overwhelmingly likely to have attended a predominantly Japanese American church as a child (if they attended any church at all). This continuity is consistent with the argument that Japanese American social organizational forms have a high degree of adaptability.

One way of appreciating how these findings shed light on the essential character of Japanese American ethnicity is to reflect on what Banton calls "cultural centrality" (1981). He suggests that some cultural elements in an ethnic group's traditions will be resistant to change over time whereas others will fade rather quickly. The most important causal factor in this regard is whether a particular cultural element hinders the economic accommodation of individuals in the New World. Thus the use of the traditional language is one of the first cultural elements to go because it limits job opportunities, while traditional ethnic norms and values pertaining to family life are usually the last to change because they have minimal impact on relating to others in the marketplace (Banton, 1981:33).

There are, however, ways in which ethnic groups vary in the degree to which they retain or give up those cultural elements not directly related to economic accommodation. Most important, in terms of the central conceptual theme of this book, is that the core elements of ethnicity in some groups are more adaptable to changing circumstances than are those in other groups.

In the case of the Japanese immigrants, their strong sense of peoplehood (Reischauer, 1981:32–37), their collective orientation, and their cultural emphasis on maintaining harmony within the group made the maintenance of interpersonal relations within the community a central goal of ethnic community life. Moreover, the strong sense of being a homogeneous people has allowed the Japanese to "borrow" elements from other cultures without losing a clear sense of their own identity. In Reischauer's words, "What distinguishes them [i.e., the Japanese] is not their imitativeness but rather their distinctiveness and their skill at learning and adapting while not losing their own cultural identity. Others have tried to do the same but with less success" (1981:33).

Further, the Japanese, in contrast to many European ethnic groups, have faced fewer of what might be called ethical dilemmas in trying to reconcile traditional ways with pressures to accommodate to new situational exigencies. Japanese culture is "socially sensitive" in that it is desirable to fit into whatever social setting one finds oneself. This "situational morality" encourages them to adopt the attitudes and behavior of the host society and thus facilitates their acculturation (Lebra, 1972; Reischauer, 1981:138–145). Religion, for instance, is viewed in a very relativistic context, with the preservation of the group clearly a more important value than a particular theological belief (Reischauer, 1981:213–224). In fact, in Japan, many individuals practice "multilayered faith" combining, for instance, Shintoism and Buddhism (Lebra, 1972; Weisz et al., 1984).

SIX	*Friendship and Voluntary*
	Association Membership in
	Ethnic and Nonethnic
	Communities

As noted in Chapter 1, the linear assimilationist and structural approaches to ethnicity suggest that there is essentially a substitutive or zero-sum relationship between ethnic group membership retention and structural assimilation. We have proposed that Japanese Americans do not fit this pattern. They show evidence of high levels of structural assimilation and yet retain high levels of ethnic group membership on several dimensions. In contrast to the mainly symbolic ethnicity found in many third generation European ethnic groups, members of this group still interact with one another in a variety of social organizational contexts.

One reason casual observers may assume that structural assimilation has led to the destruction of Japanese American community life is that many of the more visible features of the community have disappeared since the end of World War II. No longer, for example, is there a large and vital Nihonmachi, or Little Tokyo, in most West Coast cities. Despite this geographical dispersion, however, Japanese Americans have managed to retain high levels of participation in the institutional life of their ethnic community. In addition to the persistence of strong interfamily patterns of mutual aid and support, there is continued participation in a wide variety of voluntary associations such as Buddhist and Christian ethnic churches, Japanese American athletic leagues, and the Japanese American Citizens League.

In this chapter we will examine empirical data on voluntary association memberships and friendship patterns which illustrate how the ethnic community has adapted to the pressures brought on by structural assimilation. Before we look at this data, however, it will be helpful to gain some comparative perspective on the significance of different types of ethnic community involvement.

The "Ethnic Mobility Trap"

Personal relationships vary widely, ranging from transient marketplace contacts to lifelong friendships and marriage. In the next chapter, we will concentrate on economic relationships and in Chapter 8 we will deal with intermarriage. This chapter focuses on relationships that fall somewhere in between the two extremes of impersonality and intimacy. These relationships may be conceptualized as being on the continuum characterized by Granovetter (1973, 1982) as "weak" and "strong" ties.

Strong ties, such as those between best friends, are relatively intimate in character. Individuals invest more of themselves in such relationships and often expect as much (or more) from them in return. Weak ties, on the other hand, call for much lower levels of intimacy and investment and include relationships with casual acquaintances, most co-workers, and many persons with whom an individual interacts in voluntary associations such as PTAS or clubs.

The literature in psychology and sociology has long recognized the importance of strong ties in providing social support in individuals' lives. Those who do not have such ties are often portrayed as isolated, alienated, and less capable of withstanding the stresses associated with negative life events (e.g., Gottlieb, 1983; Jung, 1984). At the same time, however, Granovetter (1973) points out that persons whose social contacts are restricted to strong ties may experience limitations in securing certain types of resources, because persons with whom one has strong ties are likely to be similar to oneself. Thus a network of strong ties tends to be a clique made up of similar individuals. A person with such a network is unlikely to be able to draw upon individuals or other social networks with different resources.

On the other hand, weak ties with fellow club members, neighbors, and acquaintances can act as *bridges* to networks of individuals who are different and thus have access to different resources. Further, weak ties allow one to have access to a greater number of individuals. Granovetter found, for example, that those who were most successful in finding jobs had a greater number of weak ties. Also, he notes that weak ties can be more valuable than strong ties when the goal is to form a political coalition. Exclusive reliance on strong ties makes it difficult for persons to build bridges to other groups, and this makes them less effective politically.

In Gans's (1982) study of the Italian American community in Boston's West End, which served as the basis for one of Granovetter's examples, the subculture fostered a suspiciousness of "strangers" and an almost exclusive reliance on a small set of strong-tie relationships. This resulted in strong family cliques in the West End but posed a major obstacle to building political coalitions when the residents were faced with an urban renewal fight.

Although the structure of social relationships among Japanese Americans promotes the maintenance of strong-tie relationships among families, it also supports the development of more extensive and inclusive quasi-kin ties within the ethnic community. Most important, such ties are not as easily disrupted when individuals develop either strong-tie friendships or weak-tie associational involvements with persons outside the ethnic community. In short, the bonds of solidarity within the Japanese American community are essentially more resilient and thus more adaptable to the strains produced by the structural assimilation of its members than if they were based solely on more exclusive strong ties.

The central issue here is to identify the extent to which an ethnic group can maintain ties with both insiders and outsiders. In Chapter 8 we will consider the effect of intermarriage on the involvement of Japanese Americans in their ethnic community. Our present concern is the extent to which structural assimilation into the larger society, through friendships with nonethnics (i.e., strong ties) and involvement in clubs and voluntary associations (i.e., generally weak ties), affects their participation in the ethnic community.

The dominant theme in the literature with respect to the possibility of maintaining ties in both the ethnic and nonethnic communities is perhaps best expressed in Wiley's (1967) metaphor of the ethnic mobility trap. His argument is that ethnic group members face a choice, in fact a cruel choice, of investing in relationships in either ethnic or nonethnic worlds. From his perspective, the extent to which these relationships are "weak" or "strong" is not really the crucial issue, and in fact he does not address this matter. But Wiley does portray the lifestyle, values, and interaction patterns of the ethnic and nonethnic worlds as so different that an individual would almost have to be chameleonlike to function in both.

The classic imagery of the ethnic mobility trap dilemma is found in Whyte's (1981) *Street Corner Society*. The two main characters, Doc and Chic, represent the mutually exclusive choices of participation in the ethnic versus nonethnic worlds. The former elects to retain his lower-class Italian American lifestyle, feeling comfortable on the street corner but out of place in the larger society. Chic, on the other hand, adopts the values and lifestyle of the dominant WASP culture and gradually moves out of Cornerville into mainstream society. In both cases, individuals are portrayed as not capable of living comfortably in the two presumably distinct worlds. Similar imagery suggesting the incompatibility of ethnic and nonethnic worlds, although with a different outcome, is found in the concept of the "marginal man" who is caught between two cultures (Stonequist, 1935, 1937).

Quite a different image, however, is presented in Rose's (1959) study of small-town Jews in rural New York State. Here, apparently, individuals were able to maintain ties in the ethnic-religious community while at the same time developing friendships and associational involvements with outsiders. Rose found, for example, that small-town Jews were much more likely than big-city Jews to interact with Gentiles, yet the former were much more conscious than the latter of their Jewishness and often made a stronger effort to engage in traditional Jewish practices. In Rose's words, the small-town Jew, much more so than the urban ghetto Jew, possessed a "dual cultural membership" (p. 268). Most important, the maintenance of these different sets of ties within and outside the ethnic-religious community did not appear to produce any great amount of stress or marginality (pp. 264–280). A more recent study of Jews in Texas found a similar pattern (Rosentraub and Taebel, 1980).

Why in one instance do individuals essentially face a zero-sum choice of living in an ethnic versus nonethnic world whereas in another they are able to find an accommodation allowing a substantial amount of structural assimilation into mainstream life while maintaining interactional ties with the ethnic community? Two considerations appear to be critical in answering the question just posed: (1) the degree of value compatibility between ethnic and mainstream cultures, and (2) the extent to which the ethnic community is institutionalized in concrete organizational forms.

The issue of value and interactional style compatibility is shown in Whyte's (1981) treatment of the dilemma faced by the men on the Street Corner. The particularistic style of interaction that was carried over from the Italian peasant village was inconsistent with the more detached impersonal style of interaction of the middle-class WASP world. This conflict is also reflected in other accounts of antipathy between the ethnics and their view of legitimate relationships, as expressed in their support of the political machine, and the WASP's challenge to the legitimacy of that political form. Thus the ethnics were likely to view the middle-class WASP lifestyle as cold whereas the latter saw the ethnics' lifestyle as corrupt (e.g., Banfield and Wilson, 1963:117–118; Hofstadter, 1955).

It is not surprising that any expression of the traditional peasant ways was an impediment to upward mobility. Within this setting, structural assimilation and ethnic group membership retention inevitably became a zero-sum game. Beginning in the second generation, most persons began to give up the peasant ways and to adopt middle-class ways. The main legacy of the immigrant past by the time of the third generation was a symbolic attachment to their ethnic heritage (Alba, 1981; Alba and Chamlin, 1983; Goering, 1971; Roche, 1982).

We might expect that value incompatibility would prove to be more of a problem for the small-town Jews. After all, Jews historically have been subject to discrimination in Europe and America because of their alleged differentness. Moreover, Jews themselves frequently have made great efforts to preserve their unique religioethnic traditions and institutions. Yet these cultural differences have usually not been a hindrance to making an economic adaptation to modern-day gentile society. In fact, Jewish culture and social organization have been, in part, responsible for their being disproportionately involved in petit bourgeois activities that have served to foster and reinforce the values and skills that have enhanced their opportunities for occupational success in later generations.

Nevertheless, value compatibility by itself is not a sufficient cause for the persistence of participation in an ethnic community when individuals have become structurally assimilated. One might argue that value compatibility would lead to a quicker absorption of the group into mainstream society. Thus there must be some kind of mechanism holding persons to the ethnic community while they are being drawn into more and more involvements outside the ethnic community. Critical here is the ability to translate the belief system of the ethnic subculture into actual organizational structures.

The case of the urban ethnics described in Whyte's (1981) *Street Corner Society* and alluded to in Wiley's (1967) discussion of the ethnic mobility trap is one in which maintenance of ethnic institutions is heavily dependent on population density. This situation is addressed by Fischer's (1975, 1976:35–38, 1982:202–208) concept of an urban subculture. He suggests that ethnicity is more likely to flower in the city because of the greater likelihood of having a critical mass of fellow ethnics. When ethnic density is reduced as individuals move to the suburbs, there is no viable organizational mechanism to draw them back into the ethnic community. Thus we see the familiar pattern of low involvement with fellow ethnics despite the persistence of a symbolic ethnicity (Gans, 1979; Goering, 1971; Roche, 1982).

In the case of Rose's small-town Jews, however, organizational mechanisms did exist permitting persons to remain involved in ethnic community life even though living in low ethnic density environments. The key element in the capacity of the small-town Jews to maintain these organizational structures was their overriding sense of distinctive peoplehood and their historical experience of creating and maintaining voluntary associations to meet collective needs. As Benkin (1978) points out, American Jews brought with them from Europe this organizational capacity based on centuries of survival pressure. These organizational structures, in turn, were reinforced by their petit bourgeois experience (e.g., Bonacich, 1973; Turner and Bonacich, 1980).

With regard to compatibility of values and interactional styles, it is clear that Japanese Americans, along with other Asians, historically have been seen by majority group Americans as different from European ethnics in terms of cultural distance and "assimilability." This, in turn, has been a source of discrimination and obstacles to structural assimilation into the mainstream society. On this score, then, Japanese Americans fall into Francis's (1976) category of "secondary" ethnic groups compared with European ethnics, who are in the category of "primary" ethnic groups.

There are, however, several mutually reinforcing elements in the Japanese and Japanese American experiences that have allowed individuals to adapt to the mainstream environment while retaining critical social organizational elements of Japaneseness. The first of these is an emphasis on the long-term preservation of social relationships between group members and their families rather than an emphasis on specific religious doctrine or cultural practices. As noted earlier, Japanese Americans, like their ancestors and contemporaries in Japan, exhibit a high degree of tolerance for different religious elements and manage to combine what may appear to be quite diverse or even incompatible elements into a family's religious practices (Kiefer, 1974:37). Nonetheless, these same individuals will exert considerable effort, often driving long distances, to attend a church with fellow ethnics (Oguri-Kendis, 1979).

This means that Japanese Americans may readily adopt "American ways" and "fit in" without losing a basic sense of their peoplehood. Language, food, or even religion does not seem as central to their identity as do the social relationships between fellow ethnics (Christopher, 1983:55, 63). Thus it was not unusual when discriminatory constraints were reduced after World War II for individuals to quickly form ties with Caucasians by participating in civic, business, and even social activities, yet maintain a high level of involvement in the associational life of their ethnic community.

The second major ability critical in combining ties with outsiders and involvement in an ethnic community is also present in the Japanese American case. Like American Jews, the Japanese immigrants brought with them experience with voluntary organizational forms. Numerous studies have shown that Japanese peasant villages maintained high levels of individual involvement in voluntary associations as far back as the nineteenth century. The rate of associational involvement for the average Japanese, therefore, has long been among the highest in the world (e.g., Embree, 1939:112–157, 163–170; Norbeck, 1972). Thus, when they emigrated to the United States, they formed a host of voluntary associations to deal with various exigencies, including relationships with Japan, scientific agriculture, and various kinds of economic cooperatives. These associations, which were sometimes started with the assistance of the Japanese government, were helpful in establishing the Japanese as small-scale entrepreneurs.

Voluntary associations served somewhat different functions for the Japanese American community before and after World War II. Before the war, they were essential for the economic and social survival of the isolated ethnic enclaves. At that time, virtually all these organizations reflected the values and concerns of the first generation Issei. Some organizations, such as the ubiquitous Japanese Associations, were semi-official arms of the Japanese government. Others, such as the *kenjinkai*, which were based on emigration from a given prefecture, were general mutual assistance associations, and others, such as the farmers' and gardeners' associations, were specifically concerned with collective economic interests.

Following the war, however, the character of these associations changed dramatically. The Issei felt a need to recreate the kind of community that had existed before the war. The incarceration, however, had weakened their capacity to control the infrastructure of the ethnic community. Several features of camp life reduced their ability to socialize their Nisei children in the traditional way. Mess hall dining arrangements, for example, made it difficult for families to eat and interact socially in a traditional manner. Because the open ceiling construction of the barracks forced neighbors in "adjoining suites" to listen to all "high volume" discussions, parents could not vigorously control their children lest it be grist for the community rumor mill (Kitano, 1976:75–76). In addition, being freed from the drudgery of long hours of work on the family farm or store under the constant observation of their parents allowed the youthful Nisei to spend much of their time in age-graded cliques whose values were often at odds with those of the Issei (Bloom, 1943).

Moreover, by the end of the war, the majority of the Nisei were entering the prime of their lives. They were mainly concerned with getting on with their lives and making up for lost time. This, of course, was similar to the outlook of most Americans during this period. Besides making a comfortable living at a "clean job," most of the single individuals were interested in having an active social life, with the goal of eventually starting a family. The young married couples wanted organizations that would cater to their recreational, social, and cultural needs in a family-oriented context. Thus many active sports and religious groups were started as soon as the number of Japanese reached a "critical mass" in an area.

The development of ethnic voluntary associations in Cleveland, Ohio, following the war illustrates the capacity of the Nisei to create organizations from scratch as well the kinds of activities most suited to their, as opposed to the Issei, interests. Before the war, there were virtually no Japanese Americans in Cleveland, but several thousand persons resettled in the city when they were released from camp. By 1946 numerous Nisei softball, basketball, bowling, and golf leagues had sprung up in Cleveland, along with Japanese American Buddhist and Christian churches. A newsletter called the *Kaleidoscope,* which was put together by volunteers using borrowed equipment, provided the ethnic community with human interest stories about its members, ran a "Know Cleveland" column, and published job listings. Many of these functions are still performed today by the Cleveland *JACL Bulletin* (Fugita and Tanaka, 1987).

In the recreated postwar ethnic communities on the West Coast, the Issei typically assumed the role of elder statesmen while the Nisei provided most of the active leadership. The mix of associations that eventually emerged contained both diffuse overarching organizations, which attempted to bring together diverse elements of the ethnic community, and more specialized associations focusing on a particular social or economic interest of concern to only a segment of the community. The former types, such as the JACL or the Gardena Cultural Institute, have tended to be more persistent than the specialized sports and economic interest groups, because they can shift to different issues around which community members may be mobilized.

These more diffuse organizations are seen by members of the ethnic community as the most visible signs of the continued vitality of Japanese American traditions and lifestyle in the area. In addition, they coordinate the efforts of the more specialized groups, since those have overlapping memberships. This is helpful in avoiding conflict over the scheduling of major events so that organizations will not be competing for the same community members. In addition, the umbrella organizations can present a unified Japanese community position to the outside world.

Finally, both the more diffuse and the more specialized associations exhibit a high degree of resilience, in part because they support community friendship networks, but, perhaps more important, because of the typical Japanese American consensual approach to decision making. As Kiefer points out, they arrive at "consensus through compromise" (1974:42). He goes on to say: "The emphasis [in Japanese American voluntary associations] is on a willingness to shift points of view in order to avoid disrupting group processes. Open hostility in public groups is strongly disapproved, expressions of concern for one another's feelings are frequent, and nonverbal forms of communication are extensively used in order to avoid raising embarrassing issues."

An example of this consensual approach is found in the way that the Japanese American Citizens League (JACL) dealt with the controversy surrounding a farm-labor issue involving the Nisei Farmers League and the United Farm Workers Union (UFW) in the 1970s. The JACL, an umbrella civil rights organization, with over a hundred chapters nationally, represents a wide range of regional and ideological interests. Some of these differences in perspectives came into conflict when some liberal

Sansei wanted the organization to support Cesar Chavez's United Farm Workers while the conservative Nisei farmers in the San Joaquin Valley wanted the organization to support the growers' organization, the Nisei Farmers League. After many heated debates in the vernacular press and community forums, the JACL leaders agreed to define the issue as a purely labor-management dispute and therefore outside the purview of JACL. (See our more extended discussion in Chapter 9; see also Fugita, 1978; Fugita and O'Brien, 1977.)

Today, even though most Nisei and Sansei have moved to white suburbs, they are still involved in voluntary associations such as ethnic churches and golfing clubs (Kitano, 1976:58–62; Oguri-Kendis, 1979). Most critical for our theoretical argument is that community cohesiveness rests to a significant degree on voluntary association involvement rather than exclusively on strong-tie friendship and kin relationships. This makes it easier for individual Japanese Americans to combine ethnic community participation with mainstream community involvements.

Let us now turn to the evidence from our survey relevant to the argument we have been developing.

SURVEY FINDINGS ON FRIENDSHIP AND VOLUNTARY ASSOCIATION MEMBERSHIP

Friendship

Our measure of "strong ties" consisted of two questions that asked, in turn, about the ethnic background of the respondent's best and second best friends. Table 6:1 presents the mean number of Japanese best friends by generation and area. Not surprisingly, there is a significant difference between the Nisei and the Sansei, with the latter less likely to have all Japanese best friends. More interesting is the significant generation × area interaction. Examination of the pattern of means shows that the Nisei have approximately the same number of Japanese best friends regardless of the area in which they currently live. The Sansei, on the other hand, have more Japanese friends in Gardena, where on a percentage basis there are many more Japanese than in the other two areas sampled (see Chapter 4).

A plausible explanation is that the older Nisei are still likely to have the good friends they made during an earlier period when Japanese Americans interacted socially almost exclusively with fellow ethnics. The

TABLE 6:1. Mean Number of Japanese Best Friends, by Generation and Area (Maximum Value = 2).

| | AREA | | | | | | | |
| | Gardena | | Sacramento | | Fresno | | Totals | |
Generation	No.	N	No.	N	No.	N	No.	N
Nisei	1.59	105	1.52	103	1.45	103	1.52	311
Sansei	1.39	106	.94	108	.99	109	1.10	323
Totals	1.49	211	1.22	211	1.21	212		

Generation significant at $p < .001$; area significant at $p < .001$; interaction significant at $p < .05$.

Sansei, on the other hand, apparently are more influenced by the availability of co-ethnics in their local area. Regardless of their present class and educational differences, the Nisei, as a group, have a wealth of experiences they shared during their youth and early adult years. This would include, for example, growing up in a relatively homogeneous and "institutionally complete" (Breton, 1964) ethnic community as well as going through the internment camp experience during the war. The younger Sansei, on the other hand, generally have grown up in a much more pluralistic and integrated social environment, where the potential for interacting with whites has been much greater.

This would suggest, therefore, that the Nisei would be more drawn to one another as best friends regardless of the social milieu in which they now live, but the Sansei would be more affected by specific contextual opportunities to form friendships with fellow ethnics and persons outside the group. Put another way, the data are consistent with the interpretation that because of the salience of their shared experiences, the Nisei invest more than the Sansei in preserving strong ties with fellow ethnic group members. (For other evidence to support this interpretation, see O'Brien and Fugita, 1983a and 1984).

These findings are consistent with the basic theses of both the assimilationists and the structuralists. The fact that persons in the younger generation are likely to have Caucasian best friends when they live in a social setting with relatively small numbers of fellow ethnics is strong evidence of the propensity of the third generation to structurally assimilate into mainstream American society.

If the persistence of ethnic community involvement depended solely on the preservation of strong ethnic ties, these data would suggest that the future of the Japanese American community is very much in doubt. Indeed, as we pointed out earlier, this describes the tenuous situation of many groups in which strong ties are the principal basis of ethnic solidarity and individuals are faced with a choice between structural assimilation or involvement in the ethnic community. The data show, however, that, as argued, Japanese Americans are tied to their ethnic community by other kinds of attachments.

Voluntary Association Memberships

Involvement in voluntary associations was seen as a good measure of linkages or bridges to both the ethnic and nonethnic communities because they are not inherently as exclusive as are strong-tie relationships. Our measures of voluntary association membership are two indices that are totals of the number of memberships respondents have in Japanese American and non-Japanese American organizations. The kinds of organizations that constitute these totals include the typical range mentioned in the literature: PTAS, churches, political organizations, sports clubs, social groups, civic groups, professional organizations, and so forth (Smith, 1975).

Our data document a high overall level of activity by Japanese Americans in voluntary associations. Over 91 percent of the sample belonged to at least one voluntary association; and even when church membership is not counted, 86 percent still belong to at least one organization. This compares with a figure of 62 percent for the general U.S. population (Verba and Nie, 1972:41).

When membership in churches is included, the percentage of persons who belonged to Japanese and non-Japanese voluntary associations was almost identical: 69 percent and 70 percent, respectively. When church membership is excluded, over 69 percent of the respondents belong to non-Japanese organizations and almost 53 percent belong to Japanese organizations. The decline in the latter figure reflects the fact that most Japanese Americans who belong to a church belong to a predominantly Japanese American congregation (Oguri-Kendis, 1979).

The data just cited show that individuals in this group are more likely than the general population to belong to voluntary associations. The comparisons in terms of membership in ethnic voluntary associations are even more striking. The figures of 69 percent (including church membership) or 53 percent (excluding church membership) are over ten times higher than comparable membership figures for some European ethnic groups (see Goering, 1971; Roche, 1982). In Roche's study, for example, only 8.2 percent of first generation blue-collar Italian Americans living in a "homogeneous" (i.e., with a large concentration of Italian Americans) suburb were members of an ethnic organization. That figure declined to 2.0 percent among the second generation blue-collar group in a heterogeneous (i.e., relatively low proportion of Italian Americans) suburb and rose slightly to 3.7 percent among second generation white-collar Italian Americans in a "heterogeneous" suburb.

In fairness, it should be pointed out that the participation levels of Japanese Americans are substantially lower than those of Jews. In the survey by Rosentraub and Taebel (1980), of Jews in the Dallas–Fort Worth area, 96.1 percent of the sample belonged to non-Jewish or "secular" organizations while 94.4 percent belonged to Jewish organizations. Over 82 percent were members of synagogues and over 60 percent belonged to Jewish community centers.

Nevertheless, the data from our survey strongly support the basic thesis about the compatibility of structural assimilation and the retention of ethnic group involvement among Japanese Americans; 69 percent of the persons in our sample belonged to both ethnic and nonethnic voluntary associations. Put in terms of our earlier discussion, many members of the group currently appear quite capable of maintaining ties to both ethnic and nonethnic communities.

To examine more closely the actual amount of involvement in ethnic versus nonethnic voluntary associations, we calculated the mean number of Japanese and non-Japanese American organizations to which the respondents belonged. Tables 6:2 and 6:3 show, as expected, that Nisei are more involved than Sansei in Japanese American voluntary associations while the reverse is true with respect to involvement in nonethnic voluntary associations. The greater involvement of the younger generation in mainstream organizations and their comparatively lesser involvement in ethnic voluntary associations is, of course, consistent with the assimilationist perspective. What is most striking, however, is that the mean number of memberships in Japanese-American organizations for Sansei is still one.

Breaking down both ethnic and nonethnic voluntary association membership into specific subtypes provides some additional insight into the

TABLE 6:2. Mean Number of Memberships in Japanese Organizations, by Generation and Area.

| | AREA | | | | | | | |
| | Gardena | | Sacramento | | Fresno | | Totals | |
Generation	No.	N	No.	N	No.	N	No.	N
Nisei	1.39	105	1.92	103	2.11	103	1.80	311
Sansei	.81	106	1.06	108	1.12	109	1.00	323
Totals	1.10	211	1.48	211	1.60	212		

Generation significant at $p < .001$; area significant at $p < .001$; interaction not significant.

TABLE 6:3. Mean Number of Memberships in non-Japanese Organizations, by Generation and Area.

| | AREA | | | | | | | |
| | Gardena | | Sacramento | | Fresno | | Totals | |
Generation	No.	N	No.	N	No.	N	No.	N
Nisei	1.26	105	1.49	103	1.73	103	1.49	311
Sansei	1.42	106	1.86	108	1.88	109	1.72	323
Totals	1.34	211	1.68	211	1.81	212		

Generation not significant; area significant at $p < .05$; interaction not significant.

processes that make it possible for Japanese Americans to maintain a significant number of ties to both the ethnic and mainstream communities. As can be seen in Table 6:4, the mainstream voluntary associations the respondents belong to tend to be more "personally instrumental" in character, such as business or professional groups. Nonetheless, these organizations would seem to qualify, in part at least, as evidence of structural assimilation through "cliques, clubs, and institutions of [the] host society" although they may not be "on [the] primary group level" (Gordon, 1964:71).

On the other hand, the ethnic voluntary associations in which the respondents participate tend to have more social (or perhaps "collectively instrumental") goals and to be characterized by more intimate forms of

TABLE 6:4. Percentage of All Respondents Who Belong to Japanese
American, Asian American, and Non-Asian American
Organizations (*N* = 631).

Type of Organization	Japanese American	Asian American	Non-Japanese or Asian American	Do Not Belong
	Ethnicity of Organization			
Labor union	0.5	0.0	23.0	76.5
Veteran or fraternal	8.7	0.5	7.1	83.7
Ethnic	31.5	1.1	0.8	66.6
Political	1.7	0.5	2.7	95.1
Neighborhood	3.8	0.5	3.0	92.7
Church	45.3	0.5	3.6	50.6
Business or professional	3.5	1.3	31.4	63.9
Civic	2.1	0.3	6.8	90.8
PTA	1.1	0.3	13.8	84.8
Community center	3.0	0.6	1.3	95.1
Sports	20.1	2.7	13.4	63.8
Country club	0.3	0.0	3.2	96.5
Other	2.8	0.6	7.0	89.6

interaction. This pattern is generally consistent with our argument about
the accommodative nature of Japanese social forms and the importance of
preserving social relationships within the group.

Tables 6:5 and 6:6 show involvement in the different types of organizations by generation. Only in the case of veteran or fraternal organizations
and neighborhood association types do the Sansei belong to more mainstream than ethnic associations.

Certainly, all the associations to which the respondents belong may
contain both instrumental and social (or solidary) elements. We would be
naive not to recognize, for example, that involvement in ethnic social
associations may be good for business in the case of the small-scale entre-
preneur. The critical distinction we are focusing on, however, is between
the sort of instrumental association that facilitates the personal adaptation
of the individual to mainstream society versus the more socially oriented
organization in which the primary reason for membership is to interact
socially with other persons who are in some sense similar or like-minded.

TABLE 6:5. Percentage of Nisei Who Belong to Japanese American, Asian American, and Non-Asian American Organizations (*N* = 310).

Type of Organization	Ethnicity of Organization			
	Japanese American	Asian American	Non-Japanese or Asian American	Do Not Belong
Labor union	0.6	0.0	22.9	76.5
Veteran or fraternal	15.8	0.6	6.8	76.8
Ethnic	41.6	0.6	0.6	57.1
Political	2.3	0.3	2.6	94.8
Neighborhood	7.1	0.6	2.9	89.4
Church	55.6	0.6	3.5	40.2
Business or professional	4.8	0.3	29.4	65.5
Civic	2.6	0.6	7.7	89.1
PTA	1.0	0.6	11.6	86.8
Community center	4.2	1.0	1.6	93.2
Sports	20.9	1.3	9.3	68.5
Country club	0.3	0.0	2.6	97.1
Other	3.5	0.0	5.1	91.3

Again, recalling Banton's (1981) notion that acculturation pressures are strongest in the areas most essential to economic survival, it is not surprising that as successive generations of Japanese Americans become structurally assimilated they will join instrumental voluntary associations to help adapt to American life. What is most unusual, at least compared to many other ethnic groups, is the capacity of members of this group to retain ties in their ethnic community through voluntary association membership while pursuing greater structural assimilation into the larger society through nonethnic voluntary associations.

This capacity to live in two worlds is illustrated by the results of the regression analysis presented in Table 6:7.

The first equation shows the results of regressing the strong-ties variable—best friends—on the personal characteristics of the respondents in our sample. Moving from exclusively Japanese American best friends to at least a "mixed" set of Caucasian and ethnic friends is clearly evi-

TABLE 6:6. Percentage of Sansei Who Belong to Japanese American, Asian American, and Non-Asian American Organizations (*N* = 321).

Type of Organization	Ethnicity of Organization			
	Japanese American	Asian American	Non-Japanese or Asian American	Do Not Belong
Labor union	0.3	0.0	23.1	76.6
Veteran or fraternal	1.9	0.3	7.5	90.3
Ethnic	21.8	1.6	0.9	75.7
Political	1.2	0.6	2.8	95.3
Neighborhood	0.6	0.3	3.1	96.0
Church	35.2	0.3	3.7	60.7
Business or professional	2.2	2.2	33.3	62.3
Civic	1.6	0.0	5.9	92.5
PTA	1.2	0.0	15.9	82.9
Community center	1.9	0.3	0.9	96.9
Sports	19.3	4.0	17.4	59.2
Country club	0.3	0.0	3.7	96.0
Other	2.2	1.2	8.7	87.9

dence of structural assimilation. It can be seen that persons in the younger generation and those who have more education are more assimilated.

Other evidence of a general assimilation process is found in equation 6, in which the measure of involvement in the mainstream community, membership in nonethnic voluntary associations, is regressed on the respondents' personal characteristics. Here we find that persons who are more educated and have more income are more likely to belong to mainstream voluntary associations. Equation 6 also shows, consistent with Granovetter's (1973) argument, that having exclusive "strong ties" in the ethnic community—in this instance having only Japanese Americans as best friends—is negatively associated with building bridges to the larger society through voluntary associations.

We can also observe, not surprisingly, that the tendency to have exclusively ethnic best friends is associated with greater involvement in Japanese American voluntary associations (see equation 4). The most interest-

TABLE 6:7. Regression of Choice of Best Friends and Involvement in Voluntary Associations ($N = 614$). (Unstandardized coefficients are the top figures; standardized coefficients are in parentheses.)

Variables	Friends		Japanese Organizations			Non-Japanese Organizations			
	EQ1	EQ2	EQ3	EQ4	EQ5	EQ6	EQ7	EQ8	EQ9
Generation	-.363*	-.369*	-.759*	-.631*	-.603*	-.035	-.130	-.083	-.083
	(-.232)	(-.236)	(-.276)	(-.229)	(-.219)	(-.010)	(-.037)	(-.024)	(-.024)
Education	-.043*	-.035*	.029	.044	.031	.291*	.279*	.276*	.274*
	(-.103)	(-.085)	(.040)	(.061)	(.042)	(.320)	(.308)	(.304)	(.302)
Income	-.004	-.003	.093*	.094*	.090*	.152*	.151*	.144*	.144*
	(-.015)	(-.010)	(.189)	(.192)	(.184)	(.247)	(.245)	(.234)	(.233)
Friends				.352*	.401*		-.262*	-.288*	-.276*
				(.200)	(.228)		(-.119)	(-.130)	(-.125)
Japanese Organizations								.074	.066
								(.059)	(.053)
Sacramento[a]		-.251*			.476*				.084
		(-.151)			(.163)				(.023)
Fresno[a]		-.241*			.549*				.122
		(-.146)			(.189)				(.033)
Constant	1.69	1.823	1.135	.539	.193	-.421	.023	-.017	-.081
R^2	.082	.104	.126	.163	.193	.195	.208	.210	.211

*$p < .05$.

[a]Gardena is the reference category in relation to the dummy variables for Sacramento and Fresno.

ing result, however, is found in equation 3, in which involvement in ethnic organizations is regressed on the respondents' personal characteristics. Here we find that although education may be an impediment to the preservation of exclusive strong-tie relationships in the ethnic community, it poses no barrier to the preservation of ethnic ties through membership in voluntary associations. In other words, educated Japanese Americans are more likely to have Caucasian friends (see equation 1), but there is no evidence that they are any less likely to belong to ethnic voluntary associations.

The importance of the preceding finding cannot be overstated. If strong ties were the only kind of relationship one could maintain with the ethnic community, we would have to conclude, along the lines of the assimilationist argument, that as individuals become more structurally assimilated they will experience a commensurate loss of involvement in their ethnic community. We have seen, however, that the assimilationist argument overlooks the fact that structural assimilation does not necessarily destroy other kinds of ties to the ethnic community. In the Japanese American case, at least, the preservation of organizational ties to the ethnic community, primarily through ethnic voluntary associations, is quite compatible with the establishment of social linkages to persons in the larger society.

The ability of Japanese Americans to institutionalize ethnic community involvement through participation in voluntary associations, stems, in large measure, from characteristics inherent in their social relational forms. Because their culture combines an essentially relativistic worldview, with a strong emphasis on the preservation of social relationships between ethnic group members, Japanese American social organization has been flexible in adjusting to various exigencies, including the structural assimilation of succeeding generations. Strong support for this line of reasoning is found in equation 8, where it can be seen that having more strong ties to the ethnic community (i.e., having more ethnic best friends) is negatively associated with the development of weak ties to the mainstream community through involvement in voluntary associations, but involvement in ethnic voluntary associations does not have this limiting effect on building bridges to the nonethnic world.

Areal Differences in Social Relationships

As noted in Chapter 4, the three areas from which the sample was drawn reflect different kinds of social contexts with which individual Japanese

Americans have had to deal. The most important dimensions on which they differ are rural versus urban and the percentage of fellow ethnics in each area.

Equation 2 shows that living in Gardena, the most urbanized and densely Japanese area, substantially increases the likelihood that an individual will have exclusively Japanese American best friends. On the other hand, equation 5 illustrates that living in the less urbanized and less densely Japanese areas of Sacramento and Fresno is positively associated with the development of ties in the ethnic community through voluntary association membership. See Tables 6:1 and 6:2 for the relevant areal means.

These findings may seem somewhat surprising. Fischer's study of social networks in areas with different degrees of urbanism found that persons in the most urbanized areas had the highest levels of voluntary association membership (1982:111). Roche's (1982) study of Italian Americans shows similar results. Informal friendship networks with fellow ethnics as well as ethnic voluntary association memberships declined at a similar rate as individuals moved from areas of high to low concentrations of fellow ethnics. In our sample, however, the reverse is the case for both ethnic and nonethnic voluntary association membership (see Tables 6:2 and 6:3), although the relationship between area and nonethnic membership disappears when we control for personal characteristics, as shown in equation 9 of Table 6:7. Nevertheless, the finding that ethnic community involvement through voluntary association membership is greater in the more rural, less densely Japanese areas calls for some explanation.

Fischer's "subculture of urbanism" thesis (1975, 1976:35–38, 1982:202–208) proposes that subcultures are most likely to be sustained when they possess a "critical mass." Therefore, the expectation is that urbanized areas will be more supportive of such subcultures. One might justifiably argue that all three of the areas in this study have a sufficient critical mass of Japanese Americans, since even in Fresno or Sacramento the slightly greater than one percent of the population that is Japanese American consists of several thousand persons. Nonetheless, we would predict, following Fischer, that the much higher ethnic concentration in Gardena would be more supportive of ethnic voluntary associational life than would be the case in the other two areas. Indeed, the findings on the fate of many European ethnic subcultures as persons leave the densely settled urban enclaves for the suburbs (Goering, 1971; Roche,

1982) suggest that such a decline in the availability of fellow ethnics has a disastrous effect on the maintenance of ethnic community institutional life. The Japanese American situation with respect to ethnic voluntary association membership, therefore, stands in sharp contrast to that of these other ethnic groups.

The higher levels of ethnic voluntary association membership among Japanese Americans living in the less urban, less densely ethnic areas is probably due to the influence of Japanese culture on maintaining social relationships and the existence of the social organizational mechanisms we discussed in Chapter 2. In this regard, the somewhat lower ethnic voluntary association participation levels in Gardena may merely reflect that persons in that area can maintain ethnic contacts through strong-tie relationships without having to expend much effort in voluntary association activities. Significantly, the pattern of greater ethnic voluntary association involvement in areas that are less densely populated ethnically is also found among Jews (see Rose, 1959; Rosentraub and Taebel, 1980).

In fact, there is some evidence from the interviews that respondents in Gardena are more apt to see their ethnic community in terms of informal ties and easy availability of Japanese cultural items, such as groceries and restaurants, whereas Japanese Americans in Fresno and Sacramento are more apt to see their ethnic community in terms of formal organizational structures. Some representative comments of Gardena respondents, when asked to describe the Japanese American community, include:

"It's very closely knit, we tend to keep to ourselves, stay together, socialize together, and do things together."

"We're well liked here. Any Caucasian who doesn't like Japanese has no business living here."

"The markets carry Japanese food which you don't get in other areas. There are more stores oriented towards Japanese . . . gift shops, restaurants."

"This community has Japanese stores and shops. A lot of Japanese is spoken here. We have a Buddhist church. . . . it's almost like a little Japantown. A lot of my friends live around here. I see more Japanese Americans here than when I was living in L.A."

Some typical comments of respondents from Sacramento and Fresno, when asked to describe their ethnic community, include:

"It's related to the Buddhist Church, the culture and social events sponsored by the church."

"We have a church basketball league. We also have bazaars. There's an Asian softball league."

"It [the community] revolves around the churches . . . the Buddhist, the Methodist. . . . A natural gathering place. That's the only one Japanese have now because they're so assimilated. I'm sure there's JACL, but basically it revolves around the church."

Nevertheless, again it must be emphasized that the manner in which individuals relate to their ethnic community has substantial consequences for their involvement in the mainstream community. Persons in Gardena have fewer bridges to the larger society because of the limiting effects of ethnic strong-tie relationships. Alternatively, respondents in Sacramento and Fresno, who rely much more heavily on associational involvements to tie into their ethnic communities, are not as constrained by those linkages in building bridges to persons in nonethnic communities. This ability to be involved in networks in two different worlds has become a very important resource for persons in these communities. We will treat this matter at length in Chapter 9.

CONCLUSION

In this chapter we have examined the processes of structural assimilation and retention of ethnic community cohesion in terms of the types of linkages individual Japanese Americans have to their fellow ethnics and to the larger society. The effect of structural assimilation on strong ties to fellow ethnics appears to be very similar to what others have found in studies of European ethnic groups. Not surprisingly, the Sansei are substantially more likely than the Nisei to name a Caucasian as one of their two best friends. In addition, we saw that the availability of fellow ethnics in the local area, as measured by the proportion of residents who are Japanese Americans, has a strong effect on the maintenance of exclusively strong ties to fellow ethnics. It should be noted that it is among the

Sansei, who do not have as compelling a set of shared experiences as the Nisei, that the size of the local Japanese population exerts its greatest influence on friendship. In short, as Japanese Americans become more geographically dispersed, they develop more friendships with persons outside their ethnic community. Indeed, as we will see in Chapter 8, these same ecological and demographic processes can be expected to increase the already high rate of intermarriage with Caucasians.

The more important findings presented in this chapter, however, pertain to the ability of Japanese Americans to maintain linkages to their ethnic community through memberships in ethnic voluntary associations while becoming increasingly linked to mainstream society through membership in nonethnic voluntary associations. Perhaps the strongest empirical evidence for the capacity of this ethnic community to survive in the face of structural assimilation is the finding that membership in ethnic voluntary associations is significantly higher in Fresno and Sacramento, where the proportion of Japanese Americans in the total local population is quite small. In this regard, the resilience of the Japanese American community in such areas parallels the pattern Rose (1959) found among small-town Jews in upstate New York.

In short, these findings support our basic thesis that because of the culturally and historically reinforced bases of internal solidarity in the Japanese American community, particularly its reliance on forms of social organization other than strong ties, it can adapt to the pressures of structural assimilation without totally losing its cohesiveness.

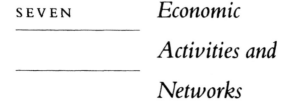

SEVEN

Economic

Activities and

Networks

A s noted in Chapter 3, historically the most distinctive economic characteristic of Japanese Americans has been their disproportionate involvement in petit bourgeois activities which have been supported by the ethnic community. Not only did the ethnic community provide customers but the businesses themselves were organized and rationalized through ethnic guilds, cooperatives, associations, and other mechanisms allowing them, collectively, to develop some of the advantages of the "center" economy, hence a competitive advantage in relation to other small producers (e.g., Light, 1972, 1979; Wilson and Portes, 1980). This adaptation, however, was dramatically altered by World War II.

The evacuation and relocation not only disrupted the petit bourgeois economic accommodation but it also changed the social and demographic characteristics of the ethnic community (e.g., Woodrum et al., 1980). When Japanese Americans began to leave the internment camps in significant numbers toward the end of the war, the War Relocation Authority discouraged them from concentrating in ethnic enclaves similar to the ones they had left (Albert, 1980:114–115; Myer, 1971). This made it difficult for them to reestablish the economic networks they had developed during the prewar era. Moreover, many of the Issei were too old to

TABLE 7:1. Self-Employed Persons, by Generation and Area (*N* = 617).

	AREA							
	Gardena		*Sacramento*		*Fresno*		*Totals*	
Generation	%	N	%	N	%	N	%	N
Nisei	31.7	104	23.8	101	59.8	102	38.4	307
Sansei	14.9	101	13.5	104	30.5	105	19.7	310
Totals	23.4	205	18.5	205	44.9	207	29.0	617

By generation: χ^2 (1, $N = 617$) = 25.45, $p < .001$.
By area: χ^2 (2, $N = 617$) = 39.5, $p < .001$.
By generation and area: χ^2 (2, $N = 617$) = 1.24, p = n.s.

rebuild their businesses. Finally, the leadership of the community had passed to the English-speaking Nisei during the war (e.g., Spickard, 1983), and this generation found postwar American society much more open to their moving into mainstream business and professional occupations. For the first time, Japanese Americans had real options with respect to the kinds of careers they wanted to pursue. No longer were they locked into the ethnic economy with its monotonous jobs on farms and in small retail operations. Not only could they train to become teachers, engineers, and managers, but they could be hired as such.

Given the massive changes that have taken place since World War II, both in the larger society and among Japanese Americans themselves, an important question is: what legacy remains of the once dynamic ethnic economic accommodation? Is its present form merely a dying remnant of an earlier era or has it been rebuilt into a different but still vital institution?

THE PERSISTENCE OF ECONOMIC NETWORKS

As shown in Table 7:1, Japanese Americans apparently are still overrepresented in small business endeavors. In 1980, 9.2 percent of the U.S. male labor force was self-employed. By comparison, 38.4 percent of the Nisei and 19.7 percent of the Sansei in our sample are in the small business sector. These figures for Japanese Americans, however, are not based on a representative sample. Our sample has a rural bias; one-third of the respondents were purposely selected from the Fresno area. For example, farmers were 8.6 percent of our sample, compared with 2.9 percent of all

TABLE 7:2. Mean Percentage of Japanese Co-Workers, by Generation and Employment Status ($N = 546$).

| | Employment Status | | |
Generation	Self-Employed	Not Self-Employed	Totals
Nisei	36.13	13.71	20.80
Sansei	23.08	15.46	16.84
Totals	31.01	14.72	

Generational effect: $F (1, N = 532) = .549, p = $ n.s.
Employment status effect: $F (1, N = 532) = 31.914, p < .001$.
Interaction status effect: $F (1, N = 532) = 6.740, p < .01$.

Japanese males living in California (U.S. Bureau of the Census, 1983a). Nevertheless, even though we cannot determine the exact percentage of Japanese in small business in the United States or even in California, we can obtain a fairly precise picture of the absolute level of self-employment among males in the three different areas in the sample as well as determine the extent of generational change in self-employment status. In all three areas, there has been a significant drop in the number of self-employed persons in the third generation. Yet, even in the area with the fewest self-employed, Sacramento, Japanese Americans are almost twice as likely to be self-employed (18.5 percent) as the national average. In short, the self-employment mode still appears more prevalent among Japanese Americans than among other Americans, although not to the extent that it was during the pre–World War II years.

Moreover, there is considerable evidence that the ethnic community still plays a significant role in supporting the petit bourgeois accommodation. Table 7:2 shows that self-employed respondents work with a higher percentage of Japanese Americans than do their nonself-employed counterparts. This pattern continues, although in a weaker form, in the Sansei generation. Similarly, the percentage of self-employed persons who have relatives working for them decreased only from 38.6 percent among the Nisei to 32.7 percent among the Sansei.

Another important piece of evidence illustrating the persistence of the ethnic economy is the high number of self-employed persons who continue to have business dealings with other Japanese Americans. These figures are 58.1 percent for self-employed Nisei and 70.0 percent for self-

TABLE 7:3. Mean Number of Japanese Businesses and Services
Patronized, by Generation and Employment Status ($N =$
599).[a]

| | Employment Status | | |
Generation	Self-Employed	Not Self-Employed	Totals
Nisei	7.67	6.63	6.96
Sansei	6.51	5.74	5.88
Totals	7.22	6.12	

Generational effect: $F (1, N = 532) = 20.731, p < .001$.
Employment status effect: $F (1, N = 32) = 14.562, p < .001$.
Interaction effect: $F (1, N = 599) = .329, p = $ n.s.

[a]The specific businesses and services include: oriental food store, grocery store, restaurant,
medical doctor, dentist, optometrist, garage, lawyer, drugstore, insurance agent, other
retail store, other professional.

employed Sansei, compared with 30.0 and 34.6 percent for their nonself-
employed counterparts. Here we see little indication of intergenerational
erosion of the ethnic business and social network for those who remain in
the small business niche. Indeed, the percentage of business dealings with
fellow ethnics is higher for the Sansei than for the Nisei.

A third set of indicators of an ethnic economic network is patronage of
ethnic businesses and services. As shown in Table 7:3, the overall frequency of dealing with fellow ethnics is quite high, with respondents
regularly patronizing an average of six or seven ethnic businesses. Although there is a slight drop-off in ethnic patronage from the Nisei to the
Sansei generations, the self-employed in both generations utilize Japanese
American establishments more than the nonself-employed do. These results strongly suggest that the ethnic economy persists.

INVOLVEMENT OF THE PETITE BOURGEOISIE IN THE ETHNIC COMMUNITY

One of the crucial features of the traditional petit bourgeois accommodation among Japanese Americans was the involvement of small-scale entrepreneurs in the institutional life of the ethnic community. To be sure,
small businessmen of any ethnic background find utilitarian reasons for
community involvement and building good will. However, the Japanese
ethnic economy, because of discrimination on the part of both nonethnic

TABLE 7:4. Mean Number of Memberships in Japanese Voluntary Associations, by Generation and Employment Status ($N = 599$).

| Generation | Employment Status | | Totals |
	Self-Employed	Not Self-Employed	
Nisei	2.03	1.35	1.61
Sansei	1.23	.90	.96
Totals	1.75	1.09	

Generational effect: $F (1, N = 599) = 42.104$, $p < .001$.
Employment status effect: $F (1, N = 599) = 33.275$, $p < .001$.
Interaction effect: $F (1, N = 599) = 3.320$, $p =$ n.s.

management and labor, was of crucial importance to the economic well-being of the ethnic group as a whole.

Since the most vigorous and talented individuals became successful small businessmen, and because the ethnic economy was built with many elements of the community dependent on one another (e.g., in agriculture a vertically and horizontally integrated ethnic economy was created), small businessmen became involved in all spheres of community life (Bonacich, 1975). They did so not only for the good will they built but because they realized the importance of making collective responses to various exigencies. The reader will recall the rather dramatic example of this in the El Monte berry strike described in Chapter 3. In addition, the more successful entrepreneurs felt responsible to support those whose efforts had been crucial to their own success.

Now that the Japanese have many employment opportunities in the center sector of the mainstream economy, an intriguing question is whether the pattern of participation and leadership exhibited earlier by the Issei petite bourgeoisie continues or whether persons in this class have become the classic loners described in the general small business literature (e.g., Bertaux and Bertaux-Wiame, 1981).

The figures in Table 7:4 show that although there is a reduction in ethnic voluntary association membership among both self-employed and nonself-employed Sansei, the former still have substantially higher rates of involvement than the latter. Indeed, the mean level of participation among the self-employed Sansei is almost as great as that of the nonself-employed

TABLE 7:5. Persons Who Read Japanese Vernacular Newspapers, by Generation and Employment Status (*N* = 615).

| | Employment Status | | | |
| | Self-Employed (%) | Not Self-Employed (%) | Totals (%) | *N* |
Generation				
Nisei	69.4	42.9	51.1	307
Sansei	28.3	18.5	20.5	308
Totals	52.2	29.1		
	(*N* = 178)	(*N* = 437)		

By generation and employment status: χ^2 (1, *N* = 615) = .654, *p* = n.s.
By generation: χ^2 (1, *N* = 615) = 61.42, *p* < .001.
By employment status: χ^2 (1, *N* = 615) = 28.592, *p* < .001.

TABLE 7:6. Persons Who Attend Japanese Community Picnics, by Generation and Employment Status (*N* = 609).

| | Employment Status | | | |
| | Self-Employed (%) | Not Self-Employed (%) | Totals (%) | *N* |
Generation				
Nisei	57.3	40.6	47.1	304
Sansei	53.3	44.1	45.9	305
Totals	55.9	42.6		
	(*N* = 177)	(*N* = 432)		

By generation: χ^2 (1, *N* = 609) = .065, *p* = n.s.
By employment status: χ^2 (1, *N* = 609) = 8.453, *p* < .01.
By generation and employment status: χ^2 (1, *N* = 609) = .639, *p* = n.s.

Nisei. A similar pattern of involvement is found with regard to reading Japanese vernacular newspapers (which commonly have both Japanese and English sections) and attendance at Japanese community picnics.

As shown in Table 7:5, Nisei are much more likely than Sansei to read Japanese newspapers, but the self-employed in both generations are more likely than the nonself-employed to read them. Table 7:6 shows a high overall level of attendance at ethnic community picnics. Again, however, self-employed Nisei and Sansei are more likely to attend than are their nonself-employed counterparts.

TABLE 7:7. Mean Number of Japanese Best Friends, by Generation and Employment Status (Maximum Value = 2).

	Employment Status		
Generation	Self-Employed	Not Self-Employed	Totals
Nisei	1.58	1.48	1.51
Sansei	1.13	1.10	1.11
Totals	1.42	1.26	

Generational effect: F (1, $N = 617$) = 40.123, $p < .001$.
Employment status effect: F (1, $N = 617$) = 1.105, p = n.s.
Interaction effect: F (1, $N = 617$) = .245, p = n.s.

It is somewhat surprising that there is no intergenerational reduction in attendance at Japanese picnics within the occupational subgroups or in the sample as a whole. The most plausible interpretation is that since these picnics are very family-oriented affairs, when one cohort does not attend it discourages attendance by the others. Normally, extended families sit and eat together. Since friends use this occasion to catch up on the fortunes and whereabouts of acquaintances and relatives, individuals feel some pressure to look their best. Having the entire family present adds credibility to the perception that the family is close and thus "successful."

It is interesting to observe in Table 7:7 that although self-employment is associated with many dimensions of involvement in the ethnic community, it is not associated with the extent to which one's best friends are fellow ethnics. The findings in Chapter 6, it will be recalled, suggested that the extent to which Japanese Americans have exclusively ethnic best friends is more a function of ethnic density than a desire to be involved with other Japanese. In fact, as shown in the earlier presentation (Chapter 6), some of the highest levels of involvement in ethnic community voluntary associations occurred in the communities that also possessed the least ethnically exclusive friendship patterns. These results, along with the finding of a lack of relationship between self-employment and friendship, reinforce the view that the Japanese American community rests on a social organizational base emphasizing not strong-tie friendships but quasi-kin ties, which are most likely to be found in ethnic voluntary associations.

TABLE 7:8. Mean Educational Attainment, by Generation and Employment Status (*N* = 599).[a]

| Generation | Employment Status | | Totals |
	Self-Employed	Not Self-Employed	
Nisei	3.48	3.27	3.35
Sansei	5.72	4.54	4.78
Totals	4.26	4.00	

Generational effect: $F(1, N = 599) = 108.824, p < .001$.
Employment status effect: $F(1, N = 599) = 14.082, p < .001$.
Interaction effect: $F(1, N = 599) = 8.700, p < .01$.

[a] Scale values: some high school (1), high school graduate (2), some technical or college (3), associate degree (4), bachelor's degree (5), some graduate or professional training (6), master's degree (7), law, medical, or dental degree, Ph.D. (8).

HUMAN CAPITAL, THE ETHNIC COMMUNITY, AND THE PETIT BOURGEOIS ACCOMMODATION

Historically, ethnic small businessmen who have had access to the resources of their ethnic community have been portrayed as having a competitive advantage in relation to other producers (e.g., Bonacich and Modell, 1980; Wilson and Portes, 1980). In the contemporary world, however, with its more open opportunity structure, an argument might be made that embedding oneself in ethnic economic relationships is not only limiting but something one does when he or she cannot seize opportunities elsewhere. Attempting to make a living in a contemporary ethnic enclave thus may be a classic example of an ethnic mobility trap. Therefore, one might predict that the contemporary petite bourgeoisie would be among the least economically successful persons in an ethnic community. Our data, which are shown in Table 7:8, however, present quite a different picture.

In both generations, the self-employed are better educated than the nonself-employed. The difference among Nisei, however, is quite small, with both subgroups averaging some college attendance. Among the Sansei, the difference between the self-employed and nonself-employed is much greater. The nonself-employed Sansei average somewhat less than a bachelor's degree, the self-employed more than a bachelor's. The difference among the Sansei is partly a function of the greater age of the

TABLE 7:9. Regression of Income on Age, Educational Attainment, and Employment Status ($N = 597$). (Unstandardized coefficients are the top figures; standardized coefficients are in parentheses.)

Variables	EQ1	EQ2
Generation	−.001	.100
	(−.001)	(.018)
Age	.073***	.063***
	(.357)	(.308)
Education	.408***	.366***
	(.357)	(.320)
Employment status		1.405***
		(.226)
Constant	.739	.920
R^2	.163	.211

*$p < .05$. **$p < .01$. ***$p < .001$.

self-employed, approximately half of whom are professionals or technical persons. Given the higher educational attainment of the self-employed, it is not surprising that they have higher incomes than those who work for others. In 1979–80 (the time of the survey) the nonself-employed Sansei had an average income of $15,000 to $20,000, while the self-employed Sansei had an average income of $30,000 to $35,000. Among the Nisei, the nonself-employed average was $20,000 to $25,000 and the self-employed average was $30,000 to $35,000. The Nisei have a greater overall income partly because they are older and thus more senior in their respective businesses and careers.

To examine the amount of unique variance in income accounted for by being self-employed, we regressed income on self-employment, controlling for age, generation, and educational attainment. As can be seen in Table 7:9, even after educational attainment is controlled, the self-employed enjoy higher earnings.

In order to obtain a clearer picture of the types of occupations Nisei and Sansei have entered, particularly with regard to the self-employment category, we aggregated the census occupational codes into seven broad categories. This is shown in Table 7:10.

As previously noted, there is a substantial drop in the percentage of

TABLE 7:10. Percentage of Respondents in Various Occupational Categories, by Generation and Employment Status ($N = 615$).[a]

Occupational Category	Nisei		Sansei	
	Not Self-Employed	Self-Employed	Not Self-Employed	Self-Employed
Professional and technical	72.5	27.5	77.3	22.7
	39.4	23.7	46.8	55.2
	(74)[b]	(28)	(116)	(34)
Managerial	63.3	36.7	92.1	7.9
	10.1	9.3	14.1	4.9
	(19)	(11)	(35)	(3)
Clerical and sales	73.2	26.8	87.1	12.9
	16.0	9.3	21.8	13.1
	(30)	(11)	(54)	(8)
Service	88.2	11.8	90.9	9.1
	8.0	1.7	4.0	1.6
	(15)	(2)	(10)	(1)
Agriculture, fishing, forestry, and related fields	15.6	84.4	46.2	53.8
	5.3	45.8	4.8	23.0
	(10)	(54)	(12)	(14)
Trades	77.1	22.9	95.5	4.5
	19.7	9.3	8.5	1.6
	(37)	(11)	(21)	(1)
Miscellaneous	75.0	25.0		
	1.6	.8	0	0
	(3)	(1)		
	61.4	38.6	80.3	19.7
	(188)	(118)	(248)	(61)

[a] First number is the row percentage; second number is the column percentage.
[b] Number of respondents is shown in parentheses.

self-employed as one moves from the Nisei to the Sansei. This is consistent with the reduction in the number of self-employed in the United States at large that has taken place over the period covered by the two generations (Goldscheider and Kobrin, 1980; Ray, 1975). Also, not surprisingly, there is a shift in type of self-employment. Among the Nisei, the largest percentage (45.8 percent) of the self-employed are in agriculture, fishing, forestry, and related occupations. Among the Sansei, the percentage in these categories falls to 23.0 percent. For the latter generation, the majority of self-employed persons (55.7 percent) are in the professional-technical category.

Taken together, the preceding analyses lead to several conclusions. The size of the petit bourgeois niche is becoming smaller, and the occupations in the niche are shifting from farming and gardening to professional and technical categories. Nevertheless, the percentage of Sansei who remain in the traditional petit bourgeois occupational categories (almost one-fifth of the sample) is quite high even if we allow for the bias introduced by sampling from the Fresno area, which contains a larger number of farmers. Moreover, the mechanisms that supported the pre–World War II ethnic economy still support Japanese American entrepreneurial activity. Not only do the self-employed work with more Japanese, patronize more Japanese businesses and services, belong to more Japanese organizations, read more vernacular newspapers, and attend more Japanese picnics, but they also earn more money. This is in sharp contrast to Ray's (1975) finding that, overall, the self-employed and nonself-employed in the United States are similar in earnings. Our data argue quite strongly that the self-employed who remain embedded in an ethnic economy, although in different occupations than their predecessors, still enjoy some unique advantages.

CONCLUSION

In this chapter we examined the extent to which the ethnic economy still exists and the degree to which its traditional form has changed. As one might expect, with the removal of the discriminatory employment barriers after World War II, Japanese Americans have moved into mainstream corporate and governmental careers in significant numbers.

We also found, however, that they, like American Jews (Goldscheider and Kobrin, 1980), continue to be overrepresented in the small business sector. In one sense, the ethnic economy has significantly changed in that the small businesses involved are no longer principally farming and shopkeeping but professional and technical in nature. Thus, not only are individual Japanese Americans currently able to utilize their generally high levels of education in this economic form but also, on average, they earn higher incomes. Continuing advantages of the ethnic economy include the ability to use ethnic community networks for contacts and to employ ethnic labor, which is likely to be more loyal. Therefore, at the individual level of analysis, our results clearly demonstrate that the ethnic economy is not a mobility trap. In fact, it still offers a number of unique advantages compared with mainstream salaried positions.

From a more macrosocial perspective, our data show that although smaller in size and less tightly bounded, the petit bourgeois accommodation has been able to adapt to new circumstances and continues to perpetuate ethnicity among Japanese Americans. Because small businessmen remain active in ethnic organizations and tend to hire fellow ethnics, they also have more opportunities for face-to-face interaction with fellow group members. The petite bourgeoisie are more likely than other Japanese Americans to patronize other Japanese businesses, read vernacular papers, and attend community picnics (see also Bonacich, 1975).

Thus, in many ways, the classic community supports for the small business accommodation continue to operate. These results are quite consistent with structural explanations of ethnicity, such as middleman minority theory (e.g., Bonacich, 1973; Bonacich and Modell, 1980). What the purely structural arguments have greater difficulty explaining, however, is that the relatively high level of ethnic solidarity is combined with a high level of structural assimilation. Although they do not directly address this point, their approach appears to suggest essentially a zero-sum relationship between ethnic solidarity and structural assimilation. Yet our findings demonstrate that this is clearly not the case with contemporary Japanese Americans. In addition to our findings on the compatibility of involvement in ethnic and nonethnic voluntary associations, reported in the last chapter, the data presented in this chapter show that even though the petite bourgeoisie are more involved than those who work for others in ethnic community life, they are no less likely to be structurally assimilated into mainstream society through friendships with Caucasians.

EIGHT

Intermarriage

In the three preceding chapters we have shown that Japanese Americans, by and large, have been able to build bridges to the majority group, establishing many kinds of contacts with Caucasians without destroying their ethnic community life. One might argue, however, that with the exception of the "best friends" measure, most of the evidence about ties to mainstream society that we have examined has involved a relatively low level of intimacy. Given the fact, as reported earlier, that Japanese Americans are increasingly intermarrying with Caucasians (Kitano et al., 1984), the critical question is: can the current relationship between structural assimilation and involvement in the ethnic community continue when more intimate forms of contact with the majority group are involved? In this chapter we will examine the effects of intermarriage on ethnic community participation and attempt to project what may be its consequences.

To gain some sense of perspective on both the current rate of intermarriage and its future consequences for ethnic community cohesiveness, it is helpful first to look at what intermarriage rates were like before World War II.

CHANGING RATES OF INTERMARRIAGE

Before World War II, Japanese American communities were, in many ways, socially and economically self-sufficient. This was the product of both widespread discrimination and the group's collectivistic adaptational strategies. By and large, they were occupationally segregated, somewhat residentially segregated, and usually, except in certain elementary schools in the Sacramento area, educationally integrated. Socially, their intimate friends were almost entirely other Japanese Americans, and most of their organizational involvements were with fellow ethnics.

The antimiscegenation laws in force in California from 1905 to 1948 made it illegal for the Japanese to intermarry. During the World War II internment years, the Nisei, whose average age at the time of evacuation was nineteen, were physically prevented from meeting members of the opposite sex from other ethnic and racial groups. Given these barriers, it is not surprising that Issei and Nisei intermarriage was an infrequent event. It is estimated that Issei men in California had an intermarriage rate of approximately 2 percent and Nisei men approximately 4 percent (Spickard, 1980). The Nisei rate was substantially lower than the approximately 20 percent intermarriage rate of second generation European ethnics (Spickard, 1980). By the late 1970s, however, intermarriage among the third generation Sansei had jumped to about 60 percent of all new marriages, including 50 percent with non-Asians (Kitano et al., 1984).

Table 8:1 shows the inmarriage-outmarriage ratio for our sample.* The intermarriage ratio for the Sansei is not nearly as high as the rates reported elsewhere. There are several reasons for this. Most of the other studies include Japanese women, who historically have outmarried at a higher rate than men. Moreover, our study includes Sansei men who married during the 1960s, when the intermarriage rate was lower. The much higher rates reported by Kitano et al. (1984) and others (Endo and

---

*These figures refer to intermarriage ratios rather than to intermarriage rates. Sklare (1964:46–52) distinguishes between intermarriage rates, which refer to new cases of intermarriage in a given year, and intermarriage ratios, which refer to the total number of intermarriages in an ethnic or religious group, or some subset of it, over time. The intermarriage rate among the Sansei generation of Japanese Americans, as previously noted, is about 60 percent of all new marriages, including 50 percent with non-Asians, (Kitano et al., 1984), but the intermarriage ratio, which we are reporting here, is much lower because it covers a much longer period, even when its point of reference is a single generation.

TABLE 8:1. Males Inmarried and Outmarried, by Generation (N = 490).

Generation	Inmarried		Outmarried	
	%	N	%	N
Nisei	93.6	264	6.4	18
Sansei	74.5	155	25.5	53
Total sample	85.5	419	14.5	71

TABLE 8:2. Intermarriage by Area for Married Sansei (N = 192).

Married Sansei	Area				
	Gardena (%)	Sacramento (%)	Fresno (%)	Total (%)	N
Intermarried	10.0	30.3	24.2	21.9	42
Not intermarried	90.0	69.7	75.8	78.1	150

χ^2 (2) = 7.911, $p < .01$.

Hirokawa, 1983; Tinker, 1982) are for those *currently* getting married. Nonetheless, the intergenerational differences in the ratios of intermarriage in our sample are substantial. The increased number of outmarriages among the Sansei reflects the dramatic reduction in prejudice and discrimination toward Japanese Americans following World War II. Another factor is that the Nisei have shown much less resistance to their children intermarrying than their Issei parents did.

Table 8:2 illustrates that today there is considerable variability between communities with respect to intermarriage. The intermarriage ratio for the Sansei is lowest in Gardena, the area with the highest density of Japanese Americans. In one sense it is not entirely appropriate to compare the density of a city, Gardena, with that of a county, Fresno, and a metropolitan area, Sacramento. Nevertheless, we should note that Japanese Americans growing up in Gardena can, if they wish, restrict their informal social contacts almost entirely to fellow ethnic group members, whereas this would be considerably more difficult in either Fresno or Sacramento. Using data from other areas, Spickard (1980) and Endo and Hirokawa (1983) report that intermarriage rates are higher for Japanese

Americans who live away from the high ethnic density areas of the West Coast. These findings suggest that if the Japanese American population becomes more geographically dispersed in the future, even higher rates of intermarriage will occur.

One might argue that the relationship between ethnic density and intermarriage may be due partly to a selective migration process. The more visible Japanese American community in Gardena may very well encourage the intermarried to move out and the inmarried to move in from other areas. Our ethnographic encounters with respondents in the different areas generally support this view. Many young Sansei couples with children reported that they lived in Gardena so that their children would be exposed to a Japanese American social environment.

Nevertheless, the most crucial question with regard to this study is: what will be the impact of increased intermarriage on the persistence of the Japanese American community? In previous chapters we found that less intimate forms of structural assimilation do not appear to have a very negative effect on ethnic group cohesiveness, but the question remains whether this very intimate form of assimilation may have consequences that will dramatically weaken the involvement of individual Japanese Americans with their fellow ethnics.

THE EFFECTS OF INTERMARRIAGE ON ETHNIC GROUP COHESION

Since the proportion of Nisei who are intermarried is very small, this phase of the analysis was restricted to Sansei men. Table 8:3 shows, as might be expected, that those Sansei who are married to Japanese American women are more involved in the formal organizational life of their ethnic communities. An inmarried couple is more likely to share common interests in Japanese American issues and friends and to have two sets of ethnic kin and friends to lead them into the formal organizational life of the community. What is perhaps most striking, however, is that even among the intermarried, fully 50 percent belong to at least one Japanese American voluntary association. This figure is many times greater than the less than 5 percent ethnic voluntary association membership reported in studies of third generation European ethnics (Chapter 6; Goering, 1971; Roche, 1982).

The relationship between intermarriage and the ethnic composition of the church the Sansei attend (Table 8:4) is similar to that of intermarriage and voluntary association membership in general. The intermarried are

TABLE 8:3. Number of Japanese Organizational Memberships, by Intermarriage for Married Sansei (*N* = 192).

| | Japanese Organizational Memberships | | | | | |
Married Sansei	None (%)	1 (%)	2 (%)	3 or more (%)	Total (%)	N
Intermarried	50.0	35.7	14.3	0.0	21.9	42
Not intermarried	33.3	28.0	22.7	16.0	78.1	150
Total subsample	37.0	29.7	20.8	12.5	100.0	192

χ^2 (3) = 10.949, p < .01.

TABLE 8:4. Type of Church Membership, by Intermarriage for Married Sansei (*N* = 191).

| | Ethnicity of Church | | | | |
Married Sansei	Asian American (%)	Non–Asian American (%)	No Church Membership (%)	Total (%)	N
Intermarried	26.2	9.5	69.3	22.0	42
Not intermarried	44.3	3.4	52.3	78.0	149
Total subsample	40.3	4.7	55.0	100.0	191

χ^2 (2) = 6.159, p < .05.

less likely than the inmarried to attend an ethnic church. At the same time, the percentage of intermarried who do attend an ethnic church is probably substantially higher than we would find in most European ethnic groups, with a few exceptions (such as Eastern Rite Orthodox groups) where the religious affiliation is unique to the ethnic group. Further, intermarriage appears to have a general dampening effect on this type of organizational involvement, as can be seen by the large number of "no church memberships" among the intermarried.

Table 8:5 shows that whether or not a Sansei has a Japanese American spouse has little effect on involvement in non-Japanese organizations. In fact, although the difference is not statistically significant, there is a tendency for the inmarried to belong to more non-Japanese American organizations than the outmarried. This finding supports our central

TABLE 8:5. Number of Non-Japanese Organizational Memberships, by Intermarriage for Married Sansei (*N* = 192).

| Married Sansei | *Non-Japanese Organizational Memberships* | | | | | |
	None (%)	1 (%)	2 (%)	3 or more (%)	Total (%)	N
Intermarried	26.2	23.8	10.0	31.0	21.9	42
Not intermarried	19.3	28.7	18.0	34.0	78.1	150
Total subsample	20.8	27.6	18.2	33.3	100.0	192

χ^2 (3) = 1.132, *p* = n.s.

TABLE 8:6. Number of Japanese Best Friends, by Intermarriage for Married Sansei (*N* = 192).

| Married Sansei | *Number of Japanese Best Friends* | | | | |
	None (%)	1 (%)	2 (%)	Total (%)	N
Intermarried	42.9	40.5	16.7	21.9	42
Not intermarried	20.7	30.7	48.7	78.1	150
Total subsample	25.5	32.8	41.7	100.0	192

χ^2 (2) = 15.357, *p* < .001.

thesis that many types of ethnic community involvement do not necessarily limit an individual's structural assimilation into mainstream American society.

The ethnic background of the respondents' friends is very much related to whether they have Japanese American spouses. As seen in Table 8:6, the intermarried Sansei are much more likely to have non-Japanese American best friends.

Finally, the generalized acceptance of intermarriage in the Japanese American community is reflected in the responses individuals gave to the question whether intermarriage produced more problems or benefits for couples. Less than one-third of the respondents in the total sample (31.7 percent) saw marriage to a non-Japanese American spouse as producing more problems than being married to a fellow ethnic, and this perception was only slightly more frequent among those who are not currently intermarried (34.2 percent).

We can summarize our findings thus far by saying that intermarriage reduces, to a moderate degree, most types of involvement in Japanese American ethnic community life. Nonetheless, the high proportion of intermarrieds who are involved in at least one ethnic voluntary association again suggests that persons in this ethnic group can maintain ethnic cohesiveness despite high levels of structural assimilation. There is, however, another possible indirect consequence of intermarriage which, in the long run, may have a more serious effect on ethnic community solidarity. This is the impact of intermarriage on the likelihood of divorce.

INTERMARRIAGE AND DIVORCE

Historically, divorce rates among Japanese Americans have been very low compared with those of other ethnic groups and those of the U.S. population as a whole (Kitano, 1976:42; Levine and Rhodes, 1981:29, 38, 53; Lind, 1964; Schwertfeger, 1982). Two explanations have been given for these low rates. First, compared with most Western traditions, Japanese American conceptions of marital roles place more emphasis on group-centered duties, obligations, and responsibilities and less emphasis on individualistic views of love and romance. Second, and perhaps more important, are the consequences of the extensive informal social networks found in Japanese American communities. There is such a high degree of knowledge about and interaction among families that it has led Levine and Rhodes to suggest that the community itself should be conceptualized as a "network of families" (1981:10).

The network of families in Japanese American communities historically has served both as a social support for family life and as a barrier against divorce. On the positive side, it has provided material and emotional assistance to couples. It has also operated as a buffer against the kinds of stresses found in all marriages. On the negative side, the network of families has served to constrain persons from committing "deviant" acts such as divorce, by enforcing sanctions such that the person not only embarrasses himself or herself but also stigmatizes his or her entire family. Gossip, which quickly flows through ethnic social networks, has been a powerful factor in producing compliance with community norms, including those pertaining to marital life (e.g., Kitano, 1976:45).

TABLE 8:7. Overall Divorce Rates (*N* = 490).

Total sample	7.1%	(35/490)
Nisei[a]	5.3%	(15/282)
Sansei	9.6%	(20/208)
Ever divorced ratio:		
1. Japanese American sample (separation not measured)	.08	
2. U.S. sample (also includes ever separated)[b]	.25	

χ^2 (1, *N* = 490) = 2.16, *p* = n.s.

[a] The chi-square shows that there is no significant difference in divorce rates of Nisei and Sansei.

[b] This ratio is taken from Spanier and Glick (1981).

TABLE 8:8. Percentage of Males Ever Divorced, by Generational and Inmarried-Outmarried Status (*N* = 490).

Generation and Status	Ever Divorced
Nisei	
Inmarried (*N* = 264)	4.2
Outmarried (*N* = 18)	22.2
Sansei	
Inmarried (*N* = 155)	5.2
Outmarried (*N* = 53)	22.6

The figures shown in Table 8:7 provide inferential evidence that traditional values and informal social networks in the Japanese American community continue to keep the divorce rate well below national norms. The ratio of ever divorced or separated to married men in the U.S. population as a whole is more than three times greater (.25) than the ratio of ever divorced (separation was not measured) to married men in our sample (.08). Although the Sansei divorce ratio is higher than the Nisei's, this difference is not statistically significant. We would expect, however, that the divorce ratio for the Sansei will go up as they get older and that it will become significantly higher than the Nisei's.

The results shown in Tables 8:8 and 8:9 demonstrate that intermarriage is associated with a greater likelihood of divorce. Moreover, as illustrated in Table 8:8, the effect of intermarriage on divorce is virtually identical across generations. Both Nisei and Sansei who are married to Japanese

TABLE 8:9. Logistic Regression of Effects of Intermarriage and Other Variables on Divorce ($N = 466$).

Independent Variables	B	Standard Error	B	Standard Error
Generation	−2.196	1.224	−2.176	1.243
Age	.005	.027	.015	.027
Education	−.206*	.102	−.223*	.108
Income	−.420*	.153	−.393**	.160
Wife's ethnic background	−1.827***	.451	−1.534**	.459
Generation × Income	.530*	.183	.525**	.189
Non-Japanese organizations			.057	.135
Japanese friends			−.014	.263
Japanese organizations			−.744**	.237
R^2	.092		.120	

*$p < .05$. ** $p < .01$. *** $p < .001$.

women have extremely low divorce rates, while those for the intermarried in both generations is four times greater. The logistic regression analysis reported in Table 8:9 shows that the effect of intermarriage on divorce remains fairly constant even when controls are introduced for generational, demographic, and ethnic community participation variables. This leads us to predict, then, that as the percentage of Japanese Americans who intermarry increases, the number of divorced persons in this ethnic group will rise substantially.

Significantly, involvement in the ethnic community through participation in Japanese organizations was found to be associated with a reduced likelihood of divorce for both the Nisei and the Sansei. Thus it appears that social integration into the ethnic community provides unique strain-reducing resources and other barriers to divorce. Since involvement in nonethnic organizations had no such effect, it is not simply social integration per se that affects the likelihood of divorce.

As in the general literature, education and income are associated with lower levels of marital dissolution for Japanese American men (Spanier and Glick, 1981). With regard to the income finding, there was a significant generation–income interaction indicating that the positive effect of income was restricted to the Nisei. Perhaps the more successful Nisei are

TABLE 8:10. Regression of Income on Inmarriage ($N = 188$).
(Unstandardized coefficients are the top figures; standarized coefficients are in parentheses.)

Education	.093*
	(.220)
Age	.018*
	(.172)
Inmarriage	.252*
	(.513)
Constant	.921
R^2	.098

* $p < .05$.

more influenced by perceived community pressure not to divorce. Finally, the fact that having Japanese friends was not associated with a lower divorce rate, but that formal ethnic community involvement was, suggests that ethnicity influences marital stability more through quasi-kin group processes than through individual-level, strong-tie friendships.

ECONOMIC CONSEQUENCES OF INTERMARRIAGE

Two questions arise with respect to the effect of intermarriage on the economic life of Japanese Americans. The first is whether intermarriage has any negative implications for the persistence of the ethnic economy. One might argue, following our discussion in Chapters 3 and 7, that men who are married to Japanese American women are better able to use the ethnic community to support their family's business. This pattern prevailed in the past and, more recently, Kitano et al. (1984) found that self-employed Japanese Americans in Los Angeles County had lower rates of exogamy than their fellow ethnics who worked for others. Our analysis, however, does not find support for this pattern. In the case of Sansei, there is no statistically significant difference between the intermarried and nonintermarried with respect to being self-employed (χ^2 (1) = 0.0, p = n.s.).

Nevertheless, as shown in Table 8:10, having a Japanese wife still appears to be an economic resource, at least as far as personal income is concerned. Even when age and educational attainment are controlled for, inmarriage has a positive association with income. Perhaps, among other things, this may indicate that those who inmarry have more traditional values, including those pertaining to economic success.

CONCLUSION

Overall, the findings presented in this chapter offer a mixed picture of the nature and consequences of intermarriage among Japanese Americans. Our data on intergenerational intermarriage ratios have the same pattern as others reported earlier in the literature. There are, however, substantial variations in intermarriage ratios from one geographic area to another. These variations are probably due to differences in ethnic density.

As might be expected, intermarriage does have a weakening effect on ethnic community involvement. Less intimate forms of structural assimilation, such as involvement in mainstream voluntary associations, do not have such a direct negative effect on ethnic community involvement. The findings reported in this chapter indicate that intermarriage is associated with a lower level of involvement in ethnic organizations and fewer ties to ethnic best friends. Intermarriage also has an indirect negative effect by creating conditions leading to greater marital instability. In an ethnic community, which is essentially a "network of families," this clearly disrupts many of the critical ties that bind community members.

On the other hand, from a comparative perspective, a striking finding is the high level of involvement of Japanese Americans in ethnic voluntary associations even when they are structurally assimilated into mainstream American life in very intimate ways, including marriage to non-Japanese. This increases our confidence in our basic thesis that although there has been significant weakening of Japanese American ethnic community life as the group has become more structurally assimilated, there remains a degree of involvement in the ethnic community surpassing that found in most other ethnic groups at similar points in their ethnic group life cycle.

NINE

Political Attitudes and Participation

In the preceding chapters we have presented evidence about the unique historical experiences and contemporary situation of Japanese Americans in relation to other ethnic groups. In this chapter we will turn our attention to the implications of this for the participation of Japanese Americans in contemporary American political life. In particular, we will attempt to explain what appears to be a paradoxical situation. Although historically the group has been excluded from many mainstream political activities, they have potential political resources which may be greater per capita than those of the descendants of many other ethnic groups.

POLITICAL PREFERENCES AND IDEOLOGIES AMONG JAPANESE AMERICANS

Our first task is to identify how the different elements in the Japanese American experience have influenced the group's contemporary political attitudes, ideologies, and affiliations. On the one hand, one can find in the historical roots of this group many elements that would support identification with the plight of others who have been subjected to racism. For example, the Asian American student movement on West Coast campuses during the late 1960s and early 1970s urged Japanese Ameri-

TABLE 9:1.   Party Identification, by Family Income, for the Japanese
American Sample (*N* = 587) and the Nation as a Whole.
(The Japanese American figures are on top; national figures
are in parentheses.)[a]

Family Income	Party Affiliation		
	Democrat (%)	Independent/Others (%)	Republican (%)
$ 0–$ 9,999	46.7 (49.0)	21.7 (32.6)	31.7 (18.1)
$10,000–$19,999	55.3 (45.7)	19.1 (35.2)	25.5 (19.1)
$20,000–$29,999	58.5 (37.0)	9.8 (40.7)	31.6 (22.3)
$30,000–$49,999	53.7 (36.0)	13.4 (31.1)	32.9 (32.9)
$50,000 and over	25.0 (23.0)	6.8 (41.0)	68.2 (35.9)
Total sample	52.4 (41.0)	13.9 (37.0)	33.7 (23.0)

[a]The national figures are taken from Sorauf (1984:148). The original source of these data is
the Inter-University Consortium for Political Studies, University of Michigan.

cans, along with other Asian Americans, to identify with other "people
of color," including American blacks, Hispanics, and third world peoples
in general. Proponents of this movement often were critical of the costs
of structural assimilation, arguing that the American experience had
forced Asians to forsake much of their culture and identity, in a fashion
similar to that described by black and Chicano nationalist advocates (e.g.,
Gee, 1976; Tachiki et al., 1971).

On the other hand, the petit bourgeois nature of their economic accommodation suggests that a conservative cast would be more characteristic
of the Japanese American community. Thus we asked our survey respondents several questions that would shed light on the relative strengths and
weaknesses of these different crosscurrents as reflected in group members' political values.

Table 9:1 provides us with some basic information about the political
affiliations of the Japanese Americans in our sample compared with the
U.S. voting-age population in 1980. The reader should note, of course,

that these comparisons are only suggestive, since we do not have a national probability sample of Japanese Americans. Overall, we can see that our sample is more likely to claim identification with either the Democratic or Republican party than is the case with a national sample of all Americans. The proportion of persons claiming to be independents or "others" is less than half that found in the national study. The effect of fewer persons seeing themselves as independents or "others" is especially pronounced in the highest income category, where the proportion of persons in our sample claiming to be Republicans is 32.3 percent greater than for persons in the same income category in the national sample. At the same time, the proportion of persons in this income category reporting Democratic party affiliation is slightly higher than for the population as a whole. In short, the smaller proportion of persons identifying themselves as independents is associated with increased partisan preferences for both the total sample and for specific income strata.

We can only speculate about reasons for the higher degree of partisanship among Japanese Americans. In our view, there are two plausible explanations for this phenomenon. The first is simply that the norms of their subculture still place a good deal of emphasis on being a "good citizen." Identifying with a party and being informed about electoral politics can be seen as being a "good citizen." The second, and more intriguing, explanation is that Japanese Americans get plugged into political networks by two mechanisms: participation in mainstream organizations and the ethnic community. This multiple set of involvements appears to increase political awareness and activity. We will elaborate on this point later in the chapter.

Table 9:2 presents a breakdown of party identification by generation and area. There are no generational differences in party affiliation, but the area in which an individual lives has a substantial impact on whether he identifies himself as a Democrat, Republican, or independent. Japanese Americans living in the conservative rural Central Valley area around Fresno are similar to their neighbors in their inclination to register more often as Republicans, while in the Sacramento area, which contains many government employees, they are heavily Democratic in party affiliation. In urban Gardena, individuals are somewhat more likely to identify themselves as Democrats.

The substantial areal effects on party affiliation affirm the notion that even though Japanese Americans are quite cohesive compared with many other ethnic groups, they are heterogeneous in their political ideologies

TABLE 9:2. Party Affiliation, by Generation and Area ($N = 603$).

| | AREA | | | | | | | | | | | | | | | |
| | Gardena | | | | Sacramento | | | | Fresno | | | | Totals | | | |
Generation	Rep (%)	Dem (%)	Ind (%)	N	Rep (%)	Dem (%)	Ind (%)	N	Rep (%)	Dem (%)	Ind (%)	N	Rep (%)	Dem (%)	Ind (%)	N
Nisei	39.2	44.1	16.7	102	22.8	72.3	5.0	101	47.5	41.4	11.1	99	36.4	52.6	10.9	302
Sansei	30.6	43.9	25.5	98	18.6	72.5	8.8	102	43.6	39.6	16.8	101	30.9	52.2	16.9	301
Totals	35.0	44.0	21.0	200	20.7	72.4	6.9	203	45.5	40.5	14.0	200	33.7	52.4	13.9	603

By generation: χ^2 (2, $N = 603$) = 5.292, p = n.s.
By area: χ^2 (4, $N = 603$) = 56.579, $p < .001$.
By generation and area: χ^2 (2, $N = 603$) = .300, p = n.s.

TABLE 9:3. Percentage of Respondents Agreeing with the Statement,
"It's Important to Support Japanese Candidates for Office."

Generation	Strongly Disagree (%)	Disagree (%)	Undecided (%)	Agree (%)	Strongly Agree (%)	N
Nisei	1.6	23.5	12.1	49.3	13.4	(306)
Sansei	5.6	31.4	20.2	36.6	6.2	(322)
Total	3.7	27.5	16.2	42.8	9.7	(628)

χ^2 (4, N = 628) = 30.786, p < .001.

and affiliations. Indeed, as we pointed out in Chapter 2, it appears that a fundamental adaptiveness in Japanese American conceptions of social relationships is that they do not rely on any specific ideological line to maintain them. Thus, being a Republican rather than a Democrat or Buddhist rather than a Christian does not matter much insofar as identification with and involvement in the ethnic community is concerned. This is in marked contrast, for example, to the historical connections between Irish ethnicity, Catholicism, and the Democratic party (e.g., Glazer and Moynihan, 1970:219–287).

The significant areal effects we have found suggest that we should exercise a good deal of caution about extrapolating from this sample to the entire population of Japanese Americans in the United States. Given the size of the areal effect, our guess is that additional variations would be found among Japanese Americans outside California or even the Orange County suburbs of Southern California.

Finally, the absence of any significant difference in party affiliation between Nisei and Sansei is consistent with many of our other findings that show a good deal of continuity between the generations. This pattern of intergenerational continuity is similar to findings reported for party identification of parents and children in national samples, suggesting that the so-called generation gap has been overstated for the population as a whole (e.g., Sorauf, 1984:142).

There are, however, some generational differences with respect to the role of ethnicity in politics. The Nisei were likely to respond affirmatively to this statement: "It's important to support Japanese candidates for office" (see Table 9:3). Alternatively, the Sansei were much more likely than the Nisei to respond affirmatively to the statement, "Japanese Americans should be encouraged to see themselves as Asian Americans" (χ^2 (2) = 7.562, p < .05). Among the Sansei, 47.1 percent thought the concept should be encouraged, 35.0 percent said it made no difference, and 17.8 percent thought it should be discouraged. The corresponding figures for the Nisei were 37.5, 45.4, and 17.1 percent. There were no areal effects. One way to interpret agreement with this statement is to say that it reflects the extent to which Japanese Americans see their interests better served by a larger political movement. Following this logic, then, the somewhat positive response of the younger generation is symptomatic of an emerging Asian American political consciousness.

In contrast to the fairly modest levels of support for the Asian American concept, respondents expressed a very high level of interest in and support for redress for the World War II incarceration. We asked them about the extent of their agreement or disagreement with the JACL-sponsored redress proposal which was then (1979–80) being considered by a congressional committee. This measure, which eventually was passed by Congress and signed into law by President Reagan (Civil Liberties Act of 1988), was designed to provide monetary compensation for all Japanese Americans interned during World War II. At the time that the respondents were asked for their opinions about the redress proposal, however, there was no certainty that it would receive widespread support in Congress. The responses to the question are shown in Table 9.4.

Almost three-quarters of the total sample agreed with the proposal, and there were no significant differences between generations or areas. The injustices associated with the World War II incarceration remain a highly salient issue for most Japanese Americans. There are, nonetheless, some differences in their support of this issue. Table 9:5 presents the results of a regression analysis addressing this point.

Income and the interaction between income and generation are significantly related to opinions about the redress issue. Those with higher incomes were less favorable toward the redress proposal (which called for a $20,000 payment to each internee). Moreover, the effect of income is much stronger among the Nisei than among the Sansei.

One explanation for the interaction effect is that Nisei with higher income have experienced a greater relative increase in their personal standard of living in the postwar era than either their less affluent peers or the Sansei who grew up in more affluent homes. Another possibility is that the wealthier Nisei are more concerned that redress will upset their com-

TABLE 9:4. Opinion on the Redress Proposal, by Generation and Area (N = 577).

	Gardena						Sacramento						Fresno						Totals					
Generation	SA (%)	A (%)	U (%)	D (%)	SD (%)	N	SA (%)	A (%)	U (%)	D (%)	SD (%)	N	SA (%)	A (%)	U (%)	D (%)	SD (%)	N	SA (%)	A (%)	U (%)	D (%)	SD (%)	N
Nisei	30.6	32.7	15.3	11.2	10.2	98	41.7	35.4	13.5	5.2	4.2	96	44.8	27.1	12.5	9.4	6.3	96	39.0	31.7	13.8	8.6	6.9	290
Sansei	34.5	44.8	8.0	3.4	9.2	87	41.2	38.1	13.4	6.2	1.0	97	37.9	37.9	10.7	9.7	3.9	103	38.0	40.1	10.8	6.6	4.5	287
Totals	32.4	38.4	11.9	7.6	9.7	185	41.5	36.8	13.5	5.7	2.6	193	41.2	32.7	11.6	9.5	5.0	199	38.5	35.9	12.3	7.6	5.7	577

By generation: χ^2 (4, N = 577) = 6.056, p = n.s
By area: χ^2 (8, N = 577) = 14.432, p. = n.s
By generation and area: χ^2 (8, N = 577) = 7.228, p = n s.

SA = Strongly agree. A = Agree U = Undecided D = Disagree. SD = Strongly disagree

TABLE 9:5. Regression of Opinions on the Redress Proposal ($N = 560$).
(Unstandardized coefficients are the top figures; standardized
coefficients are in parentheses.)

Generation	−.303
	(−.132)
Education	−.030
	(−.051)
Income	−.093*
	(−.230)
Sacramento	.320*
	(.132)
Fresno	.237*
	(.099)
Generation × Income	.074*
	(.215)
Constant	4.359
R^2	.048

* $p < .05$.

fortable relationships with the white majority. Several upper middle-class Nisei expressed the fear that the redress campaign would create a "backlash." On the other hand, the Sansei have grown up in a much more secure, pluralistic environment and would not be expected to have personal memories of severe prejudice and discrimination that might cause them to be cautious in these matters.

Since the perception of being exposed to discrimination both in the past and in the present should affect political attitudes and motivation, we asked our respondents about their experiences with and attitudes about discrimination. The results are presented in Table 9:6.

The first item inquired about the amount of discrimination the respondent had experienced as an adult. Approximately 22 percent of the total sample reported being exposed to a significant amount of discrimination during this period. Not surprising, the amount of discrimination reported by the Nisei was greater than that indicated by the Sansei. Still, two-thirds of the older group reported having been exposed to either minimal or no discrimination. The average age of the Nisei at the time of the World War II evacuation was approximately eighteen. The older

TABLE 9:6. Percentage of Respondents Agreeing with Statements About Past Experienced Discrimination and Present Social and Job Discrimination (N = 634).[a]

Generation	Amount of Discrimination Experienced as an Adult				Currently, Japanese Experience Social Discrimination					Currently, Japanese Do Not Experience Job Discrimination				
	Great Deal	Considerable	Minimal	None	SA	A	U	D	SD	SA	A	U	D	SD
Nisei	12.9 (40)[b]	18.4 (57)	60.2 (186)	8.7 (27)	7.1 (22)	68.9 (213)	11.0 (34)	12.0 (37)	1.0 (3)	5.8 (18)	32.0 (99)	7.4 (23)	45.5 (141)	9.4 (29)
Sansei	3.1 (10)	9.7 (31)	69.9 (223)	17.2 (55)	13.6 (44)	60.7 (196)	12.4 (40)	12.4 (40)	.9 (3)	4.3 (14)	31.9 (29)	9.0 (29)	43.7 (141)	11.1 (36)
Total	7.9 (50)	14.0 (88)	65.0 (409)	13.0 (82)	10.4 (66)	64.7 (409)	11.7 (74)	12.2 (77)	.9 (6)	5.1 (32)	31.9 (202)	8.2 (52)	44.5 (282)	10.3 (65)

Zero-order and partial correlations with generation

	Amount	Social	Job
r, with generation	.249*	.033	.036
r, controlling for education	.227*	.019	.099
r, controlling for Japanese organizations	.219*	.031	.069

* p < .001

[a] This table was originally published in O'Brien and Fugita (1983a).
[b] Number of respondents is shown in parentheses.

SA = Strongly agree. A = Agree. U = Undecided. D = Disagree. SD = Strongly disagree.

Nisei were in late adolescence or young adulthood during the internment, while many of the younger Nisei were in their early teens. For all the Nisei, the postwar period most likely brought a dramatic reduction in discrimination, especially in contrast to what their parents had experienced. In short, the Nisei were responding to a question about something that has changed quite dramatically during their lifetimes.

Perhaps most important for political mobilization around ethnic issues, however, is the amount of discrimination individual Japanese Americans feel they experience today. We asked two questions about this: one about social discrimination, the other about job discrimination. Three-quarters of the respondents thought that Japanese Americans currently experience social discrimination, and over half believe that employment discrimination exists. There were no significant generational differences on these matters.

The finding of such a high level of perceived discrimination suggests a potential for political mobilization based on ethnicity. It is important to note here the lack of any cleavages between generations on this issue. Nevertheless, although the presence of highly salient issues may be a necessary condition for group mobilization, it is by no means a sufficient cause of it. To better understand the latter, we will have to examine actual political participation patterns among Japanese Americans.

POLITICAL PARTICIPATION AMONG JAPANESE AMERICANS

The literature dealing with the relationship between ethnicity and political participation is complex and includes many contradictory findings (e.g., Cohen and Kapsis, 1978; London, 1975; Miller, 1982; Orum, 1983:243–245). Nevertheless, there appears to be agreement on two points bearing on Japanese Americans. First, discrimination from the majority group does not, in itself, produce a high degree of political participation by members of an ethnic group (e.g., Antunes and Gaitz, 1975; Cohen and Kapsis, 1978; Olsen, 1970; Orum, 1983:243–245). Differences in participation rates between ethnic groups appear to be due more to the extent to which different groups foster specific "participatory norms." Therefore, variations between ethnic groups in rates of political participation must be understood in terms of differences in cultural and social organizational characteristics of the groups themselves (Cohen and Kapsis, 1978; Greeley, 1974). Second, variations in political participation within ethnic groups do not exhibit any universal relationship to degree

TABLE 9:7. Percentage of Japanese Americans and Persons in a National
Sample Engaged in Different Kinds of Political
Participation.

Political Activity	National Sample[a]	Japanese American Sample ($N = 634$)
1. Report voting regularly in presidential elections	72	76.0
2. Report always voting in local elections	47	70.5
3. Active in at least one organization involved in community problems	32	24.0
4. Have ever actively worked for a party or candidates during an election	26	15.6
5. Have ever contacted a local government official about some issue or problem	20	19.4
6. Have attended at least one political meeting or rally in last three years	19	22.3
7. Have ever contacted a state or national government official about some issue or problem	18	26.4
8. Have ever formed a group or organization to attempt to solve some local community problem	14	10.1
9. Have ever given money to a party or candidate during an election campaign	13	39.1
10. Currently a member of a political club or organization	8	6.3

[a] The percentages are taken from Orum (1983:240).

of ethnic community involvement or identification, but are a function of historical, structural, and cultural specifics varying from one ethnic group to another (Cohen and Kapsis, 1978; Klobus-Edwards et al., 1978; London, 1975; Miller, 1982).

With respect to fostering general participatory norms, Japanese American ethnicity is quite supportive. The reader will recall, for example, that the participation rates of Japanese Americans in voluntary associations were much greater than those for the U.S. population as a whole (see Chapter 6).

To determine whether these general norms fostering participation are reflected in specific political activities, we compared rates of involvement in ten different political actions between persons in our sample and persons in a large national sample. The results can be seen in Table 9:7.

There is a mixed pattern of differences between our sample and the national sample. On five of the items Japanese Americans participate more than the national average and on five they participate less. These results are somewhat surprising given the relatively high levels of income and education found in our sample. Perhaps Japanese Americans are likely to be more involved in low-visibility activities such as voting and contributing money (items 2 and 9) but less involved in more "activist" activities (items 3, 4, 7, 8). It may be that their historical experiences, frequently hostile, as well as their cultural and petit bourgeois traditions, incline them to avoid more controversial kinds of political activities unless they are threatened directly (see the discussion of the Nisei Farmers League below).

EFFECTS OF ETHNIC AND NONETHNIC INVOLVEMENT ON POLITICAL PARTICIPATION

The issues of most concern to our central thesis pertain to the effects on political participation of involvement in ethnic and nonethnic communities. If, as we have been arguing, Japanese Americans are able to participate comfortably in both ethnic and nonethnic social worlds, we might expect this to be reflected in their political involvement as well. The general literature has repeatedly reported that higher levels of organizational involvement are associated with greater political activity (e.g., London, 1975; Verba and Nie, 1972). The more intriguing question, however, is the relationship between ethnic community involvement and political participation. Does, for example, ethnic community involvement (as measured by membership in ethnic organizations) operate similarly to organizational involvement in the larger society?

One possibility is that the more an individual is absorbed in ethnic community activities, the more insulated he or she will become from the issues of the larger society, including political ones. This would approximate the ethnic mobility trap (Wiley, 1967). The assumption here is that involvement in the ethnic community will satisfy most of the important instrumental and social psychological needs of the individual. Thus the more one participates in the ethnic community, the less likely one is to be involved in the larger society.

A contrasting view is that participation in the ethnic community simply provides a different kind of linkage to politics from that created by organizational involvement in the larger society. The argument here is that involvement in ethnic community organizations serves to integrate an individual into the larger political system by increasing his or her sense of efficacy, by raising salient issues, and by providing an organizational mechanism for participation in interest group politics. Rather than competing with mainstream involvement, participation in the ethnic community may provide an alternative, compatible conduit to political involvement.

As we pointed out in Chapters 2 and 6, however, a critical element in determining the effect of ethnic community involvement on participation in general would seem to be the specific kind of attachments the individual has to the ethnic community. Granovetter's (1973) argument with respect to the political impotence of the Italian community in Boston's West End was that persons in the local area had almost exclusively strong ties to small cliques of fellow ethnics but did not have "bridging" weak ties that could link the cliques to one another. While strong ties within the ethnic community tend to be exclusive in character, and keep cliques unconnected to each other and to mainstream social structures, other kinds of ties within an ethnic community may indeed be quite compatible with nonethnic involvements. The reader will recall our discussion in Chapter 2 and our findings in Chapter 6 demonstrating that Japanese and Japanese American cultural traditions and historical experiences encourage involvement in the ethnic community through membership in voluntary associations. We have shown that these involvements are quite compatible with involvement in mainstream organizations. Thus, on an a priori basis we might expect that this pattern of linkages to both the ethnic and mainstream communities would produce high levels of individual political participation. This is the focus of the regression analyses reported in Tables 9:8 and 9:9.

Our political participation dependent variable was an index made up of responses to the ten items reported in Table 9:7. The measure of involvement in the nonethnic community, or assimilation, was the total number of non-Japanese voluntary associations to which the individual belonged. This included all types of organizations, such as social clubs, PTAs, fraternal associations, civic clubs, and so on. Two analytically distinct measures of involvement in the ethnic community were used. The first was the extent to which individuals were involved in predominantly ethnic voluntary associations. This was measured by totaling the number

TABLE 9:8. Regression of Political Activity Scale on Ethnic and
Nonethnic Social Participation. Total Sample ($N = 612$).
(Unstandardized coefficients are the top figures; standardized
coefficients are in parentheses.)[a]

Variables	EQ1	EQ2	EQ3	EQ4
Generation	−.720***	−.705**	−.101	.041
	(−.152)	(−.149)	(−.021)	(.009)
Education	.311***	.204***	.202***	.196***
	(.319)	(.210)	(.208)	(.202)
Income	.178***	.111***	.111***	.085**
	(.212)	(.131)	(.132)	(.101)
Participation in non-Japanese organizations		.454***	.458**	.440***
		(.331)	(.334)	(.321)
Japanese friends			.247	.111
			(.082)	(.037)
Generation × Japanese friends			−.447*	−.412
			(−.152)	(−.140)
Participation in Japanese organizations				.306***
				(.177)
Constant	1.058	1.186	.808	.673
R^2	.175	.263	.268	.294

* $p < .05$. ** $p < .01$. *** $p < .001$.

[a] This table was originally published in Fugita and O'Brien (1985).

of Japanese American voluntary associations to which an individual belonged. The second was a measure of the extent to which an individual's
closest friends were from the ethnic community. This measure was de-
rived from items asking respondents whether their best and second best
friends were Japanese.

The first equation in Table 9:8 shows that several of the predictors of
political participation in the general population also predict the political
involvement of Japanese Americans. The negative sign of the coefficient
measuring the effect of generation (Sansei are coded 1 and Nisei are coded
0) is consistent with Verba and Nie's (1972) finding that when education
and income are controlled, participation increases gradually throughout
the life cycle up to approximately 70 years of age (the mean age for the
Sansei was 32.5 and mean age for the Nisei was 55.3).

TABLE 9:9. Regression of Political Activity Scale on Ethnic and Nonethnic Participation. (Unstandardized coefficients are the top figures; standardized coefficients are in parentheses.)[a]

Variables	Nisei (N = 297)				Sansei (N = 305)			
	EQ1	EQ2	EQ3	EQ4	EQ5	EQ6	EQ7	EQ8
Education	.275*** (2.87)	.162** (1.69)	.162** (.170)	.154** (.161)	.347*** (.310)	.252*** (.225)	.244** (.218)	.244*** (.218)
Income	.211*** (.259)	.146*** (.179)	.145** (.178)	.118** (.145)	.148** (.167)	.078 (.088)	.080 (.090)	.053 (.060)
Participation in non-Japanese organizations		.420*** (.323)	.438*** (.336)	.418*** (.321)		.487*** (.341)	.478*** (.334)	.464*** (.324)
Japanese friends			.234 (.072)	.119 (.036)			-.182 (-.060)	-.315* (-.103)
Participation in Japanese organizations				.247** (.168)				.423*** (.183)
Constant	.984	1.174	.792	.749	.297	.340	.586	.486
R²	.195	.273	.278	.303	.156	.254	.258	.288

* p < .05. ** p < .01. *** p < .001.

[a] This table was originally published in Fugita and O'Brien (1985).

In addition, persons with greater personal resources (higher education and income) were more likely to engage in the activities measured by the index. Most important, the reduction in the size of the coefficients for education and income when participation in non-Japanese organizations is introduced into the second equation indicates that persons in our sample are similar to non-Japanese Americans in that those with more personal resources have more formal ties to the larger society, which in turn are associated with greater political activity. Finally, formal ties, through involvement in nonethnic voluntary associations, have a substantial direct effect on political participation. Thus personal resources have both direct and indirect positive effects on political activity.

The impact of ethnic community involvement on political activity, however, is more complex. Besides depending on whether individuals are linked to the ethnic community via organizational involvement or friendship, it also depends on the generation of the individual Japanese American. Equation 3 in Table 9:8 shows that there is an interaction between the ethnic background of a respondent's best friends and his generational status. Looking at the separate regression runs for the Nisei and the Sansei in equations 3 and 7 in Table 9:9, we see that a higher value on the Japanese friends index is positively associated with political activity among the Nisei but has an opposite effect on the Sansei.

Equations 4 and 8 in Table 9:9 provide us with some insights into the reasons for this interaction. For Nisei, the substantial reduction in the size of the coefficient for the friends variable when participation in Japanese American voluntary associations is added in equation 4 suggests that having Japanese friends has an indirect positive impact on political participation because it is associated with involvement in Japanese American voluntary associations. The increase in the size of the coefficient of the friends variable in the case of the Sansei in equation 8, however, suggests that although having Japanese friends also pulls persons in this generation into ethnic voluntary associations, it has the stronger effect of insulating them from the larger society.

The different effects of ethnic friendship on the political activity of persons in the two generations probably reflect historical differences in the opportunities for and meanings of this kind of ethnic group membership for the Nisei and the Sansei. The Nisei, by and large, grew up in somewhat socially isolated ethnic communities. They had much less opportunity to associate with non-Japanese Americans than did the Sansei, who typically have grown up in highly integrated settings. Thus, for Nisei to have fellow Japanese Americans for best and second best friends would be expected, and their higher mean value on the friends index (1.5 versus 1.1 for the Sansei) reflects this fact. Their familial and economic links and their common internment experiences during World War II have created strong informal ties which, in turn, have increased their involvement in ethnic voluntary associations. Our open-ended questions indicate that Nisei experience feelings of trust, being understood, and comfortableness when they interact with fellow Nisei.

For the Sansei, however, the tendency to have exclusively ethnic best friends may be more a reflection of a lack of desire or comfortableness in interacting with persons from mainstream society. In other words, for persons in this generation these strong ties may have the effect of preventing the development of "bridges" to the mainstream society and, in turn, reducing political participation levels.

Equation 4 in Table 9:8 shows that ties to the ethnic community through membership in Japanese American voluntary associations have a positive effect on political activity for persons in both generations. A portion of this is an indirect effect of income, insofar as more affluent individuals are more likely to participate in ethnic voluntary associations (note the reduction in size of the income coefficient from equation 3 to equation 4). More important, however, is that the personal resource of education, which is a strong predictor of individuals' involvement in nonethnic voluntary associations, has no indirect effect on political involvement through participation in Japanese American voluntary associations. Thus the ethnic dimension is powerful enough to override the value differences associated with education.

Taken together, these results demonstrate that assimilation through mainstream organizational involvement increases the political participation of Japanese Americans. Involvement in ethnic organizational networks provides an additional complementary conduit for such activities. One potentially important implication of this pattern is that it puts persons in this group in a better position to mobilize support for their collective interests than is typically the case for ethnic groups that have similarly assimilated but have not been able to retain their ethnic group infrastructure.

Given an appropriate incentive, Japanese Americans should be able to gain access to many mainstream influentials as well as mobilize a numerically significant segment of the ethnic community. A series of events a few years ago in the Central Valley of California enabled us to examine how this potential might be actualized. In addition, the issue surrounding these events allowed us to examine the extent of political pluralism within Japanese American communities.

THE NISEI FARMERS LEAGUE

The Nisei Farmers League is a 1,500-member organization of tree fruit and grape growers in the San Joaquin Valley in Central California which was created in 1971 when the United Farm Workers Union (UFW) began an organizing campaign directed at, among others, Japanese American ranches in the area. Since that time the NFL has grown rapidly and now includes many non-Japanese members. Nevertheless, persons of Japanese ancestry constitute 40 percent of the membership and occupy the majority of key leadership positions.

The conflict between the UFW and the NFL is economic in nature. It is a classic confrontation between union and management. Initially, however, the NFL attempted to define the conflict as an "ethnic issue" and in this way tried to mobilize members of the Japanese American community throughout California and in other areas of the United States (Fugita, 1978; Fugita and O'Brien, 1977; O'Brien and Fugita, 1984).

The NFL played a highly visible role in 1976 in the California Proposition 14 campaign (its president was the chairman of the principal agribusiness political action committee). If passed, this referendum would have provided additional funding for California's Agricultural Labor Relations Act of 1975 (ALRA), and thus would have aided the organizing drive of the United Farm Workers Union. The referendum was defeated by a 2-to-1 margin. There were many other factors besides the Nisei Farmers League responsible for the defeat of this proposition. It was an economic issue in which one side broadly appealed to voters to protect the rights of workers to organize and the other side sought to protect the rights of private property. Nevertheless, since the NFL was dominated by Japanese Americans and since it initially made overt appeals to fellow Japanese Americans for support, it provided us with some valuable information on contemporary political participation patterns among members of the ethnic group (Fugita, 1978; Fugita and O'Brien, 1977; O'Brien and Fugita, 1984).

One of the most intriguing aspects of the NFL is that in many ways it reflects a continuity with the ethnic economy of an earlier period. The members of the NFL are engaged in a traditional petit bourgeois occupa-

TABLE 9:10. Percentage of Japanese and of General Population Voting in Favor of Proposition 14, by Area.[a]

| | AREA | | | | | |
| | Gardena | | Sacramento | | Fresno | |
Sample	%	N	%	N	%	N
Nisei	34.2	38	17.0	82	9.9	81
Sansei	54.2	24	36.5	63	8.3	72
Combined Japanese	41.9	64	25.5	145	9.2	153
General population	43.2		33.8		19.3	

[a] This table was originally published in O'Brien and Fugita (1984).

tion for Japanese Americans, and their appeals for support from fellow ethnics recall the earlier efforts at collective ethnic community action in the El Monte berry and Venice celery strikes described in Chapter 3 (see also Fugita and O'Brien, 1978).

At the same time, however, there are two very substantial differences between this conflict and the earlier ones. First, because they are operating with greater economic resources, fewer discriminatory barriers, and higher levels of structural assimilation, the members of the Nisei Farmers League are able to draw upon a number of social networks and influentials unavailable to Japanese American farmers during the earlier period. It is true that during the El Monte strike, local police authorities and chambers of commerce worked with the Japanese farmers, but they did so to protect the interests of the white growers.

On the other hand, even though the ethnic economy survives (see Chapter 7), a substantially smaller proportion of the Japanese American community is dependent on it today. Therefore, there was a question about the degree to which the Nisei Farmers League would be able to muster support from the ethnic community over and above what might be expected purely on the basis of economic interest.

Table 9:10 shows the results of voting on the Proposition 14 referendum for Japanese Americans and the general population in each of the three areas in the sample. Voting against Proposition 14 would curtail the UFW's ability to organize and thus was the position favored by the NFL.

Not surprisingly, both Japanese Americans and the general population were more likely to have voted against Proposition 14 in Fresno, where agriculture is the dominant industry and the farm worker referendum was more highly publicized. Even in Fresno, however, there was a substantial difference between the proportion of Japanese and the general population voting against Proposition 14. The greater degree of support for the farmers' position by Japanese Americans in the area is consistent with the argument that this ethnic group has a high potential for being mobilized on salient issues.

At the same time, the Proposition 14 data point out that there are important limits to the extent to which a Japanese American organization can use ethnicity as a resource. In the areas further removed from the issue, the ethnic effect on voting appears to be largely restricted to the Nisei. In both Sacramento and Gardena, the Nisei are substantially more profarmer than are the general populations living there, while the Sansei in those areas are somewhat less profarmer than the general population.

Table 9:11 presents the results of a regression analysis which further elucidates the sources of strength from which the Nisei Farmers League drew. Equation 2 shows that when area and the generation × area interaction are included, both generation and education have significant effects on voting on the farm labor referendum. The younger-generation Sansei and more educated persons took a less conservative position on Proposition 14. The influence of both of these variables probably has less to do with ethnicity than with differences in underlying value preferences associated with age and education.

Support for the persistence of an ethnic economy, as described in Chapter 7, is found in equations 3 and 4 in Table 9:11, where doing business with other Japanese Americans has a significant, although not very strong, impact on voting for the NFL position on the referendum. Moreover, a substantial portion of this effect is indirect, insofar as persons doing business with other Japanese Americans are more likely to have heard of the NFL (note the reduction in the size of the coefficient of the "doing business" variable from equation 4 to equation 5). The less directly economic linkages to the ethnic community—friendships, Japanese American voluntary associations, and Japanese newspapers—do not have a significant direct effect on voting, although in another analysis we found that the latter did have a significant impact on providing information about the NFL, and thus indirectly affected voting on the referendum (O'Brien and Fugita, 1984).

TABLE 9:11. Regression of Vote on Proposition 14 on Selected Characteristics of Japanese Americans ($N = 341$). (Unstandardized coefficients are the top figures; standardized coefficients are in parentheses.)[a]

Variables	EQ1	EQ2	EQ3	EQ4	EQ5
Farmer	−.120 (−.102)	.009 (.008)	.028 (.024)	.035 (.029)	.049 (.041)
Generation	.049 (.061)	.245** (.305)	.257** (.320)	.250** (.311)	.222** (.277)
Education	.015 (.092)	.020* (.126)	.021* (.125)	.020* (.124)	.024** (.151)
Self-employed nonfarming	−.105* (−.108)	−.068 (−.070)	−.043 (−.045)	−.043 (−.045)	−.044 (−.046)
Area		−.114** (−.207)	−.112** (−.204)	−.112** (−.204)	−.059 (−.107)
Generation × area		−.146** (−.292)	−.151** (−.304)	−.153** (−.308)	−.140** (−.282)
Does business with other Japanese			−.071* (−.088)	−.06*9 (−.086)	−.049 (−.062)
Japanese friends				−.021 (−.043)	−.025 (−.049)
Number of Japanese organizations				−.008 (−.027)	−.003 (−.011)
Reads a Japanese newspaper				−.018 (.022)	.036 (.043)
Heard of the NFL					−.159** (−.188)
Constant	.145	.232	.253	.290	.291
R^2	.040	.151	.156	.160	.180

* $p < .05$, one-tailed. ** $p < .01$, one-tailed.

[a] This table was originally published in O'Brien and Fugita (1984).

One-half of the areal effect on voting can be accounted for by its association with whether persons have heard of the NFL (note the reduction in the size of the coefficient for area from equation 4 to equation 5). Proximity to the issue, then, not only is important in terms of availability of information but also has an indirect effect on voting itself.

The most interesting relationship, however, is the interaction between generation and area. There may be two reasons why distance from the issue has a greater effect on weakening support for the NFL position among the Sansei than among the Nisei. First, historically and symbolically the Nisei are more closely tied to the Japanese American farming experience. Thus, even if a Nisei currently lives in Sacramento or Gardena, it is likely that either he or his father once lived on a farm. The Sansei in Fresno are living in an agricultural milieu, thus it is easy for them to empathize with the NFL position; but those Sansei living in the more urbanized areas are likely to find little in their personal experience to relate to the farm labor issue.

Second, and perhaps more significant in a general theoretical sense, there are likely to be fundamental differences between the two generations in the nature of their ethnic identification and relationship to the ethnic community. Our conversations with Nisei and Sansei, as well as our other analyses of ethnic identification using the same survey data, suggest that for persons in the older generation the role of helping fellow ethnics, although not verbally articulated, is an intrinsic part of their ethnicity. On the other hand, the Sansei's definition of ethnicity places more emphasis on sharing "common interactional styles" with fellow ethnics (e.g., Miyamoto, 1986–87; O'Brien and Fugita, 1984) and a commitment to finding out more about one's cultural and political heritage (e.g., Gee, 1976; Tachiki et al., 1971). The different bases of ethnicity reflect differences in the social, economic, and political experiences of persons in the two generations.

The Nisei, having grown up in an ethnic economy, retain more of a sense of obligation to help out their fellow ethnics even when they are not directly affected in an economic sense. The Sansei, however, have probably adopted a very different conception of ethnicity, reflecting their greater structural assimilation into a pluralistic society. Thus ethnicity for them is more likely to revolve around issues of personal identification and "fitting in" and has less to do with a sense of obligation to help fellow ethnics. However, as suggested by our findings on the redress issue, reported earlier in this chapter, the younger generation can indeed become motivated to support an ethnic issue they see as salient to ethnicity as they experience it. The Asian American movement and the creation of ethnic studies, which were supported by Asian university students in the late 1960s and 1970s, provide another example of Sansei commitment to their version of an emergent ethnicity.

Finally, the reader will recall the high overall levels of perceived social and occupational discrimination reported by both generations. This cross-cutting perception of unjust treatment that group members face because of their common ethnicity is likely to increase ethnic group solidarity and thus make it easier to mobilize the group to further their collective political interests.

Nevertheless, in following the NFL issues over the years, we have been struck by the range of views on the NFL and by the diversity of opinion within the Japanese American ethnic community that this reflects (Fugita, 1978; Fugita and O'Brien, 1977). Another issue on which there is little consensus, and that has caused serious fissures in the community, revolves around the accommodationist position the JACL took toward the World War II internment. Bitter feelings remain even today. These examples of diversity support the interpretation that the persistence of Japanese American ethnicity does not depend on the preservation of a homogeneous set of beliefs, attitudes, or actions. Indeed, one of the most intriguing aspects of the picture of this ethnic group presented so far is that its diversity of religious and political beliefs is not a significant threat to group cohesiveness.

CONCLUSION

Currently, there is considerable variation in the Japanese American community with regard to political party identification. If anything, persons in this ethnic group appear to be more partisan than an equivalent sample of Americans as a whole. Their political stands are influenced by contextual considerations, as evidenced by the substantial differences in patterns of party identification in different areas of California. There was, however, a high degree of consensus about some ethnicity-related issues. Our respondents reported having experienced significant social and job discrimination, and they showed strong support for the Japanese American Citizens League's redress proposal.

The most important findings reported in this chapter shed light on the general question of how structural assimilation and ethnic community involvement influence the political activities of individual Japanese Americans. First, ethnic friendships have different effects on Sansei compared with Nisei. Second, involvement in the organizational life of the larger society is associated, as would be expected, with increased political activity. Third, and most significant, is the finding that involvement in ethnic organizations is *also* associated with increased political activity. Ethnic organizational involvement thus acts as a complementary conduit to political activity. Therefore, in principle at least, Japanese Americans, like American Jews (cf. Gendrot and Turner, 1983), should have a greater potential political resource base than most European ethnic groups. Individuals in both groups have numerous organizational links with both their ethnic and mainstream communities.

Nevertheless, as the Nisei Farmers League experience illustrates, the potential political resources of the Japanese American community are not always utilized for concerted collective action, primarily because of the considerable diversity in values, interests, and ideologies now found among members of this group. Although there was evidence of an ethnic effect among the Nisei on the Nisei Farmers League issue, the effect was significantly weaker among the Sansei. At the same time, however, the positive reaction of most Japanese Americans to the redress proposal suggests that if an appropriate issue emerges, these potential resources can be mobilized into practical political action.

TEN | *Persistence and Change in Perceived Social Boundaries*

B arth (1969) and Alba (1985) point out that assimilation can be analyti- cally viewed from either an individualistic or a social boundary perspective. In the first case, the emphasis is on understanding the individ- ual's position in relation to the boundaries separating two groups. By and large, this has been the focus of our analysis so far. We have empirically examined the behavioral involvement of Japanese Americans in both ethnic and mainstream worlds. Our conclusion has been that Japanese Americans currently are quite involved in both social contexts; that is, they exhibit a high level of structural assimilation and yet are highly involved in their ethnic communities.

The second perspective on assimilation deals with the more complex issue of the nature of the boundaries themselves. In our earlier discussion we suggested that, paradoxically, the Japanese in Japan and Japanese Americans possess a greater sense of peoplehood and homogeneity than many other groups, yet their cultural traditions permit considerable lati- tude with respect to adapting the attitudes and behavioral characteristics of other peoples. This orientation gives rise to the interesting question: how do Japanese Americans currently view social relationships in their ethnic group compared with those in the majority group? More impor-

TABLE 10:1.   Percentage of Respondents Perceiving Differences Between
Japanese and Caucasian Ways in Four Situations.[a]

| | Situation | | | |
Generation	Business	Social	Church	Family
Nisei	39.9	38.3	66.0	60.7
	(121)[b]	(116)	(200)	(184)
Sansei	50.9	46.3	82.3	70.5
	(164)	(149)	(265)	(227)
Total	45.6	42.4	74.4	65.8
	(285)	(265)	(465)	(411)
Zero-order and partial correlations with generation				
r, with generation	.115**	.067	.082	.183***
r, controlling for education	.121**	.094*	.080	.149***
r, controlling for Japanese organizations	.094*	.091*	.137**	.190***

* $p < .05.$ ** $p < .01.$ *** $p < .001.$

[a] This table was originally published in O'Brien and Fugita (1983a).
[b] Number of respondents is shown in parentheses.

tant, to what extent do they feel comfortable operating in the two different social contexts? These questions are the focus of the empirical analyses reported in this chapter.

The respondents were first asked whether they perceived differences
between Japanese and Caucasian ways of doing things in four different
kinds of interpersonal situations. Table 10:1 shows that across both generations about half of the individuals in our study saw differences between Japanese and Caucasian ways in business, social activities, church,
and family. More respondents perceived differences in the church and
family settings, where contact between individuals is usually more intimate and more likely to be with fellow ethnics.

What is conceptually most significant is the increase in perceived differences as one goes from the Nisei to the Sansei generation. Moreover,
these differences remain significant even when education and membership in Japanese organizations are statistically controlled. This suggests,
therefore, that not only does the perception of social boundaries between
the ethnic group and the larger society persist from one generation to the

TABLE 10:2. Characteristics Distinguishing Japanese Americans from Other Americans Today. Percentages Refer to Numbers of Persons in the Sample Who See a Particular Characteristic as Distinguishing Japanese Americans from Other Americans.

Total Sample	(N = 517)	Nisei	(N = 237)	Sansei	(N = 280)
Work ethic	41.2%	Work ethic	43.5%	Work ethic	39.3%
More reserved	33.3%	More reserved	32.1%	More reserved	32.5%
Different physical characteristics	25.1%	Different physical characteristics	27.8%	Different physical characteristics	22.9%
Stick together	15.9%	Stick together	14.3%	Stick together	17.1%
Japanese preserve tradition	13.3%	Japanese preserve tradition	9.7%	Japanese preserve tradition	16.4%
Closer family ties	9.9%	Closer family ties	9.7%	Closer family ties	10.0%
Japanese are economically better off	7.9%	Japanese are economically better off	9.3%	Japanese are economically better off	6.8%

next, it may even become more prevalent among younger Japanese Americans as their structural assimilation increases.

The data also indicate that there is a remarkably high degree of consensus between Nisei and Sansei about the specific characteristics distinguishing Japanese Americans from other Americans. The results of an open-ended question inquiring about these characteristics are found in Table 10:2. It is interesting to observe here that physical characteristics rank third, behind greater work ethic and more reserved interactional style, as characteristics Japanese Americans themselves see as distinguishing their group from that of the core culture.

Perhaps the most fundamental perceptual criterion with respect to the persistence of social boundaries between Japanese Americans and the larger society, however, is whether members of the ethnic group see themselves as belonging to a distinguishable community. Given the high levels of involvement in ethnic voluntary associations reported earlier (Chapter 6), it is not surprising that the vast majority of persons in the sample report that there is a distinguishable Japanese American community in their area: 87.4 percent overall and 84.2 and 90.5 percent among the Nisei and Sansei, respectively. Moreover, most individuals (83.3 percent) reported that it was at least somewhat important for them to feel a part of the Japanese community. Here again there is virtually no difference between the generations with respect to their affective commitment to the community: Nisei, 83.0 percent; Sansei, 83.7 percent.

What is especially noteworthy about these findings is that in only one of the three areas in the sample (Gardena) is there anything even closely approximating the level of ethnic population density one would ordinarily associate with a "critical mass," necessary to sustain a distinctive subculture (Fischer, 1975, 1976:35–38, 1982:202–208). Unfortunately, we do not have any data that would allow us to directly compare the level of emotional attachment Japanese Americans have to their community with the attachment persons in other ethnic groups have to their respective communities. However, the fact that four-fifths of the Sansei generation indicated that it was at least "somewhat important" for them to feel a part of the ethnic community is strong evidence for the continued importance of the ethnic community for members of this group.

Nevertheless, it is also clear that Japanese Americans perceive significant generational erosion of their ethnic behavioral and attitudinal characteristics. Furthermore, there is a generally negative reaction to these changes. The responses to a question concerning differences between Nisei and Sansei, reported in Table 10:3, for example, show that they perceive a loss of their distinctive interactional styles and other cultural characteristics that historically have acted as markers between ethnic and mainstream communities. Again, there seems to be a relatively high degree of consensus between the generations about these issues.

Table 10:4 presents responses to a question asking respondents about their view of changes in Japanese values. These are, of course, related to perceived changes in social boundaries between their group and the mainstream. The most common response (36.9 percent) was that Japanese Americans have lost some of their traditional "family closeness" as they have become more acculturated to the more individualistic, mainstream American values.

These findings and those in Table 10:5 suggest that although Japanese Americans do not experience intense psychic cross pressures as a byproduct of living in two different social worlds, they nonetheless see significant long-term costs as well as benefits of structural assimilation and acculturation.

TABLE 10:3. Perceived Differences Between Nisei and Sansei.
Percentages Refer to Numbers of Persons in the Sample
Who Mention a Particular Difference.

Total Sample	(N = 590)	Nisei	(N = 296)	Sansei	(N = 294)
Sansei more Americanized	49.2%	Sansei more Americanized	46.7%	Sansei more Americanized	51.7%
Nisei experienced more hardship	24.1%	Nisei experienced more hardship	27.0%	Nisei follow Japanese traditions	27.6%
Sansei more aggressive	22.7%	Sansei more aggressive	24.7%	Sansei more aggressive	20.7%
Nisei follow Japanese traditions	22.0%	Nisei follow Japanese traditions	16.6%	Nisei experienced more hardship	20.7%
Nisei speak Japanese	13.1%	Sansei more educated	16.2%	Nisei more conservative	12.9%
Sansei more educated	11.2%	Nisei speak Japanese	14.9%	Nisei speak Japanese	11.2%
Nisei more conservative	9.7%	Sansei have more freedom	9.5%	Sansei lost sense of obligation to family	9.5%
Sansei lost sense of obligation to family	9.2%	Sansei lost sense of obligation to family	8.8%	Sansei more irresponsible	7.8%
Sansei more irresponsible	8.1%	Sansei more irresponsible	8.4%	Sansei have more freedom	6.1%
Sansei have more freedom	7.8%	Nisei more conservative	6.4%	Sansei more educated	6.1%

One Fresno Nisei expressed the following sentiments: "All of the [traditional] values have changed. There is reduced commitment and greater apathy. There is a tendency to disinherit ethnic relationships. The Japanese have done a good job in terms of trying to integrate and assimilate into the community they live in. This means a reduction in traditional ties, commitment, etc. and sometimes these have been lost. I feel a sense of loss, a sense of coercion. A kind of sense of disorientation."

Another Fresno respondent said: "Family ties have broken. There is no

TABLE 10:4. The Most Important Changes in Japanese Values.
Percentages Refer to Numbers of Persons in the Sample
Who Mention a Particular Value.

Total Sample	(N = 590)	Nisei	(N = 235)	Sansei	(N = 250)
Less family closeness	36.9%	Less family closeness	29.8%	Less family closeness	43.6%
Less Japanese tradition	23.5%	Less Japanese tradition	24.7%	Less work ethic	26.8%
Less respect for elders	22.9%	Less respect for elders	22.6%	Less respect for elders	23.2%
Less work ethic	22.7%	Less work ethic	18.3%	Less Japanese tradition	22.4%
Sansei more Americanized	13.6%	Sansei more Americanized	14.0%	Sansei more Americanized	12.4%
Japanese more independent	10.9%	Japanese more independent	10.2%	Japanese more independent	11.6%
Less honesty	7.2%	Less honesty	9.4%	Less emphasis on education	6.4%
Less family discipline	6.2%	Less family discipline	6.4%	Less family discipline	6.0%
Less emphasis on education	‹.2%	Less emphasis on education	3.8%	Less honesty	5.2%

TABLE 10:5. Feelings About Changes in Traditional Japanese Values.
Percentages Refer to Numbers of Persons in the Sample
Who Express a Particular Feeling.

Total Sample	(N = 506)	Nisei	(N = 246)	Sansei	(N = 260)
Negative reaction	55.3%	Negative reaction	51.6%	Negative reaction	58.5%
Positive attitude	20.9%	Change is inevitable	24.8%	Positive attitude	18.5%
Change is inevitable	20.6%	Positive attitude	23.2%	Change is inevitable	16.9%
Mixed feelings	8.8%	Mixed feelings	8.5%	Mixed feelings	10.8%
Doesn't matter	3.6%	Doesn't matter	3.6%	Doesn't matter	4.6%

strong reason for Japanese families to stay together. We don't hold as high esteem for Aunts and Uncles. I still think as individuals we cling to pride and integrity with Hakujins (white people) and among ourselves. I still see in my son part of our culture and background."

With regard to feelings about changes in these values, he related: "It's not bad or good—it occurs naturally. The War had some bearing, maybe because of camp, trying to lose ourselves faster than anyone else."

A Sacramento interviewee said: "All these things have changed [perseverance, patience, humbleness, and honesty]. People give up more easily, the Sansei are cocky, arrogant. They b.s. a lot." When asked his view of these changes, he stated: "I'm ambivalent. On the one hand, sometimes the Japanese are too patient, too loyal. I have mixed feelings. Sometimes they're just not practical. The middle way is best."

Another Sacramento Nisei explained: "By the physical dispersion of Japanese throughout the area, the identity with the community has diminished. I don't know if it's bad or not but like my kids, they aren't growing up with the same identity as I did. Also, because of affluence, they have dispersed away from the family. When we came back from the camps, we had three generations living in the home. Now we don't have that."

With regard to the changes, he said: "They are inevitable. I can't say if they are good or bad. Probably, we will feel later that kids aren't as good as we were or that they aren't having it as good as we did. We're probably wrong but that's the the way we will think. The most negative things about these changes is their loss of identity, although maybe they'll find it somewhere else. I liked the [Japanese] values but it's inevitable that they change. *Shikataganai* [water under the bridge, can't help it, what's done is done]."

The mixed feelings of many older Japanese American respondents were perhaps best expressed in the words of one respondent, who said: "Some things are good, especially advancements made by the Nisei and Sansei, they're more socially accepted. In the last 20 years there are more Japanese names in the police blotter but there are also a lot of Japanese appointed to high positions in government. So again, it is a mixture of good and bad."

The subtleties and sometimes surprises we found in talking to Japanese Americans about operating in the two different social worlds of ethnic and nonethnic community life are perhaps best seen in their responses to a question we asked about doing business with Caucasians versus fellow ethnics: "Would you say that if a person is Japanese, it is easier to do business with him or her? Why or why not?"

TABLE 10:6. Percentage of Respondents Answering the Question, "Is It Easier to Do Business with Someone Who Is Japanese?"

| | AREA | | | | | | | | | | | | | | | |
| | Gardena | | | | Sacramento | | | | Fresno | | | | Totals | | | |
Generation	No (%)	Not Sure (%)	Yes (%)	N	No (%)	Not Sure (%)	Yes (%)	N	No (%)	Not Sure (%)	Yes (%)	N	No (%)	Not Sure (%)	Yes (%)	N
Nisei	44.8	13.3	41.9	105	58.8	4.1	37.1	97	64.7	3.9	31.4	102	55.9	7.2	36.8	304
Sansei	35.3	16.7	48.0	102	42.0	7.0	51.0	100	48.6	6.7	44.8	105	42.0	10.1	47.9	307
Totals	40.1	15.0	44.9	207	50.3	5.6	44.2	197	56.5	5.3	38.2	207	48.9	8.7	42.4	611

By generation: χ^2 (2, $N = 611$) = 11.866, $p < .01$.
By area: χ^2 (4, $N = 611$) = 21.5, $p < .001$.
By generation and area: χ^2 (4, $N = 611$) = .716, p = n.s.

TABLE 10:7. Percentage of Respondents Describing Various Reasons Why It Is or Is Not Easier to Do Business with Japanese Americans.

Total Sample	(N = 389)	Nisei	(N = 181)	Sansei	(N = 208)
Similar cultural backgrounds	43.4%	Japanese are too demanding	38.7%	Similar cultural backgrounds	51.0%
Mutual trust	35.2%	Similar cultural background	34.8%	Mutual trust	38.5%
Japanese are too demanding	34.4%	Mutual trust	31.5%	Japanese are too demanding	30.8%
Japanese are more honest	8.0%	Japanese are more honest	11.8%	Japanese are more honest	3.8%

Consistent with Wiley's (1967) discussion of the attractions of making a living in an ethnic community, the majority of our respondents reported that dealing with other Japanese is easier and more comfortable. Some typical responses were:

"They're a little more honest. I trust them more. I can depend on them. They're easier to get along with and they give you greater cooperation."

"I feel more comfortable with Japanese, they're easier to talk to. If the prices are the same, you'll do business with Japanese Americans. You have more confidence."

"It is easier to do business with a Japanese knowing that you will be treated fairly, not ripped off."

"I feel more comfortable. Call it trust or whatever, it's just there."

"When I walk into a store or business and see I will be dealing with a Japanese person there seems to be immediate rapport. Maybe he knows something about my history and I know something about his."

However, a significant minority emphasized the more negative aspects of dealing with fellow ethnics. The following are some representative remarks illustrating this theme (many of them probably reflect sentiments found in any cohesive group; others appear to reflect the group-centered values of Japanese American culture):

"No, I hold back because I don't want to take advantage of them or be taken advantage of. It doesn't always work out that way."

"Because they're Japanese, I give them breaks or discounts. It's more difficult to deal with them."

"The Japanese are more demanding, more particular. They're harder to please."

"Sometimes you feel an obligation because they are Japanese. Sometimes you think you will get a better deal but you feel obligated."

"They expect too much from you. To go over backwards and do a lot of favors. For example, at donation time just because you're Japanese we get hit."

"Probably you're too conscious of what the other person feels and thinks so you feel restricted. When dealing with Japanese Americans, it's more difficult."

"The Japanese are harder to work with, more "nit picking." You can't tell him off, make him mad. With Japanese, you hold back. It's more personal."

"Maybe because we hold back more. I don't feel we have freedom of negotiation. We have 'enryo'."

"They just shy away. I guess it's jealousy on their part. They figure you're getting ahead more than they are. The Japanese people don't want anyone to be better than they are."

As shown in Table 10:6, however, Sansei were more likely than Nisei to report that it is easier doing business with their fellow ethnics. Persons in the older generation, who grew up in the highly interdependent, collectivistic ethnic community, report feeling more constrained by "obligation" to be helpful to fellow ethnics. They are also more likely to report that Japanese Americans are "too demanding."

When Nisei deal with fellow Japanese Americans in a customer-proprietor relationship, the customer is likely to expect some sign of special treatment. Although they will never publicly ask for a "break," many will feel that they have been slighted if one is not forthcoming. Nisei often will go to considerable lengths to continue to patronize a Japanese American small business once they have established a relationship with the owner, even if the goods or services are inferior or the prices higher than what could be obtained elsewhere. To stop doing business with a merchant one dealt with in the past would be seen, by both parties, as "personal." In order to minimize the risks of inadvertent slights, some of the more traditional rural Japanese American stores automatically give an unannounced discount to all fellow ethnics, even those not from the area. The more personal nature of dealing with fellow ethnics causes a minority to prefer the more impersonal interactions with mainstream persons.

On the other hand, the Sansei, who did not grow up in an "institutionally complete" (Breton, 1964) ethnic community, do not feel as constrained by norms of reciprocity and thus find it easier to do business with other Japanese Americans, simply because they "share a common culture" in which each party understands the nuances of the other's verbal and nonverbal interactional style. In turn, the resultant mutual understanding produces greater feelings of trust. The importance of these factors is reflected in the responses shown in Table 10:7.

Despite the clear perception that they share a common cultural basis of understanding with fellow ethnics, however, only about one-third (33.2 percent) of the respondents agreed with the statement, "Socially I feel less at ease with Caucasians than with Japanese" (38.2 percent among the Nisei and 28.3 percent among the Sansei). Moreover, when educational attainment was controlled, there was no significant difference between the generations on this item.

SOME POTENTIAL COSTS OF THE CONTINUED RETENTION OF JAPANESE WAYS

Despite the apparent success with which Japanese Americans have learned to live in two social worlds, it would be misleading to assume that this accommodation is totally benign. As in most adjustments in life, there are likely to be some costs involved. These costs are not, as the preceding data clearly show, anything like those supposedly experienced by the so-called marginal man (Stonequist, 1937). We do not know, for example, of any compelling evidence of unusual signs of stress among persons in this ethnic group. The main costs appear to be in certain types of social mobility. Essentially, the more collectivistic, interpersonal orientation of the Japanese is not always instrumental in some of the more individualistic settings in the larger society.

In school, teachers generally see Japanese Americans as exhibiting very positive attitudes and behavior, but difficulties sometimes arise in other settings, such as corporate management, where Euro-American norms emphasize individualistic assertiveness. Japanese American norms, which place a heavy emphasis on modesty and self-effacement, seem to impede mobility in this type of setting. Some individuals in this ethnic group may experience difficulty in situations where considerable assertiveness and verbal skills are expected. Many appear to hope that technical competence and hard work will lead to being "discovered," which would be the expected outcome in Japanese American groups. This kind of behavior, however, is likely to be interpreted by majority group individuals as showing a lack of leadership qualities. In meetings with Caucasians, Japanese American reticence and verbal modesty is sometimes perceived by core culture individuals as being quiet to the point of rudeness.

In fact, the concept of leadership is quite different in the Japanese American community and mainstream American society. Japanese American groups collectively "push" persons they see as capable and worthy into leadership positions rather than having individuals compete for the position by presenting their credentials. Leadership positions are therefore usually experienced by the Japanese as being more burdensome because there is greater perceived responsibility to the group.

CONCLUSION

The findings reported in this chapter show that Japanese Americans still see significant, although highly permeable, social boundaries between their group and mainstream American society. Moreover, this perception is remarkably similar in both the second and third generations. In fact, the Sansei often saw greater differences than the Nisei did. These views, along with the continued perception of social discrimination, and to a lesser extent the job discrimination reported earlier (Chapter 9), suggest that Japanese Americans will continue to be motivated to support the social organizational mechanisms crucial to maintaining ethnic community life.

At the same time, although they experience some real costs as a result of their accommodation, members of this group generally feel quite comfortable interacting in the nonethnic as well as the ethnic social worlds. This, coupled with our earlier findings showing similar results with respect to friendships (Chapter 6) and voluntary association membership (Chapters 6 and 9), provides powerful empirical support for the thesis that structural assimilation and ethnic community involvement are analytically separate yet compatible forms of social participation.

ELEVEN

The Japanese American

Experience and

Understanding Ethnicity

in the Modern World

The central theoretical focus of this book has been the relationship between the degree of structural assimilation of an ethnic group, in this case second and third generation Japanese Americans, and the group's cohesiveness. Historically, most social scientists have assumed that these two dimensions are directly and inversely related. For example, Gordon (1964) in his classic work implies that structural assimilation leads to the destruction of group cohesiveness. The widespread prevalence of this reasonable sounding but unwarranted assumption is partly due to the fact that the majority of investigators interested in assimilation and cohesion have studied European immigrants, who indeed generally exhibited less group cohesiveness as their members became structurally assimilated.

Not until Reitz (1980) and others pointed out that structural assimilation and ethnic group cohesiveness are two distinct, orthogonal concepts have investigators begun to consider critically the relationship between these two dimensions of ethnicity. Reitz's (1980) empirical findings document that ethnic groups do vary substantially in the extent to which they retain ethnic group cohesiveness at similar points in their life cycles. He presents evidence showing how certain variables, principally structural in nature, differentially affect group cohesiveness. However, he does not present data relevant to our central focus: the *relationship* between structural assimilation and ethnic group cohesiveness.

Our general theoretical approach to this specific but pivotal conceptual issue is that three factors constrain ethnic cohesiveness and structural assimilation—cultural predispositions, structural opportunities, and demographic opportunities (cf. Tomaskovic-Devey and Tomaskovic-Devey, 1988). Only when all three influences are examined can we truly begin to understand the complex relationship between structural assimilation and ethnic cohesiveness.

Greenstone helps to put the matter into perspective when he says that ethnicity can be seen as "an orienting variable, a source of basic cultural attitudes, which affect the way individuals *interpret* their social situation. In turn, this orientation affects the way they seek to change or preserve this situation. Ethnicity, in other words, can be examined as a major source of *cultural ideologies*—the frameworks of interpretation which are only indirectly related to an individual's status position" (1975:3).

If we hope to explain why ethnic communities vary in their capacity to survive in the face of structural assimilation, we will need to turn to the orientation and characteristics of the ethnic groups themselves. In particular, basic cultural orientations at the time of immigration, as they are modified by the changing structural requirements experienced in this country, have long-term consequences for the kinds of adaptations persons in a given ethnic group make to historically specific structural exigencies.

The most critical cultural aspect of problem solving in the long run, with respect to assimilation and group cohesiveness, is the manner in which the internal solidarity of the group is expected to be maintained. Different cultures have very different assumptions concerning choices about trusting other groups or individuals. In addition, different cultures have different sets of rules for structuring interactions between members of a group. These rules influence how attractive interaction is with fellow ethnic group members in the context of the host society.

If the internal solidarity of the ethnic group depends largely on maintaining strong-tie cliques, it is obvious that structural assimilation will take a heavy toll on ethnic cohesiveness, simply because structural assimilation, by definition, requires members of the ethnic group to establish intimate relationships with members of the larger society. Alternatively, if, as in the case of Japanese Americans, ethnic solidarity rests to a large extent on the perpetuation of less exclusive quasi-kin ties within the group, the development of primary ties to the larger society will not be as disruptive to ethnic community cohesiveness. This means, therefore, that even if we were to hold external pressures constant (e.g., the level of discrimination or other historical considerations), some ethnic groups would have a significantly easier time than others in retaining the active participation of their members under conditions of high structural assimilation.

The striking feature of the social organization that many of the European peasant immigrant groups brought with them to the United States was that they were very familistic and village-based (Handlin, 1951; Sarna, 1978; Thomas and Znaniecki, 1927). By contrast, groups like the Japanese and the Jews arrived in the New World with a history of relations with fellow ethnic group members in much more expansive forms of social organization extending beyond the boundaries of kin and village, especially through voluntary associations (e.g., Benkin, 1978; De Santis and Benkin, 1980; Embree, 1939,112–157, 163–170; Norbeck, 1972).

Previous work has shown that the familistic and village orientation of the European peasants resulted from their simply not having any experience with larger, more inclusive forms of social organization, such as the nation-state (e.g., Handlin, 1951). Nevertheless, these adaptations to structural exigencies in the European context became part of their culturally programmed responses to problems they faced in the New World. Given that they had little experience and much less culturally driven inclination to participate in more inclusive social organizational forms, it is not surprising that their responses to the American situation tended to focus on the development of strong-tie cliques (Gans, 1982; Granovetter, 1973, 1982) or parish-centered associations (Thomas and Znaniecki, 1927). The most successful "political entrepreneurs" in the various immigrant ethnic enclaves recognized this fact and based their political organizations on incentive systems providing some semblance of strong ties, such as relations with the precinct captain in the political machine (Banfield and Wilson, 1963:117–118; O'Brien, 1975:38–40, 171–173).

By contrast, the historical experiences of groups like the Jews and the Japanese prior to immigration fostered a clear sense of peoplehood (Castile, 1981) that extended beyond the boundaries of immediate kin and village. This is seen in the development of Jewish law, which specified numerous rules and relationships that set Jews as a people apart from the

Gentiles (Weber, 1952:336–355). By the same token, Reischauer (1981) and others have noted that the Japanese national and ethnic identity is more homogeneous than that of most peoples in the world and they perceive themselves as unique in many ways.

The capacity of Japanese Americans to maintain group cohesiveness in the face of structural assimilation is enhanced by another element in Japanese culture. This is their group orientation that not only stresses collective interests compared with those of the individual but supports a relativistic interpretation of specific cultural content. In essence, Japanese culture places almost everything else subordinate to the survival of the group; thus the adoption of cultural elements from others is not felt to severely compromise the integrity of the group (see Reischauer, 1981). This was seen, for example, in the shift of many Japanese Americans from Buddhist to Christian religious affiliations, but with the maintenance of a distinctively Japanese social organizational form (i.e., the Japanese church) with which to carry the religious message (see Chapter 5).

We should note that the persistence of a cohesive Jewish ethnic community life in the United States suggests that it is the sense of peoplehood rather than a relativistic ethic that is most important in their ethnic community survival. Jews, unlike the Japanese, have a cultural tradition that in many ways militates against a relativistic worldview. Yet, despite the conflicts and divisions among the various Jewish denominations, there remains a high degree of ethnic community involvement. The crucial point in the histories of all ethnic communities that manage to retain high levels of individual participation in the face of high levels of structural assimilation, however, is that the sense of "peoplehood" has been maintained by the persistence of very practical mechanisms for coping with day-to-day problems. Louis Wirth (1928), for example, illustrates that although there were serious conflicts between Jews of various national backgrounds, practical social organizational mechanisms were developed to support Jewish economic enterprises. In the case of the Japanese, the principles of quasi-kin relationships provided the blueprint for social organizational mechanisms to deal with both economic and noneconomic affairs.

The different principles that supported the internal solidarity of the respective ethnic groups upon their arrival in the New World have had two critical long-range consequences for their survival in the face of the pressures for structural assimilation. The first, and most obvious, is that ethnic groups that arrived with a clear sense of peoplehood and experience with nonfamilial social organization had a distinct advantage over groups that were principally familistic and village-oriented in developing voluntary associations serving to link the larger body of fellow ethnics together.

This is a key factor separating those ethnic groups that were successful in creating ethnic enterprises from those that were not (Light, 1972, 1979). In groups like the Japanese, the social organizational principles for developing a collective response to economic exigencies flowed quite naturally from the worldview they initially brought with them from Japan. For example, the trust and social control mechanisms necessary for the *tanomoshi* to succeed were a natural outgrowth of these quasi-kin principles.

This is not to say, of course, that other ethnic groups did not use their social networks to pursue economic and political interests. The crucial point, however, is that because their social organization was less inclusive in scope, it was less effective in an economic and political sense than that of groups like the Japanese or the Jews. This competitive disadvantage may explain some of the resentments persons in these groups have had toward groups that were able to mobilize more effective ethnic economies and lobbies for political influence.

The second, and most important, long-run consequence to emerge from the different bases of ethnic social organization pertains to their respective degrees of compatibility with structural assimilation. The strong-tie orientation that has been more central to the solidarity of many European peasant ethnic groups possesses some inherent incompatibilities with structural assimilation. In particular, persons in these groups have often had to face an ethnic mobility trap (Wiley, 1967) in which they were forced to make a choice between involvement in two incompatible social networks: the strong-tie cliques of their ethnic communities versus the weak-tie associations of the larger society. Involvement in the latter, of course, was necessary for upward mobility and structural assimilation.

In this regard, Will Herberg (1960) made the insightful observation that the structural assimilation of many European ethnic immigrant groups was facilitated by the transfer of identity from their ethnicity to their Catholicism. In effect, the Catholic Church assisted the immigrants and their children to adopt a more inclusive set of social ties. In the process, however, ethnic identification waned, and by the time of the third generation it was merely a symbolic identification (Alba and Chamlin, 1983; Goering, 1971; Roche, 1982).

The more inclusive scope of networks in the social organization of groups like the Japanese and the Jews provides more flexibility to retain relatively high levels of ethnic community involvement when individuals become structurally assimilated into mainstream American life. Persons in these groups have faced some of the same difficult choices all ethnics have faced with respect to leaving familiar environments, such as the rural ethnic enclaves of the Japanese and the urban ghettos of the Jews. Nevertheless, because ethnic community solidarity in these groups did not rest solely on strong-tie cliques, such movement of individuals away from traditional neighborhoods was not nearly as destructive to ethnic cohesiveness as it was for persons in groups depending almost entirely on strong-tie cliques.

A useful test of the capacity of different ethnic groups to survive in the face of structural assimilation is found in comparing their persistence under varying degrees of ethnic population density. It is clear that informal contact between ethnic group members and persons in the larger society is substantially affected by the number of fellow ethnics in the local area. In this respect there is support for Fischer's (1975, 1976:35–38, 1982:202–208) subcultural theory of urbanism, which argues that there is a positive association between population density and the vitality of subcultural groups. This is true even in the case of groups like the Japanese and the Jews who have maintained a high degree of ethnic community cohesion over time. Thus, for example, Rose (1959) found that his small-town Jews were much more likely than their counterparts in New York City to associate informally with Gentiles. Similarly, we found that Japanese Americans in the relatively low ethnic density areas of Fresno and Sacramento were more likely than Japanese Americans in Gardena to have Caucasians as best friends (see Chapter 6).

But the critical point is that there is substantial variation in the ability of different ethnic groups to maintain the involvement of their members in the institutional life of their respective communities in areas where they are relatively few in number. In this regard, most European ethnics do not remain involved in ethnic community voluntary associations once they move to the suburbs (Goering, 1971; Roche, 1982), but small-town Jews (Rose, 1959) and Japanese Americans in Sacramento and Fresno (see Chapter 6) maintain a higher level of involvement in ethnic voluntary associations than do their counterparts who live in urban ethnic ghettos. These findings reinforce the view that there are fundamental differences in the social organizational bases of different ethnic collectivities and that these differences, in turn, produce differences in the ability of groups to survive the pressures of structural assimilation.

THE FUTURE OF JAPANESE AMERICAN ETHNICITY

Our argument has centered on why the situation of Japanese Americans today is different from that of many other ethnic groups that have achieved similar levels of structural assimilation in American society. It would perhaps be a bit unfair to leave the reader hanging without providing some idea of what our thoughts are with respect to the future of Japanese American ethnicity, say ten, twenty, or thirty years from now.

There is every reason to expect that the processes of structural assimilation will continue into the next century. The findings in Chapter 8 certainly show that an increase in the number of Japanese Americans who are intermarried with white Americans is likely to produce significant declines in community involvement. In addition, we would expect that these liaisons will increase the overall rate of divorce in the ethnic community, further weakening community cohesiveness. Yet a significant finding on the intermarried Japanese Americans in our sample is that their level of involvement in ethnic community institutional life remains substantially higher than that of persons in other ethnic groups. If anything, our assertion here is quite conservative, given that our sample is composed exclusively of males while the role of maintaining social ties to other families in the ethnic community is typically handled by women (see Yanagisako, 1977, 1985).

The most compelling reason to expect that Japanese American ethnicity will remain viable in the foreseeable future, however, is that its social organization remains compatible with structural assimilation, and it apparently also meets a number of needs of persons in postindustrial society. The most obvious in this regard is that the social organization of the ethnic community provides a mechanism through which individuals can pursue their respective interests in American politics or in economic affairs.

An equally compelling, although more difficult to measure, reason that this social organization bolsters group cohesiveness is that it provides a basis for community in what is often a very impersonal society. This is not to say, as Japanese Americans themselves will quickly point out, that community involvement is without costs. Clearly, as in any type of social participation with commitments, there are difficulties to be faced, not the least of which involves having to interact with and accommodate to persons in ways that are not demanded in more transient, instrumental relationships. Nonetheless, there are also significant gains from such involvements. Perhaps the most important of these is the experience of relating to others who operate with the same set of assumptions about how relationships ought to be maintained and who operate with the same interactional "gear ratio" (Miyamoto, 1986–97).

REFERENCES

Alba, Richard D.
1976   "Social assimilation among American Catholic national-origin groups." *American Sociological Review* 41:1030–1046.
1981   "The twilight of ethnicity among American Catholics of European ancestry." *Annals, AAPSS* 454:86–97.
1985   "The twilight of ethnicity among Americans of European ancestry: The case of Italians." *Ethnic and Racial Studies* 8:134–158.
Alba, Richard D., and Mitchell B. Chamlin
1983   "A preliminary examination of ethnic identification among whites." *American Sociological Review* 48:240–247.
Albert, Michael D.
1980   "Japanese American communities in Chicago and the Twin Cities." Ph.D. dissertation, University of Minnesota, Minneapolis.
Altman, Irwin, and Dalmas A. Taylor
1973   *Social Penetration: The Development of Interpersonal Relationships.* New York: Holt, Rinehart and Winston.
Alwin, Duane F.
1977   "Making errors in surveys: An overview." *Sociological Methods and Research* 6:131–150.
Antunes, George, and Charles M. Gaitz
1975   "Ethnicity and participation: A study of Mexican-Americans, blacks, and whites." *American Journal of Sociology* 80:1192–1211.

Banfield, Edward C.
1958   *The Moral Basis of a Backward Society.* New York: The Free Press.
Banfield, Edward C., and James Q. Wilson
1963   *City Politics.* Cambridge: Harvard University Press.
Banton, Michael
1981   "The direction and speed of ethnic change." Pp. 32–52 in Charles F. Keyes (ed.), *Ethnic Change.* Seattle: University of Washington Press.
Barth, Fredrik
1969   "Introduction." Pp. 9–38 in Fredrik Barth (ed.), *Ethnic Groups and Boundaries.* Boston: Little, Brown.
Bechhofer, Frank, and Brian Elliot
1981   "Petty property: The survival of a moral economy." Pp. 182–200 in Frank Bechhofer and Brian Elliot (eds.), *The Petite Bourgeoisie: Comparative Studies of the Uneasy Stratum.* New York: St. Martin's Press.
Befu, Harumi
1965   "Contrastive acculturation of California Japanese: Comparative approach to the study of immigrants." *Human Organization* 24:209–216.
Benedict, Burton
1968   "Family firms and economic development." *Southwestern Journal of Anthropology* 24:1–19.
Benkin, Richard L.
1978   "Ethnicity and organization: Jewish communities in Eastern Europe and the United States." *The Sociological Quarterly* 19:614–625.
Bertaux, Daniel, and Isabelle Bertaux-Wiame
1981   "Artisanal bakery in France: How it lives and why it survives." Pp. 155–181 in Frank Bechhofer and Brian Elliot (eds.), *The Petite Bourgeoisie: Comparative Studies of the Uneasy Stratum.* New York: St. Martin's Press.
Blackford, Mansel G.
1977   *The Politics of Business in California, 1800–1920.* Columbus: Ohio State University Press.
Blalock, Hubert M., Jr.
1967   *Toward a Theory of Minority Group Relations.* New York: Wiley.
Bland, Richard, Brian Elliot, and Frank Bechhofer
1978   "Social mobility in the petite bourgeoisie." *Acta Sociologica* 21:229–248.
Bloom, Leonard
1943   "Familial adjustments of Japanese-Americans to relocation: First phase." *American Sociological Review* 8:551–560.
Bloom, Leonard, and Ruth Riemer
1949   *Removal and Return: The Socio-Economic Effects of the War on Japanese Americans.* Berkeley: University of California Press.
Bonacich, Edna
1972   "A theory of ethnic antagonism: The split labor market." *American Sociological Review* 37:547–559.

1973 "A theory of middleman minorities." *American Sociological Review* 38:583–594.

1975 "Small business and Japanese American ethnic solidarity." *Amerasia Journal* 3:96–113.

1980 "Middleman minorities and advanced capitalism." *Ethnic Groups* 2:211–219.

Bonacich, Edna, and John Modell

1980 *The Economic Basis of Ethnic Solidarity: Small Business in the Japanese American Community.* Berkeley: University of California Press.

Bottomore, T. B., and Maximilien Rubel (eds.)

1956 *Karl Marx: Selected Writings in Sociology and Social Philosophy.* Translated by T. B. Bottomore. New York: McGraw-Hill Paperbacks.

Breton, Raymond

1964 "Institutional completeness of ethnic communities and the personal relations of immigrants." *American Journal of Sociology* 70:193–205.

California Department of Food and Agriculture

1975 Principal Crop and Livestock Commodities. Sacramento: Media Office, California Department of Food and Agriculture.

Carrott, M. Browning

1983 "Prejudice goes to court: The Japanese and the Supreme Court in the 1920s." *California History* 63:122–138.

Castile, George P.

1981 "Issues in the analysis of enduring cultural systems." Pp. xv–xxii in George Castile and Gilbert Kueshner (eds.), *Persistent People: Cultural Enclaves in Perspective.* Tucson: University of Arizona Press.

Caudill, William, and George DeVos

1956 "Achievement, culture and personality: The case of the Japanese Americans." *American Anthropologist* 58:1102–1126.

Caudill, William, and Lois Frost

1974 "A comparison of maternal care and infant behavior in Japanese-American, American, and Japanese families." Pp. 3–15 in *Youth, Socialization, and Mental Health*, vol. 3 of Mental Health Research in Asia and the Pacific, edited by William P. Lebra. Honolulu: University of Hawaii Press.

Christopher, Robert

1983 *The Japanese Mind: The Goliath Explained.* New York: Linden Press.

Cohen, Abner

1981 "Variables in ethnicity." Pp. 306–331 in Charles F. Keyes (ed.), *Ethnic Change.* Seattle: University of Washington Press.

Cohen, Gary B.

1984 "Ethnic persistence and change: Concepts and models for historical research." *Social Science Quarterly* 65:1029–1042.

Cohen, Steven M., and Leonard J. Fein

1985 "From integration to survival: American Jewish anxieties in transition." *Annals, AAPSS* 480:75–88.

Cohen, Steven M., and Robert E. Kapsis
  1978   "Participation of blacks, Puerto Ricans and whites in voluntary asso-
          ciations: A test of current theories." *Social Forces* 54:1053–1071.
Cole, Cheryl L.
  1974   *A History of the Japanese Community in Sacramento, 1883–1972: Organi-
          zations, Businesses, and Generational Response to Majority Domination
          and Stereotypes.* San Francisco: R & E Research Associates.
Collins, Randall
  1975   *Conflict Sociology: Toward an Explanatory Science.* New York: Aca-
          demic Press.
Commission on Wartime Relocation and Internment of Civilians
  1982   *Personal Justice Denied.* Washington, D.C.: U.S. Government Print-
          ing Office.
Connor, John W.
  1974a   "Acculturation and family continuities in three generations of Japa-
          nese Americans." *Journal of Marriage and the Family* 36:159–165.
  1974b   "Acculturation and changing need patterns in Japanese-American
          and Caucasian-American students." *Journal of Social Psychology*
          93:293–294.
  1977   *Tradition and Change in Three Generations of Japanese Americans.* Chi-
          cago: Nelson-Hall.
Coughlin, Richard J.
  1960   *Double Identity: The Chinese in Modern Thailand.* Hong Kong: Hong
          Kong University Press.
Daniels, Roger
  1962   *The Politics of Prejudice.* Berkeley and Los Angeles: University of
          California Press.
  1969   *Concentration Camps, U.S.A.: Japanese Americans and World War II.*
          New York: Holt, Rinehart and Winston.
  1985   "Japanese America, 1930–41: An ethnic community in the Great
          Depression." *Journal of the West* 24:35–50.
Davis, Winston
  1983   "Japanese religious affiliations: Motives and obligations." *Sociological
          Analysis* 44:131–146.
Demerath, N. J., III, and Richard A. Peterson
  1967   *System, Change, and Conflict.* New York: The Free Press.
De Santis, Grace, and Richard Benkin
  1980   "Ethnicity without community." *Ethnicity* 7:137–143.
Eliot, Stephen M., and C. Edward Solberg
  1973   "Production or protection: A groundbreaking inquiry into the effect
          of wartime bureaucracy on Japanese-American agriculture." Paper
          presented to the Conference on Asian Studies, Pacific Coast Branch,
          Vancouver, British Columbia, June 14–16.
Ellis, John Tracy
  1969   *American Catholicism.* 2d ed. Chicago: University of Chicago Press.

Embree, John F.
1939   *Suya Mura: A Japanese Village*. Chicago: University of Chicago Press.
Endo, Russell, and Dale Hirokawa
1983   "Japanese American intermarriage." *Free Inquiry in Creative Sociology* 11:159–162.
Feagin, Joe R., and Nancy Fujitaki
1972   "On the assimilation of Japanese Americans." *Amerasia Journal* 1:13–30.
Fei, H. T.
1939   *Peasant Life in China: A Field Study of Country Life in the Yangtze Valley*. London: Routledge and Kegan Paul.
Fendrich, James Max
1983   "Race and ethnic relations: The elite policy response in capitalist societies." *American Behavioral Scientist* 26:757–772.
Ferguson, Edwin E.
1947   "The California Alien Land Law and the Fourteenth Amendment." *California Law Review* 35:61–90.
Fischer, Claude
1975   "Toward a subcultural theory of urbanism." *American Journal of Sociology* 80:1319–1341.
1976   *The Urban Experience*. New York: Harcourt Brace Jovanovich.
1982   *To Dwell among Friends: Personal Networks in Town and City*. Chicago: University of Chicago Press.
Fischer, Claude, Robert M. Jackson, C. Ann Stueve, Kathleen Gerson, and Lynne M. Jones, with Mark Baldassare
1977   *Networks and Places*. New York: The Free Press.
Foner, Phillip S.
1964   *History of the Labor Movement in the United States*. Vol. 3. New York: International.
Francis, E. K.
1976   *Interethnic Relations: An Essay in Sociological Theory*. New York: Elsevier.
Freedman, M.
1964   "The family in China, past and present." In A. Feuerwerker (ed.), *Modern China*. Englewood Cliffs, N.J.: Prentice-Hall.
Fugita, Stephen S.
1978   "A perceived ethnic factor in California's farm labor conflict: The Nisei Farmers League." *Explorations in Ethnic Studies* 1:50–72.
Fugita, Stephen S., and David J. O'Brien
1977   "Economics, ideology, and ethnicity: The struggle between the United Farm Workers Union and the Nisei Farmers League." *Social Problems* 25:146–156.
1978   "The Nisei Farmers League and the United Farmworkers." Paper presented at the Asian American Labor History Conference, University of California, Los Angeles, May 5.

1985   "Structural assimilation, ethnic group membership, and political participation among Japanese Americans: A research note." *Social Forces* 63:986–995.

Fugita, Stephen S., and Henry T. Tanaka

1987   "The Japanese American community of Cleveland." In D. D. Van Tassel (ed.), *The Encyclopedia of Cleveland History*. Bloomington: Indiana University Press.

Fujimoto, Tetsuya

1975   "Social class and crime: The case of the Japanese-Americans." *Issues in Criminology* 10:73–89.

Fuller, Varden

1940   "The supply of agricultural labor as a factor in the evolution of farm organization in California." In *Agricultural Labor in California*. Washington, D.C.: U.S. Government Printing Office.

Gans, Herbert J.

1979   "Symbolic ethnicity: The future of ethnic groups and cultures in America." *Ethnic and Racial Studies* 2:1–20.

1982   *The Urban Villagers: Group and Class in the Life of Italian-Americans*. Updated and expanded edition. New York: The Free Press.

Gardena Special Census

1978   Gardena, California: City of Gardena.

Gee, Emma (ed.)

1976   *Counterpoint: Perspectives on Asian America*. Los Angeles: UCLA Asian American Studies Center.

Gendrot, Sophie, and Joan Turner

1983   "Ethnicity and class: Politics on Manhattan's Lower East Side." *Ethnic Groups* 5:79–108.

Gerth, H. H., and C. Wright Mills (eds.)

1946   *From Max Weber: Essays in Sociology*. New York: Oxford University Press.

Glazer, Nathan

1975   *Affirmative Discrimination: Ethnic Inequality and Public Policy*. New York: Basic Books.

Glazer, Nathan, and Daniel P. Moynihan

1970   *Beyond the Melting Pot: The Negroes, Puerto Ricans, Jews, Italians, and Irish of New York City*. Cambridge: MIT Press.

1975   "Introduction." Pp. 1–26 in Nathan Glazer and Daniel P. Moynihan (eds.), *Ethnicity: Theory and Experience*. Cambridge: Harvard University Press.

Goering, John M.

1971   "The emergence of ethnic interests: A case of serendipity." *Social Forces* 49:379–384.

Goldscheider, Calvin, and Francis E. Kobrin

1980   "Ethnic continuity and the process of self-employment." *Ethnicity* 7:256–278.

Gordon, Milton
1964 *Assimilation in American Life: The Role of Race, Religion, and National Origins.* New York: Oxford University Press.
Goren, Arthur A.
1980 "Jews." Pp. 571–598 in Stephan Thernstrom (ed.), *Harvard Encyclopedia of American Ethnic Groups.* Cambridge: Harvard University Press, Belknap Press.
1982 *The American Jews.* Cambridge: Harvard University Press, Belknap Press.
Gottlieb, Benjamin H.
1983 "Social support as a focus for integrative research in psychology." *American Psychologist* 38:278–287.
Granovetter, Mark S.
1973 "The strength of weak ties." *American Journal of Sociology* 78:1360–1380.
1982 "The strength of weak ties: A network theory revisited." Pp. 105–130 in Peter V. Marsden and Nan Lin (eds.), *Social Structure and Network Analysis.* Beverly Hills, Calif.: Sage.
Greeley, Andrew M.
1974 "Political participation among ethnic groups in the United States: A preliminary reconnaisance." *American Journal of Sociology* 80:170–204.
Greenstone, J. David
1975 "Ethnicity, class, and discontent: The case of the Polish peasant immigrants." *Ethnicity* 2:1–9.
Haglund, Edna
1984 "Japan: Cultural considerations." *International Journal of Intercultural Relations* 8:61–76.
Handlin, Oscar
1951 *The Uprooted.* New York: Grosset and Dunlap.
Hatchett, Shirley, and Howard Schuman
1975–76 "White respondents and race-of-interviewer effects." *Public Opinion Quarterly* 39:523–28.
Hechter, Michael
1975 *Internal Colonialism: The Celtic Fringe in British National Development, 1536–1966.* Berkeley: University of California Press.
1978 "Group formation and the cultural division of labor." *American Journal of Sociology* 84:293–318.
Herberg, Will
1960 *Protestant-Catholic-Jew: An Essay in American Religious Sociology.* Rev. ed. Garden City, N.Y.: Doubleday Anchor Books.
Hirschman, Charles
1983 "America's melting pot reconsidered." *Annual Review of Sociology* 9:397–423.
Hirschman, Charles, and Morrison G. Wong
1981 "Trends in socioeconomic achievement among immigrant and

native-born Asian-Americans, 1960–1976." *The Sociological Quarterly* 22:495–513.

Hoffman, Abraham
>   1973   "The El Monte Berry Pickers Strike, 1933: International involvement in a local labor dispute." *Journal of the West* 12:71–84.

Hofstadter, Richard
>   1955   *The Age of Reform: From Bryan to F.D.R.* New York: Random House Vintage Books.

Hohri, William M.
>   1988   *Repairing America: An Account of the Movement for Japanese-American Redress.* Pullman: Washington State University Press.

Hosokawa, Bill
>   1969   *Nisei: The Quiet Americans.* New York: Morrow.

Hraba, Joseph
>   1979   *American Ethnicity.* Itasca, Ill.: F. E. Peacock.

Hsu, Francis
>   1971   "Psychological homeostasis and jen: Concepts for advancing psychological anthropology." *American Anthropologist* 73:23–41.
>   1975   *Iemoto: The Heart of Japan.* Cambridge, Mass.: Schenkman Publishing Co.

Ichihashi, Yamato
>   1932   *Japanese in the United States.* Stanford: Stanford University Press.

Ichioka, Yuji
>   1971   "A buried past: Early Issei socialists and the Japanese community." *Amerasia Journal* 1:25–37.
>   1977   "Japanese associations and the Japanese government: A special relationship, 1909–1926." *Pacific Historical Review* 46:409–438.
>   1988   *The Issei: The World of First Generation Japanese Immigrants.* New York: The Free Press.

Ichioka, Yuji, Yasuo Sakata, Nobuya Tsuchida, and Eri Yasuhara
>   1974   *A Buried Past: An Annotated Bibliography of the Japanese American Research Project Collection.* Berkeley: University of California Press.

Iwata, Masakazu
>   1962   "The Japanese immigrants in California agriculture." *Agricultural History* 36:25–37.

Jenkins, J. Craig
>   1983   "Resource mobilization theory and the study of social movements." *Annual Review of Sociology* 9:527–553.

Jenkins, J. Craig, and Charles Perrow
>   1977   "Insurgency of the powerless: Farm worker movements (1946–1972). *American Sociological Review* 42:249–268.

Johnson, Chalmers A.
>   1962   *Peasant Nationalism and Communist Power: The Emergence of Revolutionary China.* Stanford: Stanford University Press.

Johnson, Colleen Leahy
    1976   "The principle of generation among the Japanese in Honolulu." *Ethnic Groups* 1:18–35.
Johnson, Frank A., Anthony J. Marsella, and Colleen L. Johnson
    1974   "Social and psychological aspects of verbal behavior in Japanese-Americans." *American Journal of Psychiatry* 131:580–583.
Jung, John
    1984   "Social support and its relation to health: A critical evaluation." *Basic and Applied Social Psychology* 5:143–169.
Kan, Stephen H., and William T. Liu
    1986   "The educational status of Asian Americans: An update from the 1980 census." Pp. 1–12 in Nobuya Tsuchida (ed.), *Issues in Asian and Pacific American Education*. Minneapolis, Minn.: Asian/Pacific American Learning Resource Center.
Kashima, Tetsuden
    1977   *Buddhism in America: The Social Organization of an Ethnic Religious Institution*. Westport, Conn.: Greenwood Press.
Kiefer, Christie W.
    1971   "Notes on anthropology and the minority elderly." *The Gerontologist* 1:94–98.
    1974   *Changing Cultures, Changing Lives: An Ethnographic Study of Three Generations of Japanese Americans*. San Francisco: Jossey-Bass.
Killian, Lewis M.
    1975   *The Impossible Revolution Phase 2: Black Power and the American Dream*. New York: Random House.
Kitagawa, Daisuke
    1967   *The Issei and Nisei: The Internment Years*. New York: Seabury Press.
Kitano, Harry H. L.
    1976   *Japanese Americans: The Evolution of a Sub-Culture*. 2nd ed. Englewood Cliffs, N.J.: Prentice-Hall.
Kitano, Harry H. L., Wai-Tsang Yeung, Lynn Chai, and Herbert Hatanaka
    1984   "Asian American interracial marriage." *Journal of Marriage and the Family* 46:179–190.
Klobus-Edwards, Patricia, John N. Edwards, and David L. Klemmack
    1978   "Differences in social participation: Blacks and whites." *Social Forces* 56:1035–1052.
Labor Unions in American Agriculture
    1945   United States Department of Labor. Bureau of Labor Statistics. Washington, D.C.: U.S. Government Printing Office.
Lebra, Takie Sugiyama
    1972   "Acculturation dilemma: The function of Japanese moral values for Americanization." *Council on Anthropology and Education Newsletter* 3:6–13.
Leonetti, Donna L.
    1983   Nisei Aging Project Report. Seattle: University of Washington.

Levine, Gene N., and Darrel M. Montero
1973   "Socioeconomic mobility among three generations of Japanese Americans." *Journal of Social Issues* 29:33–48.

Levine, Gene N., and Colbert Rhodes
1981   *The Japanese American Community: A Three Generation Study.* New York: Praeger.

Light, Ivan
1972   *Ethnic Enterprise in America: Business and Welfare Among Chinese, Japanese, and Blacks.* Berkeley: University of California Press.
1979   "Disadvantaged minorities in self-employment." *International Journal of Comparative Sociology* 20:31–45.

Lind, Andrew W.
1964   "Interracial marriage as affecting divorce in Hawaii." *Sociology and Social Research* 49:17–26.

Lipset, Seymour M.
1981   *Political Man: The Social Bases of Politics.* Baltimore: Johns Hopkins University Press.

Liu, William T.
1976   "Asian American research: Views of a sociologist." *Asian Studies Occasional Report* 2:1–8.

Lockwood, David
1956   "Some remarks on 'The social system.' " *British Journal of Sociology* 7:134–146.

London, Bruce
1975   "Racial differences in social and political participation: It's not simply a matter of black and white." *Social Science Quarterly* 56:274–286.

Lopez, Ronald W.
1970   "The El Monte Berry Strike of 1933." *Atzlan* 1:101–114.

Lyman, Stanford M.
1977   "Generation and character: The case of the Japanese Americans." Pp. 151–176 in S. Lyman (ed.), *The Asian in North America.* Santa Barbara, Calif.: ABC.

Mason, William
1969   *The Japanese of Los Angeles.* Los Angeles: Los Angeles County Museum of Natural History.

Masumoto, David M.
1987   *Country Voices: The Oral History of a Japanese American Family Farm Community.* Del Rey, Calif.: Inaka Countryside Publications.

Mathias, Charles M. C., Jr.
1981   "Ethnic groups and foreign policy." *Foreign Affairs* 59:975–98.

Mayer, Arno J.
1975   "The lower middle class as a historical problem." *Journal of Modern History* 47:409–436.

Mayer, Kurt
1953   "Business enterprise: Traditional symbol of opportunity." *British Journal of Sociology* 4:160–180.

McCarthy, John D., and Mayer N. Zald
  1977   "Resource mobilization and social movements: A partial theory."
          American Journal of Sociology 82:1212–1241.
Mears, Eliot Grinnell
  1926   "The land, the crops and the Oriental: A study of race relations in
          terms of the map." *The Survey* 56:148–149.
Miller, Philip L.
  1982   "The impact of organizational activity on political participation."
          Social Science Quarterly 62:83–98.
Mirak, Robert
  1980   "Armenians." Pp. 136–149 in Stephan Thernstrom (ed.), *Harvard
          Encyclopedia of American Ethnic Groups*. Cambridge: Harvard Univer-
          sity Press, Belknap Press.
Miyamoto, Shotaro Frank
  1939   *Social Solidarity Among the Japanese in Seattle*. University of Washing-
          ton Publications in the Social Sciences, vol. 11, no. 2, Seattle: Univer-
          sity of Washington. Reprint, Seattle: University of Washington
          Press, 1984.
  1972   "An immigrant community in America." Pp. 217–243 in Hilary
          Conroy and T. Scott Miyakawa (eds.), *East Across the Pacific: Histori-
          cal and Sociological Studies of Japanese Immigration and Assimilation*.
          Santa Barbara, Calif.: ABC-Clio.
  1986–87 "Problems of interpersonal style among the Nisei." *Amerasia* 13:29–
          45.
Modell, John
  1969   "Class or ethnic solidarity: The Japanese American company union."
          Pacific Historical Review 38:193–206.
  1977   *The Economics and Politics of Racial Accommodation: The Japanese of Los
          Angeles, 1900–1942*. Urbana: University of Illinois Press.
Molotch, Harvey
  1983   "American Jews and the state of Israel." *The Center Magazine* 16:8–26.
Montero, Darrel
  1977   "The Japanese American community: A study of generational changes
          in ethnic affiliation." Paper presented at the Annual Meeting of the
          American Sociological Association, Chicago, August.
  1978   "Model minority: Japanese join mainstream America." *Human Behav-
          ior* 7:59.
  1980   *Japanese Americans: Changing Patterns of Ethnic Affiliation over Three
          Generations*. Boulder, Colo.: Westview Press.
Montero, Darrel, and Ronald Tsukashima
  1977   "Assimilation and educational achievement: The case of the second
          generation Japanese American." *Sociological Quarterly* 18:490–503.
Murase, Mike
  1976   "Ethnic studies and higher education for Asian Americans." Pp.
          205–223 in Emma Gee (ed.), *Counterpoint: Perspectives on Asian Amer-
          ica*. Los Angeles: UCLA Asian American Studies Center.

Myer, Dillon S.
  1971   *Uprooted Americans: The Japanese Americans and the War Reloca-tion Authority during World War II.* Tucson: University of Arizona Press.
Nahirny, Vladmir C., and Joshua A. Fishman
  1965   "American immigrant groups: Ethnic identification and the problem of generations." *Sociological Review* 13:311–326.
Nakane, Chie
  1970   *Japanese Society.* Berkeley: University of California Press.
Nee, Victor, and Herbert Y. Wong
  1985   "Asian American socio-economic achievement: The strength of the family bond." *Sociological Perspectives* 28:281–306.
Nielsen, Francois
  1985   "Toward a theory of ethnic solidarity in modern societies." *American Sociological Review* 50:133–149.
Nomura, Naoki, and Dean Barnlund
  1983   "Patterns of interpersonal criticism in Japan and the United States." *International Journal of Intercultural Relations* 7:1–18.
Norbeck, Edward
  1972   "Japanese common-interest associations in cross-cultural perspective." *Journal of Voluntary Action Research* 1:38–41.
Novak, Michael
  1972   *The Rise of the Unmeltable Ethnics.* New York: Macmillan.
O'Brien, David J.
  1975   *Neighborhood Organization and Interest-Group Processes.* Princeton: Princeton University Press.
O'Brien, David J., and Stephen S. Fugita
  1982   "Middleman minority concept: Its explanatory value in the case of the Japanese in California agriculture." *Pacific Sociological Review* 25:185–204.
  1983a   "Generational differences in Japanese Americans' perceptions and feelings about social relationships between themselves and Caucasian Americans." Pp. 223–240 in W. C. McCready (ed.), *Culture, Ethnicity, and Identity: Current Issues in Research.* New York: Academic Press.
  1983b   "Ethnic population size and the maintenance of ethnic community life: A re-examination of the subcultural theory of urbanism." Paper presented at the annual meetings of the Rural Sociological Society, Lexington, Kentucky, August 17–20.
  1984   "The mobilization of a traditionally petit bourgeois ethnic group." *Social Forces* 63:522–537.
  Forthcoming *The Japanese American Experience.* Bloomington: Indiana University Press.
Ogawa, Dennis
  1971   *From Japs to Japanese: The Evolution of Japanese American Stereotypes.* Berkeley: McCutchan.

Oguri-Kendis, Kaoru
    1979   "Ethnicity in the suburbs: The case of the third generation Japanese American." Paper presented at the Annual Meeting of the American Anthropological Association, Cincinnati, Ohio, December 1.

Olin, Spencer C.
    1966   "European immigrant and Oriental alien: Acceptance and rejection by the California Legislature of 1913." *Pacific Historical Review* 35:303–315.

Olsen, Marvin E.
    1970   "Social and political participation of blacks." *American Sociological Review* 35:682–697.

Olzak, Susan
    1983   "Contemporary ethnic mobilization." *Annual Review of Sociology* 9:355–373.

Orum, Anthony
    1983   *Introduction to Political Sociology.* Englewood Cliffs, N.J.: Prentice-Hall.

Ouchi, William
    1984   *The M-Form Society: How American Teamwork Can Recapture the Competitive Edge.* Reading, Mass.: Addison-Wesley.

Park, Robert E.
    1950   *Race and Culture.* New York: The Free Press.

Peterson, William
    1970   "Success story, Japanese American style." Pp. 169–178 in Minako Kurokawa (ed.), *Minority Responses.* New York: Random House.
    1971   *Japanese Americans.* New York: Random House.

Poli, Adon, and Warren M. Engstrand
    1945   "Japanese agriculture on the Pacific Coast." *Journal of Land and Public Utilities Economics* 21:352–364.

Portes, Alejandro, and Robert L. Bach
    1985   *Latin Journey: Cuban and Mexican Immigrants in the U.S.* Berkeley: University of California Press.

Ray, Robert N.
    1975   "A report on self-employed Americans in 1973." *Monthly Labor Review* 98:49–54.

Reischauer, Edwin O.
    1981   *The Japanese.* Cambridge, Mass.: Harvard University Press, Belknap Press.

Reitz, Jeffrey G.
    1980   *The Survival of Ethnic Groups.* Toronto: McGraw-Hill Ryerson Limited.

Renkiewicz, Frank
    1980   "Polish fraternalism and beneficial insurance in America." Pp. 113–129 in Scott Cummings (ed.), *Self-Help in Urban America: Patterns of Minority Economic Development.* Port Washington, N.Y.: Kennikat Press.

Rich, Clyde L.
  1977   "Is random digit dialing really necessary?" *Journal of Marketing Research* 14:300–305.
Roche, John P.
  1982   "Suburban ethnicity: Ethnic attitudes and behavior among Italian Americans in two suburban communities." *Social Science Quarterly* 63:145–153.
Rolle, Andrew F.
  1972   *The Italian Americans.* Belmont, Calif.: Wadsworth.
Rose, Peter I.
  1959   "Strangers in their midst: A sociological study of the small-town Jew and his neighbors." Ph.D. dissertation, Cornell University, Ithaca, New York.
Rosentraub, Mark, and Delbert Taebel
  1980   "Jewish enterprise in transition: From collective self-help to orthodox capitalism." Pp. 191–214 in Scott Cummings (ed.), *Self-Help in Urban America.* Port Washington, N.Y.: Kennikat Press.
Sandberg, Neil C.
  1974   *Ethnic Identity and Assimilation: The Polish-American Community.* New York: Praeger.
Sarna, Jonathan D.
  1978   "From immigrants to ethnics: Toward a new theory of ethnicization." *Ethnicity* 5:370–378.
Schaeffer, Nora Cate
  1980   "Evaluating race-of-interviewer effects in a national survey." *Sociological Methods and Research* 8:400–419.
Schuman, Howard, and Jean M. Converse
  1968   "The effects of black and white interviewers on black responses in 1968." *Public Opinion Quarterly* 35:44–68.
Schwertfeger, Margaret M.
  1982   "Interethnic marriage and divorce in Hawaii: A panel study of 1968 first marriages." *Marriage and Family Review* 1:49–58.
Sennett, Richard (ed.)
  1969   *Classic Essays on the Culture of Cities.* New York: Appleton-Century-Crofts.
Sklare, Marshall
  1964   "Intermarriage and the Jewish future." *Commentary* 37:46–52.
Sklare, Marshall, and Joseph Greenblum
  1979   *Jewish Identity on the Suburban Frontier.* 2d ed. Chicago: University of Chicago Press.
Smethurst, R.
  1974   *A Social Basis for Prewar Japanese Militarism: The Army and the Rural Community.* Berkeley: University of California Press.
Smith, David H.
  1975   "Voluntary action and voluntary groups." *Annual Review of Sociology* 1:247–270.

Solberg, C. Edward, and Stephen M. Eliot
>   1973   "The War Relocation Authority and the future of Japanese American
>   agriculture: A continuing study." Paper presented at the Western
>   Conference of the Association for Asian Studies Annual Meeting,
>   September 28–30.

Sorauf, Frank J.
>   1984   *Party Politics in America*. Boston: Little, Brown.

Spanier, Graham B., and Paul C. Glick
>   1981   "Marital instability in the United States: Some correlates and recent
>   changes." *Family Relations* 30:329–338.

Spaulding, Charles B.
>   1934   "The Mexican strike at El Monte, California." *Sociology and Social
>   Research* 18:571–580.

Spickard, Paul R.
>   1980   "Japanese Americans and intermarriage: A historical survey." Paper
>   presented at the Annual Conference of the Association for Asian and
>   Pacific American Studies, Seattle, November 7.
>   1983   "The Nisei assume power: The Japanese Citizen's League, 1941–42."
>   *Pacific Historical Review* 52:147–174.

Starn, Orin
>   1986   "Engineering internment: Anthropologists and the War Relocation
>   Authority." *American Ethnologist* 13:700–720.

Stonequist, Everett V.
>   1935   "The problem of the marginal man." *American Journal of Sociology*
>   41:1–12.
>   1937   *The Marginal Man*. New York: Scribner's.

Strong, Edward K., Jr.
>   1934   *The Second Generation Japanese Problem*. Stanford: Stanford University Press.

Sudman, Seymour
>   1976   *Applied Sampling*. New York: Academic Press.

Sudman, Seymour, and Norman M. Bradburn
>   1974   *Response Effects in Surveys: A Review and Synthesis*. Chicago: Aldine.

Suzuki, Bob H.
>   1980   "The Asian American family." Pp. 74–102 in M. Fantini and R. Cardenas (eds.), *Parenting in a Multicultural Society*. New York: Longman.

Szymanski, Albert
>   1978   *The Capitalist State and the Politics of Class*. Cambridge, Mass.: Winthrop.

Tachiki, Amy, Eddie Wong, and Franklin Odo, with Buck Wong (eds.).
>   1971   *Roots: An Asian American Reader*. Los Angeles: UCLA Asian American
>   Studies Center.

Thomas, Dorothy S.
>   1952   *The Salvage*. Berkeley: University of California Press.

Thomas, William I., and Florian Znaniecki
>   1927   *The Polish Peasant in Europe and America*. New York: Knopf.

Thurlings, J. M. G.
    1979   "Pluralism and assimilation in the Netherlands with special reference to Dutch Catholicism." *International Journal of Comparative Sociology* 20:82–100.

Tinker, John N.
    1973   "Intermarriage and ethnic boundaries: The Japanese American case." *Journal of Social Issues* 29:49–66.
    1982   "Intermarriage and assimilation in a plural society: Japanese-Americans in the United States." *Marriage and Family Review* 5:61–74.

Tomaskovic-Devey, Barbara, and Donald Tomaskovic-Devey
    1988   "The social structural determinants of ethnic group behavior: Single ancestry rates among four white American ethnic groups." *American Sociological Review* 53:650–659.

Trottier, Richard W.
    1981   "Charters of panethnic identity: Indigenous American Indians and immigrant Asian-Americans." Pp. 271–305 in Charles F. Keyes (ed.), *Ethnic Change*. Seattle: University of Washington Press.

Tsuchida, Nobuya
    1978   "By choice or circumstance? Japanese gardeners in Southern California, 1900–1941." Paper presented at the Asian American Labor History Conference, University of California, Los Angeles, May 5.

Turner, Jonathan H., and Edna Bonacich
    1980   "Toward a composite theory of middleman minorities." *Ethnicity* 7:144–158.

U.S. Bureau of the Census
    1983a   1980 Census of the Population. Vol. 1: Characteristics of the Population. Chapter C, General Social and Economic Characteristics, Part 1, U.S. Summary. PC80-1-C1. Washington, D.C.: U.S. Bureau of the Census.
    1983b   1980 Census of Population and Housing. Housing Tracts. Fresno, California SMSA. PHC80-2-165. Washington, D.C.: U.S. Bureau of the Census.
    1983c   1980 Census of Population and Housing. Census Tracts. Sacramento, California SMSA. PHC80-2-309. Washington, D.C.: U.S. Bureau of the Census.
    1988   Census of the Population. Vol. 2: Subject Reports. Asian and Pacific Islander Population in the United States: 1980. PC80-2-1E. Washington, D.C.: U.S. Bureau of the Census.

U.S. Department of the Interior, WRA
    1946a   The Relocation Program. Washington, D.C.: U.S. Government Printing Office.
    1946b   Summary Notes on Segregation Conference. WRA Officials, Denver, Colorado, July 26–27, 1943. Washington, D.C.: U.S. Government Printing Office.

U.S. Immigration Commission
    1911   Immigrants in Industries. Part 25: Japanese and Other Immigrant

Races in the Pacific Coast and Rocky Mountain States. Washington, D.C.: U.S. Government Printing Office.

Verba, Sidney, and Norman H. Nie
1972   *Participation in America*. New York: Harper and Row.

Watanabe, Colin
1973   "Self-expression and the Asian American experience." *Personnel and Guidance Journal* 51:390–396.

Weber, Max
1952   *Ancient Judaism*. New York: The Free Press.

Weisz, John R., Fred R. Rothbaum, and Thomas C. Blackburn
1984   "Standing out and standing in: The psychology of control in America and Japan." *American Psychologist* 39:955–969.

Whyte, William F.
1981   *Street Corner Society: The Social Structure of an Italian Slum*. 3rd ed. Chicago: University of Chicago Press.

Wiley, Norbert F.
1967   "The ethnic mobility trap and stratification theory." *Social Problems* 15:147–159.

Wilson, Kenneth L., and Alejandro Portes
1980   "Immigrant enclaves: An analysis of the labor market experiences of Cubans in Miami." *American Journal of Sociology* 86:295–319.

Wilson, Robert A., and Bill Hosokawa
1980   *East to America: A History of the Japanese in the United States*. New York: Morrow.

Wilson, William J.
1980   *The Declining Significance of Race: Blacks and Changing American Institutions*. 2d ed. Chicago: University of Chicago Press.

Wirth, Louis
1928   *The Ghetto*. Chicago: University of Chicago Press.

Wollenberg, Charles
1972   "Race and class in rural California: The El Monte Berry Strike of 1933." *California Historical Quarterly* 51:155–164.

Wong, Morrison, and Charles Hirschman
1983   "Labor force participation and socioeconomic attainment of Asian-American women. *Sociological Perspectives* 26:423–446.

Woodrum, Eric, Colbert Rhodes, and Joe R. Feagin
1980   "Japanese American economic behavior: Its types, determinants, and consequences." *Social Forces* 58:1235–1254.

Yamamoto, Joe, and Hiroshi Wagatsuma
1980   "The Japanese and Japanese Americans." *Journal of Operational Psychiatry* 11:120–135.

Yanagisako, Sylvia J.
1977   "Women-centered kin networks in urban bilateral kinship." *American Ethnologist* 4:207–266.

1985   *Transforming the Past Tradition and Kinship among Japanese Americans*. Stanford: Stanford University Press.

Yancey, William L., Eugene P. Ericksen, and Richard N. Juliani
  1976   "Emergent ethnicity: A review and reformulation." *American Socio-logical Review* 41:391–402.
Yoder, Fred R.
  1936   "The Japanese rural community." *Rural Sociology* 2:420–429.
Yoneda, Karl
  1967   *History of Japanese Laborers in the U.S.* Tokyo: Shin Nihon Shuppon-Sha.
  1971   "100 years of Japanese labor history in the U.S.A." Pp. 152–158 in Amy Tachiki, Eddie Wong, and Franklin Odo, with Buck Wong (eds.), *Roots: An Asian American Reader.* Los Angeles: UCLA Asian American Studies Center.
Zander, Alvin
  1983   "The value of belonging to a group in Japan." *Small Group Behavior* 14:3–14.

INDEX

Printed in the United States
66327LVS00001B/199-246

9 780295 973760